# Communication for the Contemporary Classroom

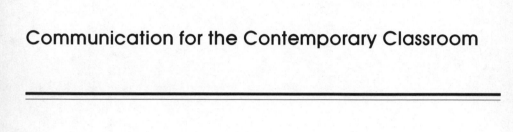

# Communication for the Contemporary Classroom

**WILLIAM J. SEILER**
University of Nebraska — Lincoln

**L. DAVID SCHUELKE**
University of Minnesota — St. Paul

**BARBARA LIEB-BRILHART**
*National Institute of Education — Washington, D.C.

* The parts of this book written by Barbara Lieb-Brilhart were done in her private capacity. No official support or endorsement by the National Institute of Education, United States Department of Education, is intended or should be inferred.

Holt, Rinehart and Winston

*New York   Chicago   San Francisco   Philadelphia*
*Montreal   Toronto   London   Sydney*
*Tokyo   Mexico City   Rio de Janeiro   Madrid*

Library of Congress Cataloging in Publication Data

Seiler, William J.
    Communication for the contemporary classroom.

    Includes bibliographies and indexes.
    1. Teacher-student relationships.  2. Interaction
analysis in education.   I. Schuelke, L. David.
II. Lieb-Brilhart, Barbara.   III. Title.
LB1033.S375   1984        371.1'022        83-8382
ISBN 0-03-059686-6

CBS COLLEGE PUBLISHING
Holt, Rinehart and Winston
The Dryden Press
Saunders College Publishing

LB
1033
S375
.1984

# Acknowledgments

Figure 1-1:    Created by Scott Baudhuin. From Seiler/Baudhuin/Schuelke, *Communication in Business and Professional Organizations,* © 1982. Addison-Wesley, Reading, MA. Figure 1.1. Reprinted with permission.

Figure 1-2:    Created by William D. Brooks. Printed with the permission of William D. Brooks.

Figure 1-3:    Reprinted with the permission of the author. Gustav W. Friedrich, "Classroom Interaction Research: The Process-Product Paradigm," unpublished manuscript, University of Nebraska — Lincoln, 1980.

Table 3-1:    Adapted from *Developing Communication Competence in Children: A Report of the Speech Communication Association's National Project on Speech Communication Competence.* R. R. Allen and Kenneth L. Brown, eds. Skokie, Ill.: National Textbook Co., 1976, pp. 182 – 185.

Figure 4-1:    From *Cultural Democracy, Biocognitive Development and Education* by Manuel Ramírez III and Alfredo Castañeda. New York: Academic Press, 1974, p. 60. Reprinted by permission of the authors.

Pages 73 – 75:    The material on learning styles is adapted from "Styles in Teaching and Learning," *Educational Leadership* 36 (January 1979) pp. 245-254. Reprinted with the permission of the Association for Supervision and Curriculum Development and Barbara B. Fischer and Louis Fischer. Copyright © 1979 by the Association for Supervision and Curriculum Development.

Pages 87 – 89:    The assumptions underlying the Iowa program are from *Guide to Implementing Multicultural, Nonsexist Curriculum Programs in Iowa Schools,* June 1980, pp.5-6, 17, and 18. Reprinted by permission of the State of Iowa Department of Public Instruction.

Figure 5-1:    From Braun, Carl. "Teacher Expectation: Sociopsychological Dynamics." *Review of Education Research,* Spring 1976, p. 206. Copyright 1976, American Educational Research Association, Washington, D.C.

Pages 133 – 148:    The material on the lecture method is adapted from Seiler, *Communication in Business and Professional Organizations,* © 1982. Addison-Wesley, Reading, MA. Pages 287 – 296 and 302 – 314. Reprinted with permission.

Page 158:    The case study is from *Business Communication Casebook.* Urbana, Ill.: American Business Communication Association, 1974. Used with permission of the American Business Communication Association.

Pages 160 – 161:    The game is from *Teaching Tips: A Guidebook for the Beginning College*

*Teacher,* 7th ed., by Wilbert J. McKeachie. Copyright © 1978 by D. C. Heath and Company. Reprinted by permission of the publisher.

Figure 9-1:   Used with permission of The Learning Line, Palo Alto, California.

Figure 10-5:   Used with permission of T. M. Visual Industries, Inc.

Table 11-1:   From *Mirrors for Behavior III, An Anthology of Observation Instruments.* Edited by Anita Simon and E. Gil Boyer. Communication Materials Center, 1974, p. 40.

Table 11-2:   From Flanders, *Analyzing Teaching Behavior,* © 1970. Addison-Wesley, Reading, MA, p. 34. Reprinted with permission.

Table 11-3:   From Amidon/Hough, *Interaction Analysis: Theory, Research and Application,* © 1967. Addison-Wesley, Reading, MA, p. 131. Reprinted with permission.

Appendix: The list of academic games is used with the permission of Games Central of ABT Associates, Inc., Cambridge, MA.

# Preface

The contemporary classroom provides educators with many challenges, some of which are unique to the decade of the eighties. This text brings together research from the fields of education and communication, applying it to problems and issues of today's classroom. Such problems as establishing a climate conducive to learning, coping with low morale and burnout, mainstreaming and other aspects of diversity, communicating attitudes through verbal and nonverbal language, using communication technology, and improving teacher communication are treated in this text as aspects of instructional communication.

While the text is intended for undergraduate students in departments or schools of communication, educational psychology, education, or any other department involved in teacher training, it may also be used in graduate courses for novice educators, in-service education programs, or training programs for those involved in instruction.

The objective of the book is to provide the reader with a basic understanding of communication as it occurs in the classroom. The emphasis falls on the relationship between communication and teaching, for the very essence of the teaching/learning process is communication; without communication, teaching and learning would be impossible. Thus, the objective of this text is not only to provide an understanding of communication, but also to show how communication affects the teaching/learning process.

This text, drawing from the fields of education, communication, psychology, child development, and others, provides a broad base of information about communication and its role in education. We combine theory, research, and applications with an abundance of examples to make the content meaningful and useful to the reader.

We have organized the book into two parts: Part 1 (Chapters 1 to 5) provides a foundation for the understanding of communication as the essential integrative component of all instruction. Chapter 1 discusses teaching as communication and includes a definition of communication, the central postulates of communication, a brief overview of the study of classroom communication, and communication as it is applied to the teaching/learning process. Chapter 2 describes communication in effective and ineffective learning climates, what teachers can do to manage learning climates, and how the teacher can use communication to establish effective learning climates. Chapter 3 presents information on the various stages of communication development and their implications for the classroom. In Chapter 4, aspects of student diversity such as cultural differences, learning styles, sex differences, handicapping conditions, and learning disabilities, and their implications for classroom communication, are discussed. Included is an examination of communication problems and opportunities in multicultural classrooms; classrooms with handicapped, mainstreamed children; and with children with diverse communication styles. Chapter 5 discusses ways in which teachers communicate attitudes to students (verbally and nonverbally), with emphasis on self-image, teacher expectancy, and other aspects of teacher behavior that influence communication.

Part 2 (Chapters 6 to 11) illustrates the important applications of communication to the teaching/learning process. Chapter 6 emphasizes characteristics that are important to effective classroom interaction. It includes a discussion of teaching competencies and teacher behavior variables; these variables include structuring, soliciting, and reacting. Chapter 7 examines two of the most widely used methods of communication in the classroom — lecture and discussion. Each method is described and its applications to the classroom are presented.

In Chapter 8, three instructional strategies that involve high student interaction — simulation, games, and role playing — are discussed. Chapter 9 concerns individualized learning and includes information on the development of self-instruction programs, programmed learning, personalized systems of instruction, learning contracts, and the instructional resources concept. Chapter 10, which discusses communication and technology in the classroom, is unique in bringing together the technology of the computer, student responders, and videotape recordings with communication in the classroom.

Finally, in Chapter 11 we focus on the communication processes involved in assessing instructional outcomes, instructional processes, and feedback. Included is a look at systematic observation and some of the procedures by which evaluation of communication in the classroom can be done. One section deals with teacher feedback as it relates to students and to their parents.

The beginning of each chapter contains a brief outline to help the reader focus on what should be learned. Whenever possible, we use illustrations and examples that directly apply communication to the classroom and the teaching/learning process. The end of each chapter has a detailed summary, discussion questions, a reference list, and a list of selected additional readings. At the end of the book are name and subject indexes.

Numerous people should receive credit for the completion of this book. We are indebted to our reviewers Ken Brown of the University of Massachusetts, Gus Friedrich of the University of Oklahoma, Ann Staton-Spicer of the University of Washington, and Andy Wolvin of the University of Maryland for their comments, which have been invaluable in helping to shape our book. We would also like to thank Thomas W. Gornick, Ellen H. Parlapiano, Carla Kay, Renee Cafiero, and the staff of Holt, Rinehart and Winston for their patience and their professional approach in publishing our text. Dave adds his special thanks and appreciation to Betty Shoultz for her help and loyalty. In addition, we thank our typist, JoAnn Wellsandt, for her excellent work under the most trying of circumstances. Finally, we thank June Rugg for her outstanding editorial comments and suggestions.

WJS
LDS
BLB

# Contents

# 4    Communication and Diversity in the Classroom                          68

# 5    Communication and Attitudes in the Classroom                          95

# part 2    APPLICATIONS     119

# 6    Communicating: Indirect Teaching Behaviors                          121

# 7    Communicating: Lecture and Discussion Methods                          132

# Communication for the Contemporary Classroom

# FOUNDATIONS

Understanding and using communication effectively in the classroom require a foundation on which to build. In Part 1, we have brought together in a unique blend the theories, principles, and concepts of education and communication as they directly relate to communication in the classroom. While specific skills are important to the success of a teacher, learning about the foundations of what communication is and means in the classroom is equally important. In this Part, we describe teaching as communication and affirm that teaching and learning are impossible without communication. We define communication, provide the central postulates, describe the essential components, illustrate a model of communication, and present a model of classroom instruction.

We examine teacher classroom behavior in the school and classroom context. We provide descriptions of effective and ineffective learning climates; aspects of climate that the teacher can manage and influence, such as instruction, discipline, student self-concept, and teacher morale; and communication behaviors that teachers can use to develop an effective climate.

We discuss the student's communication development and its implications for instruction; examine specifically how children develop sounds, words, syntax, semantics, nonverbal communication, functional communication, and strategies for learning, and how selective perception affects communication; review specific learning problems that relate to communication; and discuss the role the teacher plays in children's communication development.

We focus on the many sources of diversity in the classroom, including cultural background, learning styles, sex differences, communication styles, and handicapping conditions. We alert the teacher to potential communication problems and suggest ways of coping with diversity. Diversity is described as a positive aspect of the learning environment, which the teacher can use to promote student growth. Finally, our discussion centers on the verbal and nonverbal messages that teachers communicate in the classroom and the ways in which their communication produces attitudes affecting their instruction. The ways teachers foster images of themselves, and the ways their expectations promote student learning, are also described as foundations.

# The Role of Communication in Teaching and Learning

## chapter 1

*focus*   TEACHING AND COMMUNICATION ARE INSEPARABLE

COMMUNICATION
Central Postulates of Communication
The Essential Components of Communication

THE STUDY OF CLASSROOM COMMUNICATION

COMMUNICATION APPLIED TO TEACHING AND LEARNING
Presage Variables
Process Variables
Product Variables
Feedback Variables

Teaching and communication are inseparable. Teachers' success with students is to a large extent related to their competence and effectiveness as communicators. Many variables and factors can affect whether or not someone learns in the classroom, but there is little argument that teachers' communication effectiveness is among the most important. In fact, learning cannot occur without communication.

This book involves the relationship between communication and learning. We approach the subject from the perspective that communication is essential to teaching and learning. In this chapter we discuss what communication is, provide a brief overview of classroom communication, and apply communication to teaching and learning.

## COMMUNICATION

A review of the many definitions of *communication* quickly shows that no single definition is universally accepted by the scholars who use the term. Some definitions are long and complex, and others are brief and simple; some describe communication from the view of the initiator, some from the view of the receiver, and some from both views — those of the initiator and the receiver. Our purpose is not to discuss the differences between or among definitions of communication; however, to discuss communication's relationship to instruction, we must have a common meaning for the term. Thus, for our purpose, we define communication as *the process by which verbal and nonverbal symbols are sent and received and given meaning.*

To help you understand our approach to communication, the following sections discuss four central postulates of communication and identify the essential components that make up the communication process.

## Central Postulates of Communication

**1. Communication Is a Process.**  This implies that communication is dynamic and continuous, and has no beginning or end to it. To illustrate the notion that communication is a process, consider this question that Heraclitus, an ancient Greek philosopher, posed thousands of years ago: "Can you step in the same river twice?" If you answer *yes,* you are arguing that the river is, after all, the same river and you just stepped in at a different point in time. If you answer *no,* you are probably taking into account that the river is flowing, the water is constantly moving downstream, and the composition of the riverbed is changing, if ever so slightly, so that it is not the same river. You, too, are not exactly the same person you were just a few minutes ago.

Likewise, communication in this course may have begun the moment you stepped into the classroom, but would it have begun at all if you hadn't registered for the class in the first place? The reason you came to the class was to learn, and you probably made that decision before you even registered for the course. You see, you can keep tracing the beginning further and further back. Thus, the beginning is only a point in time and is dependent upon what preceded it. You may be asking when it all will end. Some of you are probably thinking, "Soon, I hope!" However, if you were to leave the class now, it would not be the end of its effect on you. If you can accept the idea that communication is a process, you are viewing events and relationships around you as dynamic, ongoing, constantly changing, and continuous. When something is labeled a process, it simply means that it does not have a clear beginning, precise ending, or fixed sequence of events. This can also be said about communication in every classroom.

**2. Communication Is Systemic.**  Simply stated, the communication process implies interdependence among its components. Thus, communication occurs when the components within it interact and affect one another. The human body is an excellent example of the systemic process. If something goes wrong within the body, there is a reaction; some response occurs either to correct what has gone wrong or to warn that something is wrong. All parts of the body are interdependent and work together as parts of one complex system.

In a similar sense, the communication process is systemic. The essential components include a source, a message, a channel, a receiver, feedback, and environment. Noise is a seventh component that is always present to one degree or another. Each of these components is discussed in detail later in this chapter. While the communication process is much more complex than the mere listing of seven components, the elimination of any one of these basic components (except for the reduction of noise) would prevent communication from occurring or at least make it less effective. Like communication in other contexts, communication that occurs in the classroom is systemic. The components that make up classroom communication are interdependent. Throughout this book you will see how the components of classroom communication affect and relate to one another.

**3. Communication Is Both Interactional and Transactional.**   Much debate exists concerning the definitions of interaction and transaction as to how they relate to the communication process. They are generally discussed as two separate concepts. However, since we believe that they are closely tied, we have chosen to discuss them together. Interaction is the exchanging of messages that occurs among people involved in the communication process. Transaction carries the concept of interaction one step further by viewing communication between people as a simultaneous sharing event. That is, the persons involved in the communication process are sharing in the encoding (creating) and decoding (interpreting) of messages. For example, teachers communicating to their students are not only sending information to their students, but are also receiving information in return (feedback). In addition, the teachers are simultaneously receiving their own communication. They can and do listen to themselves. Without this sharing, communication — and teaching and learning, for that matter — would be impossible. Each, therefore, is affecting the other and sharing in the process. In short, communication is the exchange by which we share our reality with others.

**4. Communication Can Be Intentional or Unintentional.**   This postulate suggests that communication can occur whether it is intended or not. Given the intent or lack of it, there are four possibilities for communication situations (see Figure 1-1).

   If communication were always in the realm of consciousness and within our control, we would have situation number one in Figure 1-1 — that is, a person intends to send a message to another person (or persons), who wishes to receive it. The teacher, for example, presents a

**FIGURE 1-1**   Intentional-Unintentional Communication

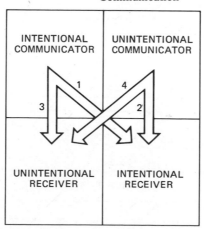

| INTENTIONAL COMMUNICATOR | UNINTENTIONAL COMMUNICATOR |
|---|---|
| UNINTENTIONAL RECEIVER | INTENTIONAL RECEIVER |

lecture with the intent of having the students receive information, and the students are listening because they want to learn the information being presented. A second possibility involves a person sending a message unintentionally to a person who is intentionally trying to receive the message (situation number two). This usually occurs when someone is purposely eavesdropping. In the classroom, for example, the teacher might be talking to one student while another student purposely listens in on the conversation. In the third possible situation, a person sends a message, but the receiver reacts unconsciously or unintentionally. This frequently happens in the classroom when the teacher is talking and students are daydreaming. Finally, in situation number four, neither party may intend that communication occur; an exchange of this type often involves nonverbal communication, such as appearance, seating arrangements, etc.

## The Essential Components of Communication

As we mentioned earlier, the communication system consists of a number of essential components: source, message, channel, receiver, environment, and feedback. Noise, which is anything that interferes with a message and thus potentially distorts its intended meaning, is also a component of communication; therefore, we have included noise as a seventh component in the communication process. The schematic model (Figure 1-2) helps to present the essential components of communication.

The communication system can be compared to the human digestive system, in which all parts interact and affect all other parts in the process of digesting food. Stopping the digestive process provides an easy way to examine, one at a time, the various parts of the system. This, of course, is unrealistic because it allows us to view the parts only in static relationship to each other. Examining communication, like examining the digestive system, must be done in a similar fashion. The process of communication must also be stopped and the system separated into its various parts so that each component can be discussed.

The *source* is the encoder (creator) of messages. The communication source in the classroom can be anyone who initiates a message — the teacher, a student, or a group of students. Because communication is considered to be both transactional and interactional,

**FIGURE 1-2 A Model of Communication**

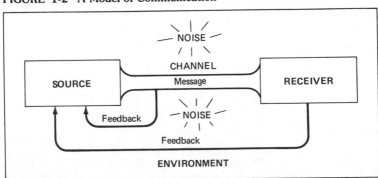

both the teacher and the students function as sources, sending messages simultaneously to one another. In communication, the source has essentially four roles: (1) to determine the meaning of what is to be communicated, (2) to encode the meaning into a message, (3) to send the message, and (4) to perceive and react to the listener's response to the message. The fourth role makes communication a transaction and an interaction as well as a process and a system. Similarly, the teacher as a source must (1) determine what is to be taught (communicated), (2) determine what is the best method of teaching the intended material (encode), (3) determine the most effective way to send the message (communicate), and (4) perceive and react to the students' responses to the message.

The *message* forms the stimulus that is produced by the source. Therefore, any verbal or nonverbal stimulus that affects a receiver (or receivers) is a message, whether it is intended or not. Messages include organization, words, grammar, and style. Each message is different from any other message. Even if the same message were created over and over, it would be different. Remember that communication is a process. The source has to make many decisions before a message can be communicated. What is the best way to organize it? Which words will make the message clear to the listener? How should the words be put into grammatical form? The teacher, as source, must consider these decisions and others when presenting information to students.

The *channel,* usually consisting of light and sound waves, is the link between the source's message and the receiver. The means by which light and sound waves travel, however, may differ. For example, when a teacher and student are talking face to face, light and sound waves in the air serve as the primary channel. If a memo is sent from the principal of the school to the students through the teacher, the light and sound waves still serve as the primary channel, but the memo and the teacher are the physical means by which the communication is conveyed. Books, films, television, computers, radios, magazines, and pictures are means by which messages can also be conveyed; nevertheless, the light and sound waves make up the channel.

The *receiver* decodes (interprets) the message. The receiver can be one or more persons (a teacher, a group of teachers, a student, an entire class of students, a parent or parents of students). A source sends messages and also receives them; thus, communication is both transactional and interactional.

Communicating with ourselves is called intrapersonal communication, for only one person is involved, and the messages begin and end with that individual. Within each of us there are all the components (source, message, channel, receiver, feedback, noise, environment) of communication. Intrapersonal communication affects all other communication transactions. Wenburg and Wilmot (1973) suggest that individual perceptions cannot be checked with someone else, but that all meanings attributed to messages are determined by individuals. Perception of self plays an important part in how one interprets messages.

All communication that takes place for us as individuals must first take place within us. Our personal differences react to the messages around us. This makes communication not only a process but a personal event as well, because we can never divorce "self" from our interactions with others, no matter how neutral or empathetic we may believe ourselves to be. The teacher who says, "I understand your feelings," really only understands them as they become internalized within the teacher's own feelings and perceptions.

Like the source, the receiver has several roles: (1) to receive (listen, see, touch, smell, or taste) the message; (2) to attend to the message; (3) to interpret (decode) and evaluate the message; (4) to store and recall the message; and (5) to respond to the source (in feedback), channel, environment, noise, and message.

The *environment* (climate) refers to the atmosphere (attitudes, status, room size, color, temperature, seating, and many other factors) that surrounds the person or persons involved in the communication. Even the distance between individuals is considered to be an environmental factor. Thus, a student who sits in the back row of the classroom experiences an environment different from that of the student who sits in the front row. The teacher's attitude as well as the students' attitudes will affect the environment or atmosphere in the classroom; for example, if the teacher is perceived to be enthusiastic about what is being taught, this will have an impact on the environment of the classroom and help to improve learning. All these factors and others can influence the effectiveness or ineffectiveness of communication and thus of teaching and learning. For example, when communication is ineffective or inefficient because of environmental factors, noise is considered to be present. The environment has a tremendous influence upon communication, as shown in Chapter 2.

*Noise* (anything that interferes with or changes the meaning of the source's intended message) is included as a component of communication because it is always present to one degree or another in every communication situation. Noise is often associated with physical sounds, but it can also be psychological: thoughts going through a person's mind that distract from the reception or creation of a message, or a visual distraction such as a person's or object's movement, which draws the attention of the receiver, even if only for a moment. There are also factors that distort rather than merely distract from the intended message. For example, a teacher wanting the attention of the students may speak louder than normal. The students, or at least some of them, may not be aware of the teacher's reason for speaking loud and may assume that the loud speaking voice is an indication of anger. Essentially, noise is anything that reduces the clarity, accuracy, meaning, understanding, or retention of a message.

In the classroom, interferences might include annoying vocal habits or physical movements on the part of a teacher or student, the room temperature, inadequate lighting, the seating arrangement, movements and sounds of others, inattentiveness, lack of listener motivation, or physical impairments of the hearing mechanism. These examples demonstrate that noises, acting either alone or in combination, may distort or reduce the effectiveness of classroom communication.

*Feedback* is the component in the communication process that allows the source to monitor the receiver's response to the message. If the purpose of communication is to share meaning accurately, to influence others, and to respond to others' needs, then some means for correcting faulty messages, misconceptions, missed meanings, and incorrect responses is necessary. Feedback supplies a means for insuring accurate communication exchanges and indicates whether or not the communication has been received and understood.

Feedback can also encourage and provide reinforcement as it is used to help the source and receiver monitor the communication. The teacher provides feedback on student progress not only to the students but to their parents as well. Students also provide feedback to the teacher on how well they are learning or what they like or dislike about what they are learning. Parents provide feedback to teachers about how they feel their children are learning. Principals provide feedback to teachers on how well they perceive them to be teaching. Not only is feedback essential for communication, but it is also vital to teaching and learning.

Now that we have defined communication, discussed communication's central postulates, and explained the components that comprise communication, let us briefly give an overview of how communication in the classroom became a concern for educators.

## THE STUDY OF CLASSROOM COMMUNICATION

Speech-communication instruction dates back to antiquity, and speaking ability has been the mark of an educated person in every civilized society. The early courses in America were concerned with oratory and public speaking. For over seventy years departments of speech communication with extensive curricula have been in existence. More recently, however, researchers and educators in the field of speech communication have expanded their understanding and knowledge of how communication relates to all aspects of life; but even though communication is responsible for making teaching and learning possible, systematic study of classroom communication has been limited or ignored.

We now recognize the need for communication competencies in business and industry, in education, and in a variety of other settings. To be successful an organization needs people who can communicate effectively and efficiently. The school as an organization needs proficient communicators. Consequently, many of the skills important for people in industry are also important for communication in the classroom.

Business and industry supply a variety of studies that demonstrate the importance of communication. Lockwood and Boatman (1975) asked participants in a conference on career communication education, "Which speech communication competencies are required in your business, industry, agency, or profession?" The conference was made up of representatives from a variety of professions, including law enforcement, religion, health, government, industry, social services, and education, among others. The following summarizes their responses:

*Small Group Facilitation.*   Ability to develop and facilitate effective functioning of small groups within an organization, both in terms of accomplishing the group's task and establishing an atmosphere of cooperation within the group.

*Interviewing.*   Ability to assess individual capabilities and establish rapport with potential employers or those already on the job.

*Problem Solving/Decision Making.*   Ability to analyze a problem, make decisions concerning specific strategies to solve the problem, and evaluate the effectiveness of the solutions.

*Public Relations.*   Ability to establish communication that invites credibility, trust, and confidence between a firm and the public.

*Listening.*   Ability to receive, interpret, understand, and respond to both verbal and nonverbal messages from clients or employees, both in terms of the information given and the feelings expressed.

*Persuasion.*   Ability to persuade clients or employees (as individuals or groups) to accept a policy, believe a claim, or take a specific course of action.

*Motivation.*   Ability to motivate others in a given job situation by being sensitive and responsive to their needs.

*Conflict Resolution.*   Ability to handle conflict between individuals or groups within an organization by diagnosing the conflict and selecting strategies to achieve resolution of the conflict.

*Speaking Competence.*   Ability to think through, organize, and present information in a concise and coherent manner.

*Relationship Building.*   Ability to facilitate positive and productive relationships between co-workers and between members of various levels of an organization.

*Questioning Techniques.*   Ability to ask questions that are precise, clear, and logical for the purpose of securing relevant and in-depth information [p. 7].

Teacher educators, according to Lynn (1976), appear to be concerned about the need to develop teachers' communication competencies. She points to such areas as verbal interaction, listening and responding, methods of inquiry, classroom dynamics, interpersonal communication, cross-cultural communication, nonverbal communication, semantics, and the evaluative nature of language as speech communication competencies that teachers should have to be successful in the classroom.

Many colleges and universities now recognize the central nature of communication in their teaching curricula; these require students wishing to enter teaching to have certain speech communication competencies. At first the requirements centered on two criteria: (1) speech clearance or proficiency testing to determine whether the student could speak clearly and effectively; and (2) at least a basic speech communication course. For the most part, this was the first effort to provide speech communication competency for students studying to be teachers.

In 1978, a committee[1] of professionals in the field of speech communication prepared a document listing the communication competency requirements for teachers of preschool through college classes, including adult education. The document suggests that teachers need to be competent cognitively and affectively in their understanding of communication as well as in the psychomotor skills of presenting messages. In the cognitive area forty-two objectives were listed; in the affective and the psychomotor areas eighteen objectives were listed for each. Some of the objectives were suggestions about what the classroom teacher should know and understand about communication, while others were suggestions as to what communication skills the classroom teacher should possess.

[1] The information discussed here was taken from a working draft of a report prepared by a select committee of members of the Instructional Communication Division of the International Communication Association.

Swinton and Bassett (1981) provide a profile, based upon teachers' perceptions, of competencies needed by the teacher of speech communication and drama. While the competencies they suggest are for a very specific type of instruction, we believe that these same competencies may be generalized to all teachers in all types of instruction. The first category consists of *personality characteristics*: "enthusiasm for the students and the subject matter; integrity, honesty, fairness, openmindedness, and sincerity combined with a sense of humor; and a positive, patient, and realistic attitude toward student efforts and personalities (p. 152). The second category is *interpersonal skills and relationships*. The effective teacher is a "sensitive, empathetic listener who seeks to establish an open, comfortable, nonthreatening constructive rapport with students; who demonstrates understanding of the students as individuals; and who fosters an atmosphere of mutual respect as he or she assists them in developing strong self-concepts leading to self-awareness and self-confidence" (p. 152).

The third category is *planning skills*. In this category, the teacher should demonstrate the ability to organize and plan the classroom curriculum. The fourth category is *professional attitudes and activities,* wherein the competent teacher should, "above all, enjoy teaching" (p. 153). This category further implies that the competent teacher is active professionally, as reflected in a desire to continue to learn. The fifth category is *teaching strategies.* A competent teacher is described as one who can communicate instructions clearly and who can effectively use a variety of communication abilities and skills, including audiovisual devices.

*Evaluation abilities,* the sixth category, suggests that teachers should be able to provide feedback that is positive, constructive, and immediate, either orally or in writing. The seventh and last category is *management skills.* This includes the ability to control the classroom environment by the establishment of fair and consistent discipline as well as of expectations for student behavior in the classroom. As indicated earlier, these categories were intended for a very specialized teacher; but as you can see, these same categories are also relevant to all teachers and require effective communication by the teacher.

## COMMUNICATION APPLIED TO TEACHING AND LEARNING

To gain a better understanding of communication and the teaching/learning process, we present the following model (Figure 1-3), which illustrates the perspectives and the topics involved in our study of the role of communication in teaching and learning. The model is a modification of those developed by Dunkin and Biddle (1974) and Friedrich (1978, 1980, and 1982). You will notice that there are four major components: presage variables, process variables, product variables, and feedback variables. Like the components in the communication model (Figure 1-2), these four variables are interdependent; the lines (both solid and dotted) indicate the relationships between and among them. The solid lines illustrate the direct relationships, and the dotted illustrate additional relationships in the learning process that are outside the classroom.

### Presage Variables

Presage variables help to predict possible outcomes in the instructional process. Several factors are included in the presage variables, including teacher experiences, teacher proper-

**FIGURE 1-3 A Model of Classroom Learning**

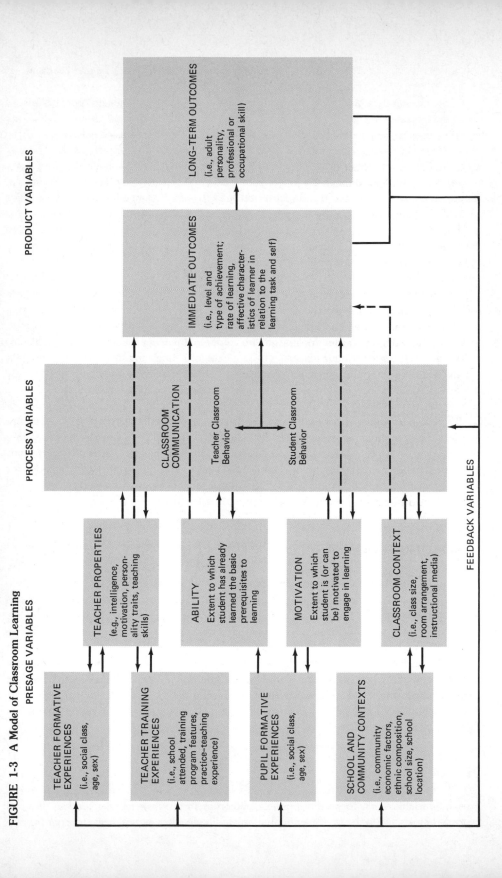

ties, student experiences, student ability, student motivation, school and community contexts, and classroom context.

The teacher experiences involve the teacher's teaching and learning situation, which has an effect upon the learning process. For example, the teacher's social class, race, sex, and age can all have an effect on students. A second category of variables includes what the teacher brings into the situation; this involves the training of the teacher and includes, among other things, the courses that the teacher has taken. If you were to ask experienced teachers about the influence of their training on their teaching, we believe that almost all of them would say that it had a major impact. Of course, such factors as the teacher's knowledge, experiences with students, motivations, communication skills, personality traits, experiences as a student teacher, and role models all relate to the teacher's training and properties, and do have an effect in the classroom. Specific teacher traits such as openmindedness, self-concept, receptivity, trustworthiness, friendliness, and likableness all can affect classroom communication and, ultimately, learning.

Student factors, under presage variables, involve the student and what the student brings to the teaching/learning situation. First, there are the formative experiences just as there are for the teacher; each student's social class, age, sex, and race have all helped to form a unique individual. Second, the student's ability is affected by previous training—for example, courses taken, past successes and failures both in and out of school, past successes and failures with peers, and the student's traits and skills; all of these can influence and affect the teaching/learning process and the communication behaviors in the classroom and in the school. Finally, motivation of the student is critically important, not only to student behavior but ultimately to student learning also.

The school and community also contribute to the model of classroom learning. These factors are often outside the control of the teacher, but they are nevertheless extremely important and cannot be ignored. Such factors as school leadership, the economic condition of the community, its ethnic composition and size, the size of its schools, the condition and location of the schools, and the school's physical aspects can all influence the teaching and learning process.

## Process Variables

The second major component in the model focuses on the classroom factors that are created when the teacher and the students are brought together. This is when communication in the classroom occurs. Two major factors are included in the process variables: the teacher's classroom behavior and the student's classroom behavior.

## Product Variables

The third major component in the model consists of the product variables. Achievement in terms of cognitive, affective, and psychomotor development are the product variables of almost all classroom learning. These variables, which are the criteria for the entire teaching and learning process, help to determine if teaching has been successful or not. All other aspects of the model result in the product. Any aspect in the process that has no effect on the product variables, or that produces a negative impact on them, should be changed or removed from the process. These variables divide into immediate outcomes — those often observed during class or shortly after a class has finished — and long-term outcomes — those manifested in each individual long after the classroom experience is over.

## Feedback Variables

The fourth major component in the model is feedback. In our earlier discussion of feedback as well as in later ones in the book, we suggest that feedback is necessary for the process of teaching/learning to exist. Feedback continually occurs from teacher to student, from student to student, from student to teacher, from teacher to parents, from student to parents, from parents to student, and from parents to teacher. Feedback is one of the most important parts of the teaching/learning process and occurs through communication.

Our argument to this point has been that teaching cannot occur without communication; we believe this argument is fully supported by the competencies suggested in the research presented earlier in this chapter. Through classroom observations and tape recordings, Bellack, Kliebard, Hyman, and Smith (1966) and Flanders (1970) found that 66% of the time in the average classroom is spent in some form of talk. In many classes this figure is much higher, and can reach 95%. This applies particularly to classes where the lecture is the primary means of communication, as in some college and university classrooms. While these figures are approximations of the amount of talk that takes place in the classroom, it must be pointed out that some instructional methods, as discussed later in this book, require less talk by the teacher and more by students. Regardless of the amount of talk that takes place, the effectiveness of what is being communicated determines the learning outcome.

Herbert (1967) provides further evidence that teaching involves communication when he suggests that most of what is referred to as classroom teaching consists of lessons in which the teacher and students communicate with one another and with some form of subject content. Nuthall and Snook (1973, p. 52), in summarizing a number of research studies, identify four lesson forms in which the average teacher spends approximately the following time:

1. 18 to 22% lecturing or lecturing and demonstrating or exhibiting materials
2. 20 to 30% engaging in the question-answer type of recitation or discussion with students (often interspersed with short lectures)
3. 14 to 23% combining demonstration or exhibition of materials with question-answer type discussion
4. between 25 and 45% supervising students who are engaged in individual seat or laboratory work

It is apparent from the above percentages that the teacher is in constant communication, either directly or indirectly, with students.

Friedrich (1980, p. 12), in an explanation of what contributes to student achievement, suggests the following three variables that are central to the understanding of classroom cognitive achievement:

1.  *Student Ability.*   The extent to which the student already possesses the basic prerequisites for instruction

2.  *Student Motivation.*   The extent to which the student is (or can be) motivated to engage in the learning process

3.  *Quality of Classroom Communication.*   The utility of teacher-student and student-student interactions for learning

Friedrich concludes that 65% of the learning occurring in the classroom is dependent upon student ability and student motivation. The remaining 35% includes quality of classroom interaction, measurement error, and a variety of other possible variables. He further states that "it is teaching, not the teacher, and classroom environment, not physical characteristics, that influence school learning" (p. 16). The quality of classroom communication, according to Friedrich, may account for about 25% of what students achieve in the classroom. Thus, while researchers still have not convincingly determined the effects of the quality of classroom communication, some evidence suggests that it does play a significant role in learning as well as in satisfaction with the learning experience.

Communication in the classroom is more than talking, and teaching is more than just talk. While talking often comprises a large portion of such communication, it is not the only kind. Teaching occurs even without talking: Learning can take place when students individually work problems, or study quietly from programmed learning texts, or read from a book, or use a computer to learn their lessons.

Classroom communication may be talk; it may be listening; it may be oral or written; it may be verbal or nonverbal; it may be intentional or unintentional. Learning in the classroom occurs through communication between and among the teacher and student, student and student, and student and learning materials. Thus, our application of communication to teaching and learning involves more than just the teacher learning to be an effective speaker or learning to be an effective discussant. It involves applying communication to teaching and learning in all its aspects.

# SUMMARY

In this chapter, we explained what communication is and described it as a process and a system. We also explained that it is interactional and transactional in nature and that it can be intentional or unintentional. Communication was defined as a process by which verbal and nonverbal symbols are given meaning. The components of communication were discussed as including the source, message, channel, receiver, environment, noise, and feedback.

We briefly reviewed the study of classroom communication as a way of explaining the importance of communication in the classroom. Descriptions of communication competencies, derived from a variety of contexts including business and education, were presented. We then presented a model of classroom learning so as to depict the role of communication in the classroom. The model included four major components: presage variables, process variables, product variables, and feedback variables. Finally, we applied communication to the teaching and learning situation.

# Discussion Questions

1. Which communication postulate do you think is the most significant to the understanding of communication in the classroom? Why?
2. Why is it important for a teacher to understand that communication can be both intentional and unintentional?
3. If you were to create your own model of communication, is there anything you would include in the model that we didn't? Why? What other modifications would you make?
4. What communication skills do you think are the most important for a teacher?
5. What formative experiences have had the greatest effect on you as a student, either to enhance or inhibit learning?

# References

Bellack, A. A., H. M. Kliebard, R. R. Hyman, and F. L. Smith. *The Language of the Classroom.* New York: Teachers College Press, Columbia University, 1966.

Dunkin, M. J., and B. J. Biddle. *The Study of Teaching.* New York: Holt, Rinehart and Winston, Inc., 1974.

Flanders, Ned A. *Analyzing Teacher Behavior.* Reading, Mass.: Addison-Wesley Publishing Company, Inc., 1970.

Friedrich, Gustav W. "Classroom Interaction." In *Communication in the Classroom,* Larry L. Barker, ed. Englewood Cliffs, N.J.: Prentice-Hall, Inc., 1982, pp. 55–76.

Friedrich, Gustav W. "Classroom Interaction Research: The Process-Product Paradigm." An unpublished paper, University of Nebraska — Lincoln, 1980.

Friedrich, Gustav W. "Effects of Teacher Behavior on the Acquisition of Communication Competencies." An unpublished paper presented at the AERA Convention, Toronto, Canada, 1978.

Herbert, J. A. *A System for Analyzing Lessons.* New York: Teachers College Press, Columbia University, 1967.

Lockwood, D., and S. Boatman. "Marketability: Who Needs Us and What Can We Do for Them?" Unpublished paper presented at the Central States Speech Association Convention, Kansas City, Mo., 1975.

Lynn, Elizabeth M. *Improving Classroom Communication: Speech Communication Instruction for Teachers.* Falls Church, Va.: Speech Communication Association and ERIC/RCS, 1976.

Nuthall, Graham, and Ivan Snook. "Contemporary Models of Teaching." In *The Second Handbook of Research on Teaching,* Robert M. W. Travers, ed. Skokier, Ill.: Rand McNally & Company, 1973, pp. 47–76.

Seiler, William J., E. Scott Baudhuin, and L. David Schuelke. *Communication in Business and Professional Organizations.* Reading, Mass.: Addison-Wesley Publishing Company, Inc., 1982.

Swinton, M. M., and Ronald E. Bassett. "Teachers' Perceptions of Competencies Needed for Effective Speech Communication and Drama Instruction." *Communication Education,* Vol. 30, No. 2 (1981): 146–155.

Wenburg, John, and William Wilmot. *The Personal Communication Process.* New York: John Wiley & Sons, Inc., 1973.

# For Further Reading

Barker, Larry, ed. *Communication in the Classroom*. Englewood Cliffs, N.J.: Prentice-Hall, Inc., 1982.

Bassett, Ronald E., and Mary-Jeanette Smythe. *Communication and Instruction*. New York: Harper & Row, Publishers, 1979.

Bloom, B. S. *Human Characteristics and School Learning*. New York: McGraw-Hill, Inc., 1976.

Civikly, Jean M., ed. *Contexts of Communication*. New York: Holt, Rinehart and Winston, Inc., 1981.

Cooper, Pamela. *Speech Communication for the Classroom Teacher*. Dubuque, Ia.: Gorsuch Scarisbrick Publishers, 1981.

Friedrich, Gustav W., Kathleen M. Galvin, and Cassandra L. Book. *Growing Together: Classroom Communication*. Columbus, Oh.: Charles E. Merrill Publishing Co., 1976.

Hurt, H. Thomas, Michael D. Scott, and James C. McCroskey. *Communication in the Classroom*. Reading, Mass.: Addison-Wesley Publishing Company, Inc., 1978.

Klopf, Donald W., and Ronald E. Cambra. *Speaking Skills for Prospective Teachers*. Englewood, Colo.: Morton Publishing Company, 1983.

Phillips, Gerald M., Robert E. Dunham, Robert Brubaker, and David Butt. *The Development of Oral Communication in the Classroom*. Indianapolis, Ind.: The Bobbs-Merrill Company, Inc., 1970.

# Communication and the Learning Climate

*focus*    THE PROCESS OF TEACHER/STUDENT INTERACTION AND CLIMATE

**EFFECTIVE VS. INEFFECTIVE LEARNING CLIMATES**
**Openness vs. Defensiveness**
**Confidence vs. Fear**
**Acceptance vs. Rejection**
**Belonging vs. Alienation**
**Trust vs. Suspicion**
**High Expectations vs. Low Expectations**
**Order vs. Chaos**
**Control vs. Frustration**

**MANAGING THE CLASSROOM CLIMATE**
**Influencing Instruction**
**Maintaining Discipline**
**Influencing Students' Self-Concepts**
**Maintaining Teacher Morale**

**COMMUNICATION BEHAVIORS FOR AN EFFECTIVE CLIMATE**
**Reducing the Frequency of Negative Messages**
**Increasing the Frequency of Positive Messages**
**Using "You-Related" Messages That Teach**
**Using "I" Messages That Take Responsibilities for Feelings**
**Using Feedback Constructively**
**Criticizing the Behavior and Not the Pupil**
**Maintaining Awareness of the Impact of Nonverbal Behaviors**

In the previous chapter we described a model of instructional communication that includes the major elements in the teaching/learning process — presage variables, process variables, product variables, and feedback variables. This chapter focuses on the process of teacher-student interaction, specifically on one aspect important for learning—the climate established in the school and the classroom. Our major focus, therefore, is on that aspect of the model that we call "process." We discuss the different climates established in effective and ineffective schools, the aspects of climate that can be managed by the teacher, and ways in which the teacher uses communication to establish the learning climate.

# EFFECTIVE VS. INEFFECTIVE LEARNING CLIMATES

Many definitions have been used to describe the school or classroom climate. For our purposes, climate means *the perceived atmosphere of the school or classroom that manifests itself in the feelings or opinions of observers or participants in the education process.* Every school or classroom generates an atmosphere, which is often not articulated explicitly, but which leaves a distinct impression of the interrelationships of the educators and the students. Consider these contrasting schools:

> Students are arriving by bus at the elementary school. The principal, staff, and students represent a variety of racial and ethnic groups present in the community. The principal greets each of the children entering the school, and occasionally asks, "How's your mother, Tim? Is she out of the hospital yet?" or, "How's the new baby sister?" The principal seems to know each child and each family. Children proceed in an orderly fashion to their rooms. The teachers are smiling as they greet the children. Some children tell a teacher, who listens with interest, about a television show that they have watched the previous night. The staff seems happy to work there, and the children seem to like school.

In another school, we see the following:

> The buses arrive at the school. The bus driver is furious at two boys who have caused problems during the trip. The assistant principal is waiting with pink slips to punish those whom the driver reports. Students seem sullen as they enter the school. In the classroom the teachers are demanding quiet and "get to work." Some students wander in late and are sent to the principal's office to be disciplined. Teachers rarely smile, and the principal is in the office dealing with those who have misbehaved.

In observing these two schools, we come away with differing impressions of the atmosphere and the relationships among people. We are reacting to the "climate" that has been established over a period of time through the interactions and expectations of the faculty, principal, staff, students, and parents. Research on school climate and its various aspects shows that some climates appear to foster and facilitate learning, while others seem to inhibit or detract from learning. Evidence shows that effective and ineffective schools differ in the climates that they have established in a number of characteristics: openness vs. defensiveness, confidence vs. fear, acceptance vs. rejection, belonging vs. alienation, trust vs. suspicion, high expectations vs. low expectations, order vs. chaos, and control vs. frustration. While this list, which is discussed in the following paragraphs, does not present all the positive and negative factors that comprise climate, it does present those that have strong implications for communication and learning.

## Openness vs. Defensiveness

Perhaps the best indicator of an open climate occurs when pupils freely admit to and seek help from teachers for problems. Likewise, teachers feel free to seek feedback, to be evaluated for the purposes of improvement, and to ask for help. In a school or classroom environment where teachers frequently criticize or send negative messages, students will develop hostility and eventually act defensively even when they are not accused. Open climates seem to be characterized by respect, trust, caring, and a chance for input into decision making, while the opposite is true of closed climates (Howard, 1974; Phi Delta Kappa, 1974). A classroom or a school, like any organization, will have a productive work climate if communication is honest, especially about work performance. Students and teachers want honest feedback on how they are doing and how their performance can be improved. Teachers should schedule time to discuss with students their problems and ways in which their performance can be improved. Likewise, principals should openly discuss teacher evaluations with teachers and work with them to find ways of improving performance. In an ideal climate, there is "upward communication," that is, communication that permits teachers to evaluate the performance of principals and students to evaluate performance of teachers, and opportunities are provided for feedback to be discussed and utilized.

## Confidence vs. Fear

Strongly related to the openness factor is the degree of fearfulness that is present in the climate. In a positive climate, students seem to feel capable of learning and teachers feel capable of teaching. Time is spent more on instruction and less on "control." In a negative climate, the status barriers of principal, teacher, and students seem prevalent, and people feel intimidated and afraid of making mistakes. When administrators have positive self-concepts, their subordinates are usually not afraid to express ideas or dissatisfaction related to the job (Bogue, 1972). Gibb (1961) studied characteristics of supportive and defensive climates in organizations. He found that people in defensive climates felt they were frequently being evaluated or subjected to "good" and "bad" judgments. They also felt manipulated and subject to many rules and procedures. The climate seemed cold and impersonal, with superiors talking down to people. In a supportive climate (one in which people felt more confident than fearful) leaders took more of a problem orientation, i.e., they tried to get at the causes of difficulties rather than using rules to cope with difficulties. There was also more descriptive rather than evaluative language, and more empathy and fairness. These findings can be applied to classrooms and schools. If teachers feel that the principal is constantly judging them, that rules and regulations are interfering with teaching, and that nobody cares about them as people, they are likely to feel fearful and negative. If they treat their students in a similar manner, the classroom will be pervaded by a climate of fearfulness and learning will be impaired.

Many teachers feel that they must create an atmosphere of fear in order to control a classroom. They are afraid that if they smile, students will "walk all over them" and not see that they are tough. However, most authorities on classroom discipline agree that preventive measures in which guidelines and limits of behavior are communicated early are better and will prevent the atmosphere of fear that goes with punitive (after-the-fact) messages (Kindsvatter and Levine, 1980).

## Acceptance vs. Rejection

In a positive environment, students feel accepted in their classrooms and feel that they are a part of the total school. In a fourth-grade class observed by one of the authors, the children individually expressed the notion that they were the teacher's favorite; no child felt unaccepted by the teacher. The teacher knew each one's capabilities, deficiencies, and personality characteristics and accepted each child unconditionally. This attitude spilled over to the children, who expressed sympathy or encouragement to one another or who gave each other help when necessary. There was an absence of the ridicule or conflict often found in classrooms where children vie for the teacher's acceptance. Closely related to feelings of acceptance are feelings that a supervisor (teacher or principal) is fair and equitable. For example, Timm (1980) set up a series of experiments in an organization where supervisors responded differently (unfairly) to one half of a work group from the way they did to another half. Those workers who recognized unfair treatment produced less and tended to withdraw psychologically from participation in the task.

In a classroom, children are quick to perceive inequities through communication behaviors similar to those used by Timm's "unfair" managers. For example, if the teacher answers questions for some children and not for others or compliments some and not others, the children will soon draw their own conclusions about which ones the teacher accepts or rejects. Those who feel rejected may behave by disrupting activities or withdrawing from them.

## Belonging vs. Alienation

Recent studies suggest that many high school students feel alienated from school life. In reviewing the literature on alienation and adolescence, Galbo (1980) conceptualized alienation to include separation or loss as "a form of disintegration in which life is seen as fragmentary, incomplete, and not whole" (p. 27). Hartley and Hoy (1972) found less alienation among adolescents in schools with open climates than in those with closed climates.

One factor affecting alienation may relate to the changing nature of adolescence. At the turn of the century, very few people attended high school. Now states have compulsory attendance laws enacted simultaneously with child labor laws, which keep students in school until they are in late adolescence. Students today mature earlier physically, sexually, and intellectually than those of previous generations. Those who in earlier times might have been members of the work force at age fifteen now find themselves in school, often feeling confused about the paradox between their mature bodies and their dependency on parents and the school system. Some find escape in drugs, alcohol, or vandalism — all expressions of their growing alienation that affect the climate of the school and classroom. In noting these factors, Moberly (1980) has called for increased alternatives within the schools, such as joint work programs with industry. Certainly a realistic approach to contemporary adolescents is necessary if the climate is to be a positive one.

Such an approach was described by Maynard (1976), a principal who changed the climate of his Seattle high school. Students felt alienated, skipped class, and were generally negative toward school. Maynard formed a school climate team, consisting of students and faculty, who developed projects to improve the school. Through shared decision making, which included having teachers and students make budget decisions and interview prospective staff, students and staff became proud of their school and absenteeism decreased. In other words, "ownership" and participation in decisions that affected them decreased the feeling of alienation for teachers and students.

A similar example occurred in a community where an architect involved students, teachers, and other community members in the design and building of a creative playground. Parents and children raised money, gathered donations of materials, and, with the help of school staff and the community, built the playground in a single weekend. The playground over the years was never vandalized, was well maintained, and was perceived by everyone in the school and community as their property. Thus, a feeling of belonging involves ownership and sharing in an activity or project.

## Trust vs. Suspicion

Students who mistrust teachers, or vice versa, often find themselves in a vicious spiral. If they feel that they are mistrusted, they are likely to act in an untrustworthy manner. Rotter (1980) offers evidence that people with low trust of others are often less trustworthy than people who trust others more. In classrooms or schools characterized by low trust, individuals were more liable to be looking for opportunities to take advantage of one another. Also, a climate characterized by suspicion and mistrust is apt to detract from learning.

In a climate where principals allow teachers, and teachers allow pupils, to communicate openly about dissatisfactions, trust is likely to be built. But such a climate usually occurs when the administrator has a positive self-concept (Bogue, 1972) and is willing to share in decision making. For example, in one district where teachers, principals, and superintendent met together to choose school goals and classroom practices, student achievement, commitment, and trust improved (Bonney, 1972).

Johnson and Johnson (1975) emphasize the need for teachers to encourage trust among students during periods of cooperative activities, and provide the following suggestions:

1.  Encourage students to contribute openly their information, ideas, thoughts, feelings, intuitions, hunches, and reactions to the group's discussion and work.
2.  Encourage students to share materials and resources.
3.  Ensure that the students have the skills to express acceptance, support, and desire to cooperate.
4.  Encourage students to express cooperative intentions, acceptance, and support toward each other during their cooperative interactions.
5.  Point out rejecting and nonsupportive behaviors that shut off future cooperation, such as silence, ridicule, superficial acknowledgement of an idea [pp. 105–106].

## High Expectations vs. Low Expectations

In schools with positive climates, teachers somehow communicate to students that they can succeed. Squires (1980) notes that "if teachers believe that all of the students in their classroom will succeed in passing the grade, learning to read, or graduating from high school, then it appears that the teacher is more likely to structure the environment in accordance with that expectation" (p. 34). There is abundant evidence (presented in Chapter 5) that teachers who expect little of their students will communicate these expectancies through verbal and nonverbal cues. Students will behave accordingly, and teachers will then have their expectations confirmed. In the positive learning climate, there is the belief that each child can succeed, that the teacher and the school have a responsibility to discover the means of communicating with each child, and that problems are not the child's fault. On the other hand, the negative learning climate seems permeated by messages of failure and blame and attributions of causes for failed learning that lie outside of the school. Intelligence levels, home environments, cultural stereotypes, and poor motivation are just some of the reasons given to justify low expectations for pupils.

## Order vs. Chaos

Part of an effective school climate is reflected by the extent to which rules are explicit and children understand them. Among other indicators, Squires (1980) notes that an effective school has a focus or direction supported by its administration, staff, and students, and that the principal provides opportunities for staff to coordinate their actions in the areas of instruction and discipline. At the classroom level time is used effectively, students master academic work, teachers plan lessons in advance, teachers start the lesson on time without interruptions, and students bring books and pencils to class. It is easy to detect the chaotic climate where rules are ambiguous, classroom time is used on activities other than instruction, and teachers and students are frequently unprepared. Communication in the orderly, goal-oriented classroom focuses primarily on instruction, while communication in the chaotic classroom focuses primarily on problems of management.

## Control vs. Frustration

Evidence indicates that in effective schools both students and teachers believe their actions can affect their futures. In fact, achievement appears to be positively related to students' sense of control over their environment (Miller and Crano, 1980; Squires, 1980). If students believe that luck is more important than hard work and that their lives have been predestined by their parents' situations or environment, they will feel little motivation to improve their lot. Likewise, if teachers feel that they have little input into decision making, a sense of hopelessness may develop. The school and classroom that are permeated with such beliefs will be characterized by frustration on the part of both students and teachers.

It is apparent from this discussion that factors which distinguish positive and negative classroom climates are influenced by the overall climate of the school. Evidence shows that in schools with positive climates, the principals serve as leaders and role models in establishing the learning environment. After examining more than 1,200 research studies, Brodbelt (1980) described leadership among the important factors that are positively related to learning, regardless of the socioeconomic status of the school. He described leadership as "the ability of the principal to frame goals and objectives, initiate programs, and obtain resources" (p. 9).

The principal is also essential in assessing needs, setting and delimiting goals for the school, and establishing a positive school climate through effective communication (Phi Delta Kappa, 1974). Principals who foster positive school climates demonstrate such characteristics as open communication (Bogue, 1972), decentralized decision making and sharing of results (Bonney, 1972), and openness to alternatives rather than "pat answers" (Doak, 1970). However, there is also evidence that some school climates are subject to many forces and may remain stable over time despite the principal; after a while negative climates may adversely affect even the good principal (Wiggins, 1972).

## MANAGING THE CLASSROOM CLIMATE

Although the principal can serve as an instructional leader in the school and is a key person in establishing the school climate, the teacher establishes the climate for the classroom. We have probably all been in schools where the climate appeared to be warm and friendly in the hallways or in the office, but where an individual classroom had an atmosphere of negativism and unfriendliness. Conversely, even in the most negative of school climates, we often find the gem of a teacher who can manage to create a positive classroom environment where students are involved in learning. Such a teacher maintains a productive, work-oriented climate, at the same time demonstrating positive interpersonal communication between teacher and students.

Admittedly the teacher is not always fully in control of some aspects of climate that affect students' classroom behaviors, since these may be strongly affected by the principal, community attitudes toward school, and the previous experiences of students. However, there is a great deal that the individual teacher can do through managing communication to establish a positive learning climate and to overcome negative factors. Four aspects that are influenced by teacher communication behaviors related to classroom climate are: (1) instruction, (2) discipline, (3) students' self-concepts, and (4) teacher morale.

### Influencing Instruction

Research findings indicate that once instructional goals are clarified and instruction is successful, many other problems, such as discipline, poor student self-concept, low teacher morale, etc., disappear. We will consider three instructional behaviors that affect the learning climate and can be influenced by the teachers's communication: (1) management of time; (2) relevance of subject matter; and (3) goal interdependence.

**Management of Time.**   People communicate a great deal through their use of time. In the United States, we tend to stick to schedules and to exert great efforts to manage and control time. Our schools are managed on the basis of time, so that children enter school at a certain age and move through designated curricula according to prescribed time patterns. Excluding education for exceptional children, few allowances are made for aptitudes and interests that permit students to learn some concepts faster than others, regardless of age. Contemporary students appear to be even more time bound than were students of the past; television with its slotted programs may be fostering children's expectations of activities occurring within given time slots. Thus, children enter school in our culture perceiving the use of time as a potent nonverbal message:

> The teacher who spends unequal amounts of time with different students and on different subjects is telling the child, "I like some students more than others, I like some topics more than others." The time provided for each student and topic thus indicates the teacher's priorities. Though subtle, this teaching of time-consciousness has powerful and long-lasting effects [Rosenfeld and Civikly, 1976, p. 199].

In recent years many research studies have been devoted to determining the amount of time that teachers allocate for given academic tasks such as reading or mathematics. Researchers also have observed classrooms to determine the amount of time students are actively engaged in the learning task. Stallings and Kaskowitz (1974) studied over 600 classroom variables and found student-engaged time to be the most important for effective classrooms. In relation to classroom climate, however, teachers often overestimate the amount of time that their students are engaged in the learning task. They may think that they have spent one hour on math, when their time was actually spent on passing out materials or disciplining students. They may think their students are listening, when they are actually daydreaming or otherwise not engaged in learning. The teacher who constantly monitors the classroom and becomes sensitive to nonverbal cues that indicate whether students are learning (or at least engaged in the learning task) will likely do the best job of managing time. When students are engaged in learning, other aspects of the climate tend to be positive.

**Relevance of Subject Matter.** While the research literature does not focus specifically on ways of adapting subject matter to students, this is an essential aspect of effective communication. If students perceive that the content does not pertain to them, their involvement remains low, and engaging them in specific learning tasks will be difficult. In classrooms with positive climates the teacher relates the subject matter to the interests and experiences of pupils.

In the authors' experiences with teachers, awareness of two principles — *concreteness* and *familiarity* — helped involve students in the classroom content, thereby changing the classroom climate. By *concreteness* we mean taking concepts that are at a relatively high order of abstraction and describing them in concrete terms, whenever possible, at the sensory levels of seeing, hearing, touching, smelling, etc. For example, teachers of social studies who teach about the Civil War might want students to role play what life was like on the southern and northern sides; they might also use pictures, field trips, descriptions from literature, and so on, to make the experiences of the Civil War concrete to children. Another principle is *familarity,* where teachers explain the unknown in terms of the known. Comparing conflict in class with conflicts in the Civil War, or describing how nerve impulses travel, using the analogy of falling dominoes (assuming students have used or seen dominoes), will help to involve students in learning. The more the teacher focuses messages on "you may remember . . ." or "imagine that you . . ." the more the child is likely to relate to new concepts.

**Goal Interdependence.** Positive classroom climates tend to be characterized by clear goals and teacher communication that helps students to attain them. Johnson and Johnson have conducted research and compiled findings on the ways in which teachers structure student learning goals and the impact of their strategies on classroom communication. Their findings are extremely important for teachers seeking to promote a productive learning climate. They define a *goal* as "a desired state of future affairs (such as completion of a math assignment)" and a *goal structure* as "the type of goal interdependence existing among students as they work toward goal accomplishment" (1978, p. 3). *Interdependence* refers to "the ways in which students will relate to each other and to the teacher in working toward the accomplishment of instructional goals" (1975, p. 7). Johnson and Johnson have described three types of goal structures:

1. ***Cooperative or Positive Interdependence.***  Exists when students perceive that they can obtain their goals when other students with whom they are linked can also obtain theirs. Examples are: When a group attempts to measure the furniture in the classroom during a math unit; when students work in teams to survey their neighborhood for opinions on political issues; when students work together to create a garden for the school yard.

2. ***Competitive or Negative Interdependence.***  Exists when students perceive that they can obtain their goals only if other students with whom they are linked fail to obtain their goals. For example, if one student wins because he or she measures classroom furniture faster than the others, all others have failed to achieve the goal. If there is a gardening contest and an individual student who gardens best wins a prize, all other students who have gardened have failed to achieve their goals.

3. ***Individualistic or No Interdependence.***  Exists when the achievement of a goal by one student is unrelated to the achievement of goals by other students — that is, whether or not a student achieves a goal has no bearing upon whether other students achieve their goals. For example, a student learns measurement, does a survey, or gardens, and does not relate to other students in the process.

   Johnson and Johnson (1975) describe the classroom climate as consisting of "the ways in which the people within the classroom interact with each other" (p. 26). Their research indicates that each of the three goal structures promotes a different pattern of interaction among students, resulting in a different learning climate. They believe that the interpersonal processes that are important for learning are: "interaction among students, mutual liking, effective communication, trust, acceptance and support, utilization of personal resources, sharing and helping, emotional involvement, coordination of effort, division of labor, divergent and risk-taking thinking" (pp. 26–27).

   While Johnson and Johnson believe that the ideal classroom should emphasize the cooperative approach, they also emphasize the need for teachers to use all three goal structures appropriately for the learning outcomes desired. They state:

> In the ideal classroom all three goal structures would be appropriately used. All students would learn how to work cooperatively with other students, compete for fun and enjoyment, and work autonomously on their own. Most of the time, however, students would work on instructional tasks within the goal structure that is most productive for the type of task to be done and for the cognitive and affective outcomes desired. It is the teacher who decides which goal structure to implement within each instructional activity. *The way in which teachers structure learning goals*

*determines how students interact with each other and with the teacher. The interaction patterns, in turn, determine the cognitive and affective outcomes of instruction* [pp. 3–4].

It is possible to use the three goal structures in combination during the course of instruction. For example, one of the authors, while teaching a methods class, asked each student teacher to review literature on communication and to list those concepts that seemed to represent a sound research base (individual goal structure). The student teachers then worked in teams to consider individual lists and to compile a master list that could be used by the class. Each team worked on a different content area, so that each team product was viewed as a needed contribution to the class (cooperative goal structure). In another context, one of the authors worked with junior high school students who were several years behind grade level in reading. She divided students into teams in which each student tried to earn points for the team (cooperative) by recognizing a word on a flash card before a member of the other team could do so (competitive). The task was skill practice; students were on the same level and had an equal chance of winning or losing; and the goal was of minimal importance. Also, since any student on the team could "yell out" the word, no one was embarrassed by the wrong answer. Therefore, the competitive approach was appropriate.

The teacher needs to use appropriate communication for all three structures. Johnson and Johnson (1975, p. 85) describe communication in the cooperative structure as encouraging the student to use other students as resources and as promoting interaction among them; the individualistic context utilizes statements that encourage the child to use the teacher as a resource; communication in the competitive structure asks "closed" questions that encourage the student to plan for strategies of winning. The cooperative structure uses nonverbal communication or spatial aspects to promote sharing of materials and "groupness," while the individualistic structure promotes the isolated space where there is the invisible "bubble" around each student that prevents intrusion by others. The teachers should learn to identify the verbal and nonverbal behaviors that promote appropriate use of each goal structure.

## Maintaining Discipline

We believe that discipline problems will be minimized if teachers can communicate so that students use time for learning, so that subject matter is adapted to the needs and interests of students, and so that students interact appropriately to achieve goals. However, managing student behavior for achieving instructional goals is one of the main concerns of teachers. Bassett and Smythe (1979) identify power discrepancies between teachers and students as a source of conflict and note that "discipline is the exercise of a teacher's power, and the strategies of discipline chosen determine much about the social climate for the classroom group" (p. 227).

We view discipline as a process of stimulating ordered, motivated behavior in students. What the teacher communicates verbally and nonverbally is the primary means of ordering and motivating. A classroom in which the teacher is indecisive about strategies for coping with deviant behavior and disruptions, or one in which teachers and students are constantly engaged in a struggle for power, is one in which teacher and pupil morale and productivity are likely to be low.

Classrooms with poor disciplinary strategies are often characterized by inconsistency in applying rewards and consequences; attempts by the teacher to become "one of the kids," thereby abandoning the leadership position; rigid rules; an atmosphere of fear and hostility; or frustration on the part of teacher and students.

Some students come to school poorly motivated or unable to participate in class activities because they cannot perform basic skills or because they are hostile toward school. These students challenge some teachers to the point at which discipline becomes the major classroom activity (Brodbelt, 1980).

While we admit that there is no cookbook available for perfecting discipline in the classroom, there are some behaviors supported by research and experience (in addition to those described in the previous section), which can be used by teachers.

**Diagnosing the Cause of Problems.**   In his analysis of research reports and other commentary on the causes of disruptive student behavior in classrooms, Swick (1977, p. 9) cites the following as major causes of disruptive student behavior:

- teacher-student value conflicts
- physical, mental, and social status of the students
- lack of teacher in-service and preservice training in classroom management
- negative influences of hostile home and community environments
- inexperience on the part of the teacher in coping with discipline problems
- malnourished children, who appear to be more prone to be disruptive than properly nourished children
- differences between teachers' expectations and students' behaviors
- teachers with insufficient self-understanding who are unable to perceive the unique personalities of individual students

In his studies of inner-city schools, Brodbelt (1980) cites problems related to classroom discipline problems. These include pupil perceptions of their parents as unsuccessful and a high turnover rate for principals and teachers. Some principals blame teacher education programs for the discipline problems, since some teachers have not been given experiences in "tough" school environments where they could develop "survival skills and strategies for remaining calm and handling street-wise pupil behavior" (p. 7). On the other hand, teachers believe that many principals neither support them in discipline problems nor enforce school rules and regulations.

In an attempt to help principals and teachers conceptualize the nature of discipline problems in their schools, Brodbelt cited pupil behaviors that are most severe — physical aggression (violence, aggression, theft, vandalism, threats, and racism) — and that are less serious — sullen and moody attitudes, smart mouthing, swearing (profanity and obscenity), clowning and showing off, restlessness, talkativeness (boisterousness, loudness), inattentiveness, lack of respect, absenteeism, and tardiness. A separate category of psychological and physical problems revolves around alcohol, drugs, hyperactivity, psychological disturbance, smoking, and bullying.

In addition, causes of continuous disruptions may lie in a handicapped student's inability to learn in a large group, inability to process large amounts of auditory or written information at once, poor self-concept, or a variety of other difficulties. If a teacher encounters such a student, the special-education person in the school or district may be a valuable resource.

Other causes of discipline problems may lie in the alienation previously mentioned or students' feelings that the subject matter does not relate to their own needs and experiences. One of the authors had occasion some years ago to supervise a student teacher who was teaching a speech class in the English curriculum. Students were ninth graders in the inner city who had long ago been turned off by school. The curriculum included reading the classics, memorizing large segments of plays, and writing themes from a list of teacher-assigned topics. The student teacher formulated a new program with a career education thrust, permitting students to develop their speaking skills by interviewing prospective employers and informing and persuading the class on a variety of careers they had explored in the library or through visits to local industries. Students also wrote themes to express their changing career aspirations. The overall goals of the English program were not changed, but they were incorporated into a new, more meaningful context for the students. In the process, they learned to communicate, stopped skipping the class, and became more interested in the total school program.

Causes of deviant behavior often lie in the prior learning problems of students. Teachers assume that because students have been passed through previous grades or curricula, they can adequately utilize the prerequisite skills for their current classes. Several researchers, such as Bloom (1976) and Bracht and Hopkins (1972), found that achievement at one grade level could be predicted from previous grade levels. Huitt and Segars (1980) stress that "unless low-scoring students are provided instruction that is responsive to what they currently know and can do, their pattern of achievement is unlikely to change" (p. 4). If a teacher does not provide learning that is appropriate to the individual, it is likely that the student will "get lost" in the instructional setting. Some may cause disruptions, while others may become nonparticipants.

**Communicating for Effective Management.**  Most writers agree that it is very ineffective for the teacher continually to threaten students, especially when those threats cannot be carried out. Others point out that when teachers work with individual students, they communicate with the entire class: Class members are witnesses to what the teachers say and do, deciding on future behaviors based on what they observe. Gnagey (1968) describes the value of control techniques that are (1) *clear,* that is, specifying the deviant, the deviancy, and the preferred alternative behavior; (2) *firm,* that is, communicating through tone of voice, facial expression, and gestures that the teacher means business; (3) *task focused,* that is, connecting the teacher's demand and the work to be accomplished. Thus, instead of saying, "I want you to be quiet during this film," the teacher might say, "You must be quiet during the film or else you will not be able to rate it afterward. We don't have time to see it a second time" (pp. 51–52).

Kounin (1970), in his studies of various classrooms, concluded that certain dimensions of teacher communication behaviors are significantly related to children's behavior in learning settings. In summary, these dimensions are:

*Awareness.*  Refers to communication that indicates the teacher knows what is going on regarding children's behavior. For example, two children in the back of the room are throwing paper airplanes while the teacher is involved in leading a reading group. The teacher continues focusing on the group, but says, "John, Vera, I see you. Get back to work now!"

*Overlapping.*  Refers to the teacher's handling of two matters at the same time. For example, the teacher is listening to a student recite, while another student is passing notes in the back of the room. The teacher, whose manner continues to indicate a listening attitude to the student, moves closer to the desk of the misbehaving student and removes the note.

*Smoothness and Momentum.*    Refers to the teacher's management of movement and activity in the classroom. Problems of movement can occur when the teacher exhibits the following nonverbal behaviors:

*Jerkiness.*    Teacher actions that produce sudden stops in the activity flow. For example, the teacher asks Joan to explain to the class how she solved an arithmetic problem. While Joan is speaking, the teacher sees some crayons out of place and asks, "Who left crayons out of the box?" After engaging in a talk about the need for neatness in the classroom, the teacher returns to Joan's explanation, but has broken the flow of activity in the classroom.

*Slowdowns.*    Teacher actions that hold back activity in the classroom, as in the following dialogue recorded by Kounin (1970, p. 95):

> The teacher is starting a lesson about telling time and is walking toward the blackboard, saying: "I have some times on the board I would like you to designate on the clocks that you're going to make yourself." Margaret groaned softly. The teacher turned to Margaret and *slowly* said: "Now, Margaret, did you come to school to learn?" The teacher paused for about three seconds, looking at Margaret. "Is it so painful, Margaret?" Another pause. "No, I don't think so. Your parents are going to want you to tell time." Pause. "And you're going to be very happy to learn telling time, Margaret. You don't have to make all those groans because you don't want to tell time. But, after all, if your mother sees you can tell time you might get a watch of your own." The teacher then turned to the whole class, saying: "Let us all sit up tall," and resumed the lesson.

In discussing discipline, we have emphasized the need for development of an appropriate communication style. This implies that successful classroom management, while based upon some scientific (that is, regularly occurring) principles, is an art that develops over time. Kindsvatter and Levine (1980) have emphasized that successful discipline cannot be based upon quick solutions or gimmicks, but must be based upon principles of teacher and student behavior that underlie classroom management. They also believe that many teachers have difficulty with defiant children because of their personalities and that not all teachers can learn effective discipline:

> Effective classroom discipline grows out of the teacher's leadership qualities, group process skills, and the mutual respect that exists in the classroom. However, the extent to which a teacher can be an effective leader, can acquire and employ principles of group process, and can promote a condition of mutual respect depends upon the existence of that potential within the teacher's personality [p. 691].

However, we maintain that the group process skills needed for effective discipline can be learned and applied by most people who are motivated to become teachers.

**Communicating to Promote Long-Range Changes in Behavior.**    Some of the most successful strategies for behavior change come from the area of behavior modification that works on principles of positive reinforcement for desired behaviors. We are not advocating that a classroom be established using a pure behavior modification model. Such a model is often necessary in classrooms for learning-disabled or emotionally disturbed children, where the goal is to change many inappropriate behaviors. However, many of the principles of behavior modification can be adapted to the regular classroom to change specific undesirable pupil behaviors. We now discuss several of these principles.

*Positive Reinforcement Principle.   To improve or increase a child's performance of a certain activity, immediately reward the correct performance and ignore incorrect perform-ances.*

For example, if a child is continually late to class, the teacher may not only comment on how nice it is to have the child there on time, but also may make that child attendance monitor. There are many reinforcers the teacher can use, such as permitting individual children to do something they enjoy (recess, reminding the teacher that it is lunchtime, playing a game, and so on). However, many of the most potent reinforcers can be given through the teacher's verbal and nonverbal behaviors.

Some verbal responses that teachers might use are: "that's super, good point, good for you, thank you for _____, good thinking, I really like the way you are working" (Hayes and Stevenson, 1980, p. 62).

Some nonverbal signs of approval that might serve as reinforcers are: "sitting on a desk near a student, patting on the back or shoulder, signaling O.K., winking, smiling" (Hayes and Stevenson, 1980, p. 62).

*Satiation Principle.   To stop a child from acting in a particular way, allow them to continue (or insist that they continue) performing the undesired acts until they tire of them.* (Krumboltz and Krumboltz, 1972, p. 139).

For example, in a class that was noisy and refused to settle down to work, the teacher made it clear that students should continue their behavior and that she would return when they were ready to work. Students continued their noise for a period of time, but eventually became bored. When the teacher returned, they were quiet and ready to work. Using the same principle, a father whose children were fighting in the backseat of the car stopped the car and insisted that they go on fighting. For a time the children continued their fighting; every time they stopped, the father insisted that they continue, and made it clear that he would not drive while they fought. After a while the children became tired of staying in a parked car and begged their father to drive so that they could get to their outing.

*Extinction Principle.   To stop children from acting in a particular way, arrange conditions so that they receive no rewards following the undesired act* (Krumboltz and Krumboltz, 1972, p. 155).

If children scream when they want something and parents pay no attention whatsoever to the children at the time the screaming occurs (later responding only when appropriate requests are made), eventually the children will find no rewards in this behavior and will stop screaming. In the classroom, however, it is difficult to stop all reinforcers, since other children might respond to the offender even if the teacher does not. A wise teacher used the following strategy:

> Ginger would not wait her turn to share ideas in the third grade classroom but would interrupt whoever was talking whenever she thought of something to say. The teacher discussed with the class the rules for sharing ideas, and the class agreed on a "courtesy rule" of raising hands and waiting turns before sharing ideas during class discussion. Even though she had taken part in establishing the new courtesy rule, in the next class discussion Ginger again broke the rule.

The class then agreed that they simply would not listen to anyone who broke the courtesy rule. When Ginger interrupted, the teacher and the class would try not to look at her or give any indication that they heard but would continue to devote their attention to the person who had permission to speak. After being ignored three times in a row, Ginger stopped interrupting, raised her hand, and waited her turn to speak [Krumboltz and Krumboltz, 1972, p. 160].

*Positive Practice Principle.*   *To change a behavior, have the student practice a corrected behavior when a mistake has been made* (Azrin and Besalel, 1981).

This practice involves stopping all activities when a mistake has been made and carefully performing the correct behavior several times. It differs from punishment because the child is given an explanation of why the practice is needed, and it is established as a routine method of dealing with problem behavior. The child is given feedback when the correct behavior is practiced. The teacher's verbal and nonverbal behavior should communicate guidance rather than anger and criticism. For example, Joe was a third grader who constantly blurted out and interrupted other students when they spoke. Joe knew that he was supposed to wait his turn because he had done it on several occasions. The teacher decided to try positive practice by discussing with Joe what the new rules would be. Whenever Joe interrupted, the teacher had him stop and practice raising his hand and listening to find out whether another student was speaking. He had him practice that five or ten times. The practice started immediately after Joe blurted out. The teacher was always calm and nonpunishing in tone. It became easier for Joe to raise his hand than to go through the practice. When Joe stopped blurting out and started raising his hand on his own, the teacher was careful to call on him to reinforce the behavior.

There are many other aspects to behavior modification, with strategies too numerous to describe here. The teacher wishing to establish an orderly climate for learning would do well to read one of the numerous books on the subject or to take a course that offers applications to classroom behavior. The important point to remember when attempting to change behavior is to *be consistent* and to *promise only those reinforcers or consequences that you can deliver.*

## Influencing Students' Self-Concepts

Among the most important aspects of school and classroom climate are the students' self-concepts, which include their feelings about themselves as learners and as human beings in general. Many writers have noted the relationship between climate and students' self-concepts (Clark, 1977; Howard, 1974). Beane, Lipka, and Ludewig (1980), in reviewing research on self-concept, report that variables related to self-concept are "school achievement, perceived social status among peers, participation in class discussions . . . and self-direction in learning" (p. 85). We have summarized some of their findings that have implications for communication:

The custodial climate (characterized by concern for maintenance of order, preference for autocratic procedures, student stereotyping, punitive sanctions, and impersonalness) seems to have a negative effect on self-concept, while the *humanistic climate* (characterized by participation in decision making, respect, fairness, self-discipline, interaction, and flexibility), seems to have a positive effect.

Self-concept appears to be positively affected by *multi-age interactions,* such as tutoring of younger children or involvement of elderly people in the schools, whereas age isolation may have a detrimental effect.

*Working with parents* seems to help in self-concept development, especially through parenting workshops, conferences, and the promotion of parent teaching at home.

*Cooperatively made rules,* as opposed to imposed rules, have a more positive effect on self-concept because they enhance students' sense of control over their lives.

*Pupil self-evaluation,* rather than exclusively adult evaluation, tends to foster positive self-concept. (Logs, personal journals, and reports that include statements by the students of what they have learned are examples.)

Evidence demonstrates that students' success rate in the classroom is a factor in distinguishing between ineffective and effective schools (Huitt and Segars, 1980) and thus can have an impact on the students' self-concepts and attitudes toward learning. Fisher, Marliave, and Filby (1979) found that, on the average, students spend only 50% of their time on tasks that provide for high success and that students in high success activities achieve better than expected in reading and mathematics. Thus, to influence the self-concepts of students, teachers might structure their learning activities so that students experience the least amount of errors. This does not mean that learning should be made too easy, but that students should be able to experience the "right answers" most of the time because content is appropriately adapted to their prior learning levels and their current ability levels. The more success students experience, the more they are likely to want to learn and the greater the level of achievement will be. The most important aspect, however, is that success is likely to develop positive feelings of self.

Some ways of improving students' self-concepts have already been suggested, namely, well-prepared lessons, adapted to individual student levels, that produce frequent opportunities for success. Believing that students can learn and caring about their success are important attitudes that are quickly communicated to students. Most students, even the ones about to drop out, really *want to learn.* The belief that they never will learn prompts their disruptive behavior and their wish to "drop out." Del Polito (1973) has described the way in which an individual's self-concept develops through interactions with others, primarily the significant others who provide rewards and punishments and who can forge the individual's perception of self. Obviously, the teacher serves that role for students.

Belief in a child's ability can be expressed in many ways. The daughter of one of the authors was blessed with a fourth-grade teacher whose pupils felt especially cared about in her class. During an illness that kept the teacher out of class for over a week, some of the children sent her cards and letters. The teacher answered each of them, one in the following manner:

Dear Marla,

Returning to school on Monday and receiving your greeting card and poem made me feel very special.

I love to read your poetry — you are truly very talented.

Please let's keep in touch after this year. I am going to follow your achievements with interest and love.

Thank you, dear Marla
Margaret J.

## Maintaining Teacher Morale

In recent years, a great deal has been written about the effects of teacher morale, stress, and burnout in relation to the school and classroom climate. While we cannot present an exhaustive review of the literature on this topic, within the context of this chapter we will attempt to summarize some of the reasons for lowered morale and some communication strategies that have been used in coping with burnout.

**Evidence of a Morale Problem.**   Burnout involves "physical, emotional and attitudinal exhaustion generated by excessive demands upon the individual's energy, emotion or resources" (Georgia Professional Standards Commission, 1980, p. 3). Some symptoms attributed to burnout are diminished pleasure in teaching, increased use of sick leave, drug and alcohol consumption, irritability, fatigue, depression, insomnia, and physical problems such as migraine headaches, ulcers, and back pain. Other articles ("Teacher Burnout," *NJEA Review,* 1979; Bloch, 1978) have compared teacher burnout to combat fatigue experienced by soliders in battle.

Walsh (1979) reported that 56.6% of 5,500 respondents in a Chicago teachers' union stress survey claimed physical and/or mental illness as a direct result of their jobs. In Tacoma, Washington, the teachers' association won stress insurance for its members.

In a case history of her own "pain" of burnout, Bardo (1979) describes her feelings of frustration with teaching:

> Yet, no matter how brilliant the lessons I prepared, no matter how much I personally cared for learning, no matter how expensive the tools I brought to my classroom, little learning could occur when the students didn't care to learn. Unable to learn for them, unable to sit at my desk and ignore them, I found the only solution for me was to quit teaching [p. 253].

**Reasons for Morale Problems.**   Many educators have described the reasons for teacher burnout (Georgia Professional Standards Commission, 1980; Keef, 1979; Mazer and Griffin, 1980; Mead, 1980; Truch, 1980; Wilhelm, 1980). Among the most frequently cited reasons are:

- fear of physical and psychological harm — that is, responses to threats of violence and unsafe schools
- professional and personal disillusionment with the teaching profession
- discipline problems, that is, feelings of being unable to manage the students in the classroom
- lack of support from superiors, especially the principal
- public criticism of education and attitudes of low esteem for teachers
- poor teacher preparation to face the reality of the classroom
- staff imbalance caused by shifting enrollments, leading to a stagnant older staff and too many inexperienced teachers
- insecurities caused by economic factors such as teacher layoffs, collective bargaining issues, involuntary transfers to other schools, and low salaries
- lack of opportunities for teacher participation in decision making
- classes that are too large
- lack of job mobility
- poor student motivation

Other writers have also noted the added conditions of stress for special education teachers who must deal with especially difficult learners (Ingram, 1980; Shaw *et al.,* 1980). In an editorial, NEA President Willard H. McGuire (1979) reported:

> Violence and vandalism are just two of the many problems teachers face. No wonder fear, insecurity, and anxiety are replacing the joy of teaching. The ultimate result is teacher dropouts. Too many teachers are feeling burned out and ignored. They want to teach. They want their classrooms to crackle with excitement. But they face too many students who won't do their homework and too many parents who say they can't control their children's home study habits and many school boards who cut supplies and equipment from the budget and too many supervisors who say "live with it" when teachers try to get special help for a disruptive child [p. 5].

Problems of low morale and burnout seem to be increasing as resources diminish and the public demands better accountability.

**Improving Morale Through Better Communication.**   Despite the difficulties described in the foregoing section, some positive approaches have been taken to help solve problems of burnout.

*Establishing Support of the Administrator.*   Most observers of the burnout problem indicate that the administrator can help by allowing teachers to feel more of a sense of control and to have greater input into decision making in the schools.

The Safe School Study sponsored by the National Institute of Education (1977) found that effective school governance, particularly by the principal, can help greatly in reducing school crime. The leadership of the principal and the establishment of a structure of order differentiated safe schools from those having trouble. Principals who were available to students and staff and who had fair and consistent styles of governance seemed to be able to change schools experiencing violence.

Bruscemi (1979) suggests that stress can be reduced by creating an atmosphere of calm and order; avoiding unclear and unexpected messages; maintaining high expectations of staff; adopting good listening techniques; and using a systematic and constructive feedback system.

*Establishing Support from Professional Organizations.*   The American Federation of Teachers has taken action on several fronts to meet the problems of teacher burnout, including design of local programs to increase teacher input and studies of the problems of stress (Newell, 1981). The National Education Association (1979) has undertaken similar activities for its members and has passed a resolution on Stress on Teachers and Other School Personnel, urging "its local affiliates in cooperation with local school authorities, to develop stress-management programs that will facilitate the recognition, prevention, and treatment of stress-related problems" and further urging that effects of stress be recognized, demanding "procedures that will ensure confidentiality and treatment without personal jeopardy" (p. 36).

*Establishing Assistance for Teachers in Stress Management.*   Sparks (1979) describes an excellent teacher program at the Northwest Staff Development Center for helping teachers to reduce feelings of isolation, to identify sources of job-related stress, and to identify professional strengths and successful work experiences that they can draw on to increase their satisfaction with teaching and to form a plan to prevent or alleviate distress.

Teachers themselves have described productive approaches to stress reduction, such as yoga, meditation, and biofeedback. Moe (1979) suggests getting exercise and enough sleep, doing things you enjoy in your spare time, and setting realistic goals. Others emphasize the importance of identifying and facing problems and developing a sense of humor in the classroom. One teacher, responding to problems of burnout, stated: "For me at least the challenge and the delight of teaching remain as valid and fulfilling as I found them. But after all, change is one good definition of being alive" (Freeman, 1979, p. 56).

## COMMUNICATION BEHAVIORS FOR AN EFFECTIVE CLIMATE

Much of the content in this chapter has focused on factors that influence effective learning climates. We now focus on those aspects of the individual teacher's communication behavior that can have a positive influence on the learning climate.

### Reducing the Frequency of Negative Messages

Blame, criticism, and constant evaluative comments tend to produce withdrawal and defensiveness on the part of students. Classrooms where the teacher's messages are mostly negative are characterized by conflicts, tension, and poor productivity.

### Increasing the Frequency of Positive Messages

As indicated earlier, the more verbal reinforcement the student gets for good behavior, the more likely is that behavior to increase in frequency. As a teacher, you might ask a colleague to observe your teaching and to count the number of negative and positive comments you make within a period or portion of the day. Then consciously try to increase the number of positive messages and to decrease the number of negative messages. You should note a change in the climate of your classroom.

### Using "You-Related" Messages That Teach

Think of the students as an audience that you wish to involve in the subject matter you are teaching. The effective teacher provides the link between the subject matter and the students. In rhetorical theory, this process is called "audience adaptation."

### Using "I" Messages That Take Responsibilities for Feelings

Human relations programs typically advocate direct rather than indirect expressions of feelings. Statements such as "I feel annoyed when you touch my things" (direct expression) are better than "You are always in places where you shouldn't be. You are so stubborn about obeying my rules" (an indirect expression of feeling). Direct expressions of feelings show that the speaker is taking responsibility for feelings, and that the other person has the choice of whether or not to continue the behavior that is bothersome. Statements such as "I feel angry" (frustrated, happy, sad, or whatever) help children to learn empathic responses and the nonverbal cues that indicate emotions in others.

## Using Feedback Constructively

Johnson (1972) suggests many principles for giving nonthreatening feedback that are of use to teachers. These include: (1) focusing feedback on behavior rather than on the person — for example, "John talked a great deal during class today," rather than "John is a loudmouth"; (2) focusing feedback on observations rather than inferences — for example, "You hit three children on the playground," rather than "You don't seem to like your classmates today"; and (3) focusing feedback on behavior related to a specific situation, preferably to the "here and now" rather than on behavior in the abstract or the "there and then." For example, statements such as "You have always been a troublemaker in this class" are not very helpful; it is better to say, "Sally, you are interrupting and making it difficult for others to talk."

## Criticizing the Behavior and Not the Pupil

In an effective learning climate, pupils must feel they can change behavior; to attack personality or inherent characteristics is to leave a pupil feeling frustrated and likely to be more of a behavior problem. Labeling children as "poor spellers" or "class clowns" will lead to reinforcement of those images. It is better to analyze with the pupil any spelling errors or disruptions, and help to eliminate them, than to have the pupil attain a reputation for a pattern of behaviors.

It is better to say, "Your homework isn't done. You know the rule; must stay after school to do it," than to say, "You are so lazy. You just aren't trying to get through this course."

It is better to say, "We cannot learn in this class because you are being too noisy. You will have to leave until you can learn with us," than to say: "Why are you always disrupting this class? If you want to be the class clown, fine! But don't expect to amount to much in this life."

## Maintaining Awareness of the Impact of Nonverbal Behaviors

Throughout this chapter, we have mentioned teacher behaviors such as touching, voice cues, use of furniture arrangements, and other nonverbal aspects that affect climate. Much of the climate in the classroom and the school is established through *how* we say something, how we look when we say it, where we stand in relation to others, and so on. You may wish to have a colleague videotape you while you are teaching. You may be surprised at the number of times you smile or frown, your degree of movement around the room, or the tone of your voice. The more you become aware of the impact of the nonverbal message, the more you can do to improve classroom climate.

# SUMMARY

This chapter discussed aspects of the school and classroom climate that can be influenced through the teacher's communication. Climate was defined as *the perceived atmosphere of the school or classroom that manifests itself in the feelings or opinions of observers or participants in the education process.* Effective climates are characterized by openness, confidence, acceptance, a sense of belonging, trust, high expectations, order, and a sense of control; ineffective climates are characterized by defensiveness, fear, rejection, alienation, suspicion, low expectations, chaos, and frustration. The principal is a key person in establishing a positive school climate through behaviors such as open communication, decentralized decision making and sharing of results, and openness to a variety of alternatives to problems.

Four aspects of classroom climate that are directly influenced by teacher behaviors are instruction, discipline, students' self-concept, and teacher morale. The teacher's verbal and nonverbal communication behaviors affect these aspects of climate and establish positive or negative conditions for learning. Since the teacher is responsible for the classroom climate and the principal is responsible for establishing the school climate, the whole staff must work together to implement strategies for productive communication.

# Discussion Questions

1. What communication behaviors of the teacher foster characteristics of effective school and classroom climates? Conversely, what communication behaviors of the teacher foster characteristics of ineffective climates?
2. How can effective teacher communication alleviate instructional problems such as insufficient time spent on the learning task, irrelevant subject matter, expectations of failure, and unclear goals?
3. Contrast two teachers: one exemplifying effective disciplinary strategies and the other ineffective disciplinary strategies. What are the differences in their verbal and nonverbal communication behaviors?
4. Describe an actual or hypothetical case of a child who exemplifies disruptive behavior in the classroom. Identify the probable causes for the behaviors. How might you employ behavior modification strategies to change specific behaviors? What communication behaviors might you, as the teacher, use to change the child's behavior?

5. Describe either a school that you believe fosters positive self-concepts in children or one that fosters negative self-concepts. Using the research synthesis on self-concept by Beane, Lipka, and Ludewig (1980), describe those factors that appear to be present in the school you have described.

6. After reviewing the reasons for poor teacher morale and burnout, discuss those factors that might be alleviated through improved communication in the classroom, school, community, or teaching profession. Develop a plan that will help you to prevent burnout and to maintain your productivity.

# References

Azrin, Nathan, and Victoria Besalel. *How to Use Positive Practice.* Lawrence, Kan.: H & H Enterprises, Inc., 1981.

Bardo, Pamela. "The Pain of Teacher Burnout: A Case History." *Phi Delta Kappan,* Vol. 61, No. 4 (December 1979): 252–254.

Bassett, Ronald E., and Mary-Jeanette Smythe. *Communication and Instruction.* New York: Harper & Row, Publishers, 1979.

Beane, James A., Richard P. Lipka, and Joan W. Ludewig. "Synthesis of Research on Self-Concept." *Educational Leadership,* Vol. 38 (October 1980): 84–89.

Bloch, Alfred. "Combat Neurosis in Inner City Schools." *American Journal of Psychiatry* Vol. 135, No. 10 (October 1978): 1189–1192.

Bloom, B. S. *Human Characteristics and Student Learning.* New York: McGraw-Hill, Inc., 1976.

Bogue, E. G. "One Foot in the Stirrup," *Phi Delta Kappan,* Vol. 53, No. 8 (April 1972): 506–508.

Bonney, Lewis A. "Changes in Organizational Climate Associated with Development and Implementation of an Educational Management System." 1972. ERIC Document #066790.

Bracht, G. H., and K. D. Hopkins. "Stability of Educational Achievement." In *Perspectives in Educational and Psychological Measurement,* G. H. Bracht, K. D. Hopkins, and J. C. Stanley, eds. Englewood Cliffs, N.J.: Prentice-Hall, Inc., 1972, pp. 254–261.

Brodbelt, Samuel. "Effective Discipline: A Consideration for Improving Inner City Schools." *Clearing House,* Vol. 54, No. 1 (September 1980): 5–9.

Bruscemi, John N. "Reducing Stress in Classroom Teachers: An Administrative Model." Paper presented at the Annual Meeting of the National Middle Schools Association, Dearborn, Mich., October 31–November 3, 1979. ERIC Document #184244.

Clark, Frank J. "Improving the School Climate: Operations Notebook 19." Association of California School Administrators, October 1977. ERIC Document #145567.

Del Polito, C. M. "The Development, Implementation, and Evaluation of Self-Concept Enhancement Programs." Doctoral dissertation, Purdue University, 1973.

Doak, E. Dale. "Organizational Climate: Prelude to Change." *Educational Leadership,* Vol. 27, No. 4 (January 1970): 367–371.

Fisher, C., R. Marliave, and N. Filby. "Improving Teaching by Increasing 'Academic Learning Time.'" *Educational Leadership,* Vol. 37, No. 1 (1979): 52–54.

Freeman, Jayne. "The Joy of Teaching: Another Case History." *Phi Delta Kappan,* Vol. 61, No. 4 (December 1979): 254–256.

Galbo, Joseph J. "It Bears Repeating: Adolescent Alienation in Secondary Schools: A Literature Review." *High School Journal,* Vol. 64, No. 1 (October 1980): 26–31.

Georgia Professional Standards Commission. *Teacher Satisfaction in Georgia and the Nation: Status and Trends. Teacher Burnout: Causes and Possible Cures.* Issues for Education Series. Atlanta, 1980. ERIC Docment #194515.

Gibb, Jack. "Defensive Communication." *Journal of Communication,* Vol. 11, No. 2 (1961): 141–148.

Gnagey, William J. *The Psychology of Discipline in the Classroom.* New York: The Macmillan Company, 1968.

Hartley, M. C., and W. K. Hoy. "'Openness' of School Climate and Alienation of High School Students." *California Journal of Educational Research,* Vol. 23, No. 1 (1972): 17–24.

Hayes, Rosa P., and Merice G. Stevenson. *Teaching the Emotionally Disturbed/Learning Disabled Child: A Practical Guide.* Vol. I: *Developing Behavior, Instructional and Affective Programs.* Washington, D.C.: Acropolis Books, 1980.

Howard, Eugene R. "School Climate Improvement." *Thrust for Educational Leadership,* Vol. 3, No. 3 (January 1974): 12–14.

Huitt, William G., and John K. Segars. *Characteristics of Effective Schools.* Philadelphia: Research for Better Schools, Inc., October 1980.

Ingram, Leslie A. "Teacher Burnout in Special Education: The Personal Perspective of a Classroom Teacher." Paper presented at the Annual International Convention of the Council for Exceptional Children, Philadelphia, Pa., April, 1980. ERIC Document #187073.

Johnson, David W. *Reaching Out.* Englewood Cliffs, N.J.: Prentice-Hall, Inc., 1972.

Johnson, David W., and Roger T. Johnson. "Cooperative, Competitive and Individualistic Learning." *Journal of Research and Development in Education,* Vol. 12, No. 1 (1978): 3–15.

Johnson, David W., and Roger T. Johnson. *Learning Together and Alone: Cooperation, Competition and Individualization.* Englewood Cliffs, N.J.: Prentice-Hall, Inc., 1975.

Keef, James L. "Teacher Restlessness and Decision Making." *Clearinghouse,* Vol. 52, No. 9 (May 1979): 410–412.

Kindsvatter, Richard, and Mary Ann Levine. "The Myths of Discipline." *Phi Delta Kappan,* Vol. 61 (June 1980): 690–693.

Kounin, Jacob S. *Discipline and Group Management in Classrooms.* New York: Holt, Rinehart and Winston, Inc., 1970.

Krumboltz, John D., and Helen B. Krumboltz. *Changing Children's Behavior.* Englewood Cliffs, N.J.: Prentice-Hall, Inc., 1972.

Maynard, William. "A Case Study: The Impact of a Humanistic School Climate." *National Association of Secondary School Principals Bulletin,* Vol. 60, No. 399 (April 1976): 16–20.

Mazer, Irene R., and Marjorie Griffin. "Perceived and Experienced Stress of Teachers in a Medium Sized Local School District." Paper presented at the Annual Meeting of the American Educational Research Association, Boston, Mass., April 7–11, 1980. ERIC Document #186379.

McGuire, Willard H. "Teacher Burnout." *Today's Education,* Vol. 68, No. 4 (November–December 1979): 5.

Mead, Ramsay O. "A Teacher's Tale: Why We Are Miserable." *American School Board Journal,* Vol. 167, No. 9 (September 1980): 37–40.

Miller, Stephen K., and William D. Crano. "Raising Low-Income/Minority Achievement by Reducing Student Sense of Academic Futility: The Underlying Theoretical Commonalities of Suggested Strategies." Paper presented at the Annual Meeting of the American Educational Research Association, Boston, Mass., April 7–11, 1980. ERIC Document #186575.

Moberly, David. "Compulsory Attendance: A Second Look." *High School Journal,* Vol. 63 (February 1980): 195–199.

Moe, Dorothy. "Teacher Burnout: A Prescription." *Today's Education,* Vol. 68, No. 4 (November–December 1979): 35–36.

"National Education Association Resolution E79–81: Stress on Teachers and Other School Personnel." *Today's Education,* Vol. 68, No. 4 (November–December 1979): 36.

National Institute of Education. *Violent Schools — Safe Schools.* The Safe School Study Report to the Congress, U.S. Department of Health, Education and Welfare, Washington, D.C., 1977.

Newell, R. C. "Teacher Stress and Burnout: Learning to Survive in the Classroom." *American Teacher,* Vol. 65, No. 5 (February 1981): 6–7.

Phi Delta Kappa. *School Climate Improvement: A Challenge to the School Administrator.* An occasional paper. Bloomington, Ind., 1974. ERIC Document #102665.

Rosenfeld, Lawrence B., and Jean M. Civikly. *With Words Unspoken: The Nonverbal Experience.* New York: Holt, Rinehart and Winston, Inc., 1976.

Rotter, Julian B. "Trust and Gullibility." *Psychology Today,* Vol. 14, No. 5 (October 1980): 35–42, 102.

Shaw, Stan, *et al.* "Preventing Teacher Burnout: Suggestions for Efficiently Meeting PL 94–142 Mandates and Providing for Staff Survival." Paper presented at the Annual International Convention of the Council for Exceptional Children, Philadelphia, Pa., April 1980. ERIC Document #187048.

Sparks, Dennis. "Teacher Burnout: A Teacher Center Tackles the Issue." *Today's Education,* Vol. 68, No. 4 (November–December 1979): 37–39.

Squires, David A. *Characteristics of Effective Schools: The Importance of School Processes.* Philadelphia: Research for Better Schools, Inc., October, 1980.

Stallings, J. A., and D. Kaskowitz. *Follow Through Classroom Observation Evaluation, 1972–1973.* Menlo Park, Cal.: Stanford Research Institute, 1974.

Swick, Kevin J. *Maintaining Productive Student Behavior.* Reference and Resource Series. Washington, D.C.: National Education Association of the United States, 1977.

"Teacher Burnout." *NJEA Review,* Vol. 53, No. 1 (September 1979): 10–13.

Timm, Paul R. *Managerial Communication: A Finger on the Pulse.* Englewood Cliffs, N.J.: Prentice-Hall, Inc., 1980.

Truch, Stephen. *Teacher Burnout and What to Do about It.* 1980. ERIC Document #194464.

Walsh, Debbie. "Classroom Stress and Teacher Burnout." *Phi Delta Kappan,* Vol. 61, No. 4 (December 1979): 253.

Wiggins, Thomas W. "A Comparative Investigation of Principal Behavior and School Climate." *Journal of Educational Research,* Vol. 66, No. 3 (1972): 103–105.

Wilhelm, David. "A Proposal for the Professional Entries and Exits of Classroom Teachers." *Clearinghouse,* Vol. 54, No. 2 (October 1980): 63–65.

# For Further Reading

Anderson, Carolyn S. "The Search for School Climate: A Review of the Research." *Review Educational Research,* Vol. 52, No. 3 (1981): 368–420.

Lindelow, John, and JoAnn Mazzarella. *School Climate: Another Perspective.* Burlinga Foundation for Educational Administration under the auspices of ERIC Clea Educational Management, 1982.

Reynolds, Maynard C., ed. *Social Environment of the Schools.* Reston, Va.: The C Children, under the auspices of the ERIC Clearinghouse on Handicap 1980.

Sparks, Dennis, and Janice Hammond. *Managing Teacher Stress and Burnout*. Reston, Va., and Washington, D.C.: American Alliance for Health, Physical Education, Recreation and Dance and the ERIC Clearinghouse on Teacher Education, February 1981.

# Communication Development: Implications for Instruction

*focus*   STUDENT COMMUNICATION SKILLS THAT INFLUENCE THE TEACHING/LEARNING PROCESS

THE PROCESS OF COMMUNICATION DEVELOPMENT

ASPECTS OF COMMUNICATION DEVELOPMENT
Development of Sounds
Development of Words
Development of Syntax
Development of Semantics
Development of Nonverbal Communication
Development of Functional Communication
Strategies for Learning
Impact of Selective Perception

SPECIAL PROBLEMS
Organic Problems
Learning Disabilities
Communication Apprehension

THE TEACHER'S ROLE IN COMMUNICATION DEVELOPMENT

This chapter focuses on student communication skills that influence the teaching/learning process. The focus is specifically on the ways in which children develop the communication skills that enable them to participate in social and instructional processes. If the ability to speak and listen or to interact with others is impaired, the child will experience difficulty in learning in most academic areas, and will suffer in social relationships and career contexts. To explain how the child develops communication, we examine (1) the processes by which children develop communication, (2) aspects of communication development, (3) special problems in development, and (4) the teacher's role in fostering communication development.

# THE PROCESS OF COMMUNICATION DEVELOPMENT

The small baby hears many sounds from the environment — doors closing, mother or father speaking or singing, the dog barking. At first, these sounds apparently merge one into the other in what has been called a "booming, buzzing confusion." It takes some time before the baby can interpret the sounds, sort them out, and give them meaning. However, evidence suggests that at birth the child can distinguish speech sounds from other acoustic signals. The brain is apparently "programmed for speech," even though the baby cannot yet produce speech sounds. Because of the high positioning of the vocal folds at birth and the large size of the tongue in relation to the rest of the oral cavity, the child cannot at first produce speech (Wood, 1981). However, as the physiology changes and speech reproduction is possible, a typical course of speech development will occur, *providing the child has opportunities for interaction with other human beings.*

Well-documented cases illustrate what happens to speech development when children are not able to interact with other human beings. One case occurred in the early nineteenth century and involved Victor, "the wild boy of Aveyron," who was found in a French forest at about age twelve, having survived with animals in the wild, apparently from infancy. At an institution for deaf-mutes, he came under the care of a physician, Jean Itard, who diligently tried to teach him to speak. Although he was not deaf, Victor was not able to learn to speak. A possible throat injury might have prevented speech learning, but the primary difficulty lay in the total lack of human interaction during the boy's critical years of development (Lane, 1976).

Cases like this and other evidence led some researchers to believe that humans may have a potential for language built into their brains, and that this potential must be stimulated by exposure to language at critical times in the child's development and well before puberty. If these critical moments are lost, it is thought, the child can never develop mature communication skills. However, the notion of critical learning periods is not entirely clear from current research evidence. Another case of an isolated child involved Genie, who was found in 1970 in California at the age of thirteen. She had apparently been imprisoned by her mentally ill father in a small room and had not been spoken to since infancy. She was described by Pines (1981) as follows:

> When Genie arrived in Children's Hospital in November 1970, she was a pitiful, malformed, incontinent, unsocialized, and severely malnourished creature. . . . She could not straighten her arms or legs. She did not know how to chew. She salivated a great deal and spent much of her time spitting. And she was eerily silent [p. 29].

From 1970 to 1980 Genie became the subject of intense efforts by psychologists, linguists, neurologists, and others who study brain development to teach her to speak and to learn about human communication in the process. Eventually, Genie could utter simple sentences, but she never learned to ask questions; and her speech was often garbled. While Genie proved that some language could be learned after critical periods had passed, she failed to master the grammatical principles of speech. However, she was good at such tasks as recognizing facial features and color, shape, and size of objects. While Genie made little progress on the tasks governed by the left-brain hemisphere (such as grammatical rules, auditory memory, and abstract thinking), she did perform well on tasks governed by the right-brain hemisphere (such as visual memory, facial recognition, drawing). Thus, on the basis of this case and other evidence, it is possible that there are critical periods for the development of the left hemisphere, which governs language, and that if such development fails, learning of another sort can still proceed in the right hemisphere, although language disorders will prevail.

Evidence also reinforces the importance of human interaction in speech and communication learning. While children are born with the ability to hear speech and with the potential for reproducing it, they must imitate and interact with human models in order to learn to communicate. Furthermore, it is important for teachers to understand that children will speak the dialect, with its phonology, grammar, and syntax, that they have heard. Value judgments about intelligence, creativity, and communication competence based upon dialect are therefore never justified. Furthermore, while language learning can occur if models are imitated, *communication* learning (the use of speech for specific functions) occurs in relation to others through interactions in daily contexts.

Children learn language in the context of communicating, and, conversely, learn communication strategies while they are learning the fundamentals of language and connected speech. For example, a fourteen-month-old child who accompanied his mother to a health club engaged in the following dialogue:

CHILD:    Ooh, fowa (as he notices the flowered wallpaper).
MOTHER:    Yes, those are pretty flowers.
CHILD:    (excitedly, hitting various flowers on the wall) Fowa, fowa, petty fowa.
MOTHER:    (pointing) Look! Here's a yellow flower. Here's a blue flower. Lots of flowers.
CHILD:    Boo fowa.
MOTHER:    Yes, those are just like the blue flowers in our kitchen.
CHILD:    (thoughtful) Fowa, tshen. Wan' fowa.

The child most probably could not make the connection to the flowers at home, but through interaction he was expanding his knowledge of colors and of language structure at the same time that he was learning to communicate his feelings and wants.

Many writers have described the process that children go through in developing speech and language abilities (see, for example, Hopper and Naremore, 1978; Wood, 1981). Unlike the processes of reading and writing, speaking and listening are biological heritages; that is, as long as the child's physical development is normal and there are communicative human beings in the environment, the child will learn to speak. Other people act as prods to the child's learning, but imitation and interaction occur naturally.

# ASPECTS OF COMMUNICATION DEVELOPMENT

Major aspects of language and communication that have implications for classroom learning include sounds, words, syntax, semantics, nonverbal communication, and functional communication, all of which develop simultaneously in the growing child. In addition, teachers must understand communication development in relation to strategies for learning and the impact of selective perception.

## Development of Sounds

Linguists describe the sounds of any language in units called *phonemes*. Through studies of phonemics, linguists can describe and record the sound systems of any language, compare languages or dialects, and study language changes in a given culture over time. Children learn most of the speech sounds they need for communication in their language within the first few years of life, with the more difficult and less frequently occurring sounds learned last.

The child is still likely to be mastering such sounds as *l*, *r*, and *th*. However, if by the age of seven children exhibit confusion among *l*, *r*, and *w*, and similar *th/s* confusion, or difficulty with all of these sounds individually, they may have articulation problems and should be referred to speech therapy. Saying "wadder" for "ladder" or "thilly" for "silly" would be examples of an articulation problem.

Learning about sounds embodied in the dialect differences of children represents an important aspect of teaching. If a child comes from a Spanish-speaking culture or from one in which black English is spoken, that rather than incorrectness may be the basis on which phoneme substitutions are made. Wood (1976) points out:

> Asking a black or Spanish-speaking child to discriminate or produce phonemes not representative of the phonology of his target language is an issue very different from asking English-speaking children to change English phonemes that are misarticulated [p. 101].

The community, the school, and the classroom teacher need to decide how to approach differences apart from articulation errors and how they wish to approach instruction. Bidialectical approaches, sometimes called "English as a second language," in which the child keeps the first language intact and adds standard English (without having to feel that one form is superior to the other), are usually best.

## Development of Words

Although a five-year-old child may be able to produce over 2,000 words, it is difficult to know how well that child understands their meanings in connected speech. The child learns by *expanding* meanings for words and by later *contracting* them. At first the child may call all men "Daddy" or a large dog a "horse"; these are examples of expansions of meanings. At twelve months one of the authors' children called a stalk of broccoli a "tree." Gradually, the child contracts word usage so that each word is used with the appropriate referent.

Berko (1958) studied children's understandings of compound words such as blackboard, sunshine, Thanksgiving. She identified four stages in the child's acquisition of meanings for these words. Stage 1 involves *identity*, i.e., the child believes that a thing is called a thing because it is a thing. For example, young children when asked why something is called *breakfast* are likely to answer, "Because." Older children typically give few of these responses unless, as recent evidence indicates, they have learning disabilities associated with language. Stage 2 involves *salient feature or function*— the child responds with a function associated with the meaning of the total compound word and not to the two separate words. For example, a blackboard is a blackboard "because you write on it" (p. 168). Stage 3 involves *word-related salient feature;* in this stage the child (by about first grade) responds with a function associated with one of the words in the compound structure. A fireplace is called that because "there is fire in it"; a merry-go-round "goes around." Stage 4 is the *etymological stage,* in which the child begins to take into account both the names of things and their meanings. For example, a ten-year-old might respond to *breakfast* with "We break our fast from overnight," but Berko's young subject, not yet in this stage, responded, "Breakfast is called *breakfast* because you have to eat it fast when you rush to school" (p. 170).

Youngsters may also make false connections and misuse words as a result; for example, a four-year-old knew the word *appointment* meant *date.* When a friend broke a date, she reported, using another big word she had no doubt heard without understanding, that she had had a "disappointment."

The teacher needs to understand that all these stages are likely to persist to some degree as the child learns language, and that the child may have private meanings for many words. One of the goals of instruction might be to help the child respond more frequently at the etymological level.

By age five, the child appears to have learned the rules for using plurals, possessives, and verb tenses. The teacher may want to test a child's knowledge of these rules by duplicating Berko's use of nonsense words. Using a "wug" to stand for a fat bird and "ricking" for a man swinging an object, Berko (1958) elicited responses as follows:

This is a wug (picture of one wug).
Now there is another one (picture of two wugs).
There are two of them. They are two _____ .

This is a man who knows how to rick.
He is ricking. He did the same thing yesterday.
    What did he do yesterday?
Yesterday he _____ [p. 155].

To date little research has been done on the contribution of vocabulary development or word knowledge to the development of effective communication skills, or the use of language for interactive purposes (Asher and Wigfield, 1981, p. 108).

## Development of Syntax

Syntactical development refers to the rules for relating and combining words in a sentence. Awareness of this aspect of development gives great insight into children's thinking and their relationship to their environments. Wood (1981) describes six major stages in the development of syntax in children. These stages are based on the work of Roger Brown, who observed and recorded the speech and language development of three children over a period of several years.

*Stage 1: Basic Relations.*  In this stage, children develop multiple word utterances that depict relationships. For example, "Mommy laugh" or "hit car" or "silly doggies."

*Stage 2: Modulated Relations.*  The child develops nuances of meaning that are more specific in communicating intentions or desires, for example, "I want two candies." Utterances demonstrate more precise meanings that are adapted to a context, for example, "Mommy is silly."

*Stage 3: Simple Sentence Modalities.*   The child can use the basic predicate structure and change it to a question or negative structure, for example, "What time is it?" and "It's not loud enough."

*Stage 4: Advanced Sentence Modalities.*   The child can combine clauses to form more complex structures, for example, "Remember how we sneaked up on her?" or "Look at the kid throwing the ball" or "I like the kind you bought yesterday."

*Stage 5: Categorization.*   This stage, beginning in the late preschool years and continuing through the early elementary years, involves more complex categorizations of words, especially nouns, verbs, and prepositions. For example, with age the following errors in standard-English speakers become less frequent: "My sister, she gots red hair." or "Give me some moneys."

*Stage 6: Complex Structures.*   In this stage, children are developing meanings and usage of subtleties, like the differences among. "I told Bill to leave," "I asked Bill to leave," and "I promised Bill to leave." They are overcoming such difficulties as the following:

> "Ask her the time" may be interpreted as "tell her the time." "I don't think she has the ball" may be interpreted as "She doesn't have the ball."

## Development of Semantics

Whereas syntax refers to the relationships among words in sentences, semantics refers to meaning or the relationships of words to ideas and contexts. The process of developing meanings apparently parallels the processes in the development of children's thought processes. However, Carroll (1973) points out.

> There are those who believe that language development leads and guides mental development, and there are those who believe that, on the contrary, mental development leads language development. There is no *a priori* way of resolving this question, and it is difficult even to interpret the few empirical studies that bear on it. On the basis of  . . .  available evidence, I incline to the belief that mental development tends to lead and proceed in advance of language development [pp. 180–181].

Two researchers, Jean Piaget and Lev Vygotsky, have contributed most to our understanding of developmental periods in children. Gruber and Voneche (1977, pp. 456–463) describe Piaget's stages of development:

*Sensory-Motor (0–2 Years).*   The stage before language, during which the child develops from undifferentiated to adaptive behavior, and adjusts to the environment primarily through perceptual-motor rather than symbolic activity.

*Preoperational Thought (2–7 Years).*   The "prelogical" period, during which the child attempts to deal with symbols, but shows many contradictions and errors of logic.

*Concrete Operations (7–11 Years).*   When logical operations appear, including the conceptions of time, space, and reversibility of actions; thinking becomes less egocentric, and rules of logic are applied to concrete events.

***Propositional or Formal Operations* (11 – 15 Years).**   When the adolescent can deal with hypotheses and propositions and understands basic principles of casual and scientific thinking.

Central to an understanding of semantic development is Piaget's notion of egocentrism:

> Children, he observed, frequently make no real attempt to take the role of the listener or to adapt a message to the listener's informational needs; they are caught up in their own point of view and are unaware that others see things differently. Piaget describes the young child's talk as primarily egocentric and the mature adult's talk as primarily socialized. Hence more of the young child's talk than the adult's is for the self, even when in the company of others [Allen and Brown, 1976, p. 67].

Vygotsky (1962) argued that egocentric speech does not disappear as the child grows older, but withdraws inward at school age to become nonvocal inner speech. He believed that egocentric speech serves as the basis for autistic and logical thinking in adults. After observing children's thought and language, Vygotsky argued:

> The primary function of speech in both children and adults is communication, social contact. The earliest speech of the child is therefore essentially social. At first it is global and multifunctional; later its functions become differentiated. At a certain age the social speech of the child is quite sharply divided into egocentric and communicative speech. . . . From our point of view, the two forms, communicative and egocentric, are both social, though their functions differ. Egocentric speech emerges when the child transfers social, collaborative forms of behavior to the sphere of inner-personal psychic functions. . . . Egocentric speech, splintered off from general social speech, in time leads to inner speech, which serves both autistic and logical thinking [p. 19].

Robinson (1981) states that "Piaget's egocentric child does not *understand* that for communication to be successful, the message must meet the listener's information requirements" (p. 168). Robinson's studies of children indicate that young children (around five years) commonly blame the listener for message inadequacies, whereas older children (around seven years) commonly blame the speaker; however, eleven-year-olds blame the speaker when appropriate. Robinson also presents evidence that children, with prompting by adults, can learn to improve messages that are too general rather than blame listeners (pp. 182 – 83). He suggests that adults might be able to enhance communication development (thereby decreasing egocentric viewpoints) if they become more aware of the child's need to be informed explicitly about the success or failure of communications.

Wood (1981) summarizes three phases in children's development of meaning. In phase one, which occurs before the first birthday, the child uses sounds to communicate needs, to ask someone for something, to relate to others, to express feelings, to ask questions, and to show curiosity about the social world. Children use their voices, bodily movement, and sounds to accomplish these communication goals. In phase two, children seem to recognize the boundary between themselves and their environment and use language to demand responses from others, to initiate actions, and to make statements or inquire about what they know or want to know. They develop dialogue and grammar for meanings and interactions with others. In phase three, children develop choices in communication; that is, among many possible meanings, they learn to choose the one that fits the context at that moment. "The environment affects their choices of meaning, but communication practices (meaning choices) affect their new view of the environment" (p. 159). In this last phase, children also learn that there are "scripts" or appropriate modes of communication for various social contexts. For example, they learn rules of dinner-table talk, patterns of behaviors for the "good guys" and the "bad guys" in stories, and hundreds of other "scripts" for social contexts.

## Development of Nonverbal Communication

The child is mastering nonverbal communication along with the verbal. Some developmental aspects of nonverbal communication are kinesics (body language); proxemics (the use of space); paralanguage, or the use of voice, facial expressions (for example, smile, frown, brow movements), and visual responses (for example, length and direction of gaze). These develop in an integrated way as the child learns communication skills.

The young child is constantly on the move, wriggling, squirming, jumping, and flinging the body about. Just as there seems to be the biological urge to speak, there also appears to be a need for motion. While this constant motion declines during the school years, early-childhood educators will tell you that young children find it difficult to sit still for long periods of time. Some of the earliest communication behavior of the child is through body motion — pointing, gesturing, and movements of the whole body.

To understand how we develop and use body language, researchers studied the relationships of body movements to meanings in various cultures. The task is difficult because one gesture does not relate to one isolated meaning. For example, folding the arms across the chest may mean that a person feels hostile, relaxed, cold, or doesn't know what to do with the arms. Careful interpretation would depend upon related motions of the legs, head, face, feet, and other parts of the body as well as verbal language. Thus, the study of kinesics must be implemented in a communication context.

Teachers need to remember that gestures and facial expression (a part of kinesics) are culturally learned through interactions along with speech. Likewise, eye contact in communication is learned very early in life and is part of the child's overall reaction to smiling behavior in infancy. Knapp (1978), in describing the early eye-to-eye contact between mother and child, notes that "the mutual gaze, the breaking of gaze, and facial responsiveness are crucial elements in establishing primitive bases for social relationships — even though the gaze duration may be fairly short" (p. 68).

The child learns to use distances that are appropriate to conversation with the adult norm stabilizing at around third grade (Knapp, 1978). Knapp points out that differences in spatial preferences between boys and girls may be established early through differential patterns of adult behavior. Boys seem to be given toys (trucks, cars, footballs) that encourage them to expand their space, while girls are given domestic toys directed at the home environment.

Evidence indicates that the child can differentiate vocal characterisitics (pitch, quality, loudness, rate, duration) within the first few months of life. Furthermore, during the early stages of making sounds, the infant seems to imitate perceived differences in pitch levels, with lower pitch for the father and higher for the mother (Knapp, 1978, p. 70). As the child grows older, pitch tends to get lower; and pausal patterns, tempo, and loudness features become well established by the time children enter kindergarten. While children are very good at communicating a number of different emotions with their voices and bodies at a very young age, they have a harder time interpreting emotions from vocal cues alone. During the elementary school years, children develop intonation patterns that support the more complex syntactic structures that they are learning.

As children develop, the nonverbal cues become very potent in communication. Somehow we learn, as we develop, that nonverbal cues are less within our control than verbal ones, and that they are more apt to express true feelings than are verbal cues. We tend, when faced with conflicts between verbal and nonverbal cues, to trust the nonverbal. Thus, if a parent is feeling tense or anxious, the child is often able to sense this despite the "happy face" and words that the parent manufactures.

Teachers should recognize that a wide range of differences exists among individuals in their ability to encode and decode nonverbal cues, and that research has not yet adequately accounted for these differences (Allen, 1981). Part of communication education should focus on the development of nonverbal behavior.

## Development of Functional Communication

As children grow older, all the aspects of development that we have been discussing become integrated into a system whereby they relate to others through oral communication. The Speech Communication Association's National Project on Speech Communication Competence (Allen and Brown, 1976) described five categories of communication acts in which human beings develop varying degrees of competence:

1.  *Controlling.*   Acts that include such behaviors as commanding, offering, suggesting, permitting, threatening, warning, persuading, and responses to the foregoing behaviors.

2.  *Feeling.*   Acts in which the main purpose is to express affective responses, including expressions of feelings or attitudes, commiserating, exclaiming, and responses to the foregoing behaviors.

3.  *Informing.*   Acts dominated by offering or seeking information, including questioning, justifying, naming, explaining, and responses to the foregoing behaviors.

4.  *Ritualizing.*   Acts that serve to maintain social relationships such as greeting, leave-taking, turn taking, and various cultural amenities.

5.  *Imagining.*   Acts that cast participants in imaginary situations, including creative behaviors such as role playing, fantasizing, theorizing.

These acts represent the interactive nature of communication — that is, human beings both express feelings and receive feelings from other people, engage in controlling behavior and are controlled by others in the course of interaction, and must learn the skills associated with both the sending and receiving roles involved in each act.

The National Project on Speech Communication Competence also described communication competence as involving four features: (1) an available repertoire of experiences—that is, the capability to perform a wide range of communication acts (within the five categories previously described) required by the social environment; (2) selection of strategies from the repertoire based upon appropriateness for a specific social context; (3) implementation of strategies—that is, the use of verbal and nonverbal behaviors to accomplish a given intent in social interaction; (4) evaluation of communication performance—that is, the ability to judge the effects of one's communication and its satisfaction to self and others in a given situation.

In other words, children in acquiring adult behavior learn a number of communication strategies that can help perform certain functions; they select the strategy that will best fit the context, implement the strategy, and then evaluate performance based on the achievement of purpose or on the level of satisfaction from the communication.

For example, a thirteen-year-old boy, seeking to get a raise in his allowance, might learn to use a variety of communication strategies to accomplish this goal. He might use reasoning and cite evidence of peer-group allowance levels, he might shout and bully to get what he wants, or he might bring along a friend to help him plead his case. Having chosen the strategy based upon his parents' mood, the probability of agreement by the parent, the reasonableness of the request, etc., he might try to implement the strategy and become aware of how the parent responded, whether he or she felt coerced or positive about the interaction, whether he achieved his goal, etc.

Delia, Kline, and Burleson (1979) have demonstrated that children's persuasive strategies become increasingly sophisticated with age. The greater the sophistication, the more they reflect high levels of social perspective taking, i.e., the children can see things from others' points of view. Older children also have more complex interpersonal constructs than younger children; this complexity is apparently necessary for the formulation of messages that are sensitively adapted to listeners. In their study of children's persuasive strategies, Delia, Kline, and Burleson demonstrated that young children (on the K–12 spectrum) give unelaborated requests when persuading; for example, "Could I have a party, please?" An older child would elaborate more on the necessity and desirability of the request: "I've never had this before or anything so why don't you let me really have a party 'cause I've been wanting to do this for a long time" (p. 248). A still older child would try to alleviate the effects of anticipated counterarguments: "There wouldn't be a lot of running around and there would only be about five people" (p. 249). At the highest level of complexity, the child takes the listener's perspective in articulating an advantage, as in attempting to persuade someone to take a puppy: "If I were you and I lived alone, I'd like a good watchdog like this one" (p. 249). Delia, Kline, and Burleson conclude that the "development of the ability to produce listener adapted messages proceeds through a series of phases" (p. 255) of first seeing the relevance of listener qualities to communication efforts and ultimately producing messages that take into account those characteristics.

Higgins, Fondacaro, and McCann (1981) present evidence of various skills involved in the development of speaking and listening in functional communication. While speaking and listening seem to have some skills in common (verbal comparison and "taking the characteristics of one's communicative partner into account" [p. 306], for example), the skills required for the speaking role and the listening role appear to be different, with each process involving distinct communication rules. While we have advocated instruction on the interactive nature of communication throughout the curriculum, such research evidence strongly suggests the need for additional separate instruction in speaking skills and listening skills.

Are children already competent at functional communication when they enter school? A teacher who is familiar with both the linguistic research and the communication research is likely to become confused by seeming contradictions. Linguistic research tends to demonstrate that children are very competent at using speech to meet social demands (Shuy and Griffin, 1981), but as Dickson (1981) points out, there appears to be a developmental trend for development of specific competencies, and we have yet to understand "how task demands, cognitive development, and experience interact to produce a level of performance for an individual" (p. 196).

It is important for the teacher to understand, at the level that we now know, the various stages in which the child develops communication behaviors necessary for performing the various communication acts. Table 3-1 presents behaviors that tend to occur at various stages of development, organized according to aspects of code behaviors (the verbal and nonverbal language that a child uses), adaptation to culture (relating to the expectations of the groups in which the child communicates and in which language develops), and functional communication (using language for specific purposes). We must emphasize that children display wide variations in their abilities to perform these behaviors at various ages. It is the role of education to intervene and to assist the child in developing those behaviors required for communicating competently as an adult.

## Strategies for Learning

Hopper and Naremore (1978) describe five methods by which children learn to communicate. The first is *operant conditioning,* which occurs when behavior is repeated because it is reinforced. Thus, if the child says "wan cookie" and is given a cookie, the child has been reinforced and will likely repeat the phrase again. When an older child, speaking in front of the class, finds that to be a pleasurable experience, that child will likely want to repeat the behavior. Another way speech is learned is by *imitation.* Most of the sounds and words of the language are learned by children imitating what they hear. An effective way of teaching children to speak appears to be through *modeling,* in which the adult models communication patterns so that children can emulate them without giving word for word playback. Another way in which children learn to speak is by what is called *self-motivated practice.* The very young child appears to practice sounds and to make noise because it is enjoyable. This may help communication, although the child is not consciously practicing in order to learn to communicate. A means of learning that has been given more prominence in recent research is *rule induction.* The child hears a number of sentences that use similar syntactic constructions. Through a process of generalization, the child unconsciously realizes what rules are followed. In the process of learning, children often overgeneralize the rule, as in the mistake of calling all men "Daddy" or all furry animals a "bow-wow." As children learn plural rules and exceptions, they may say "feets," or for the past tense "threwed" or "ranned."

## Impact of Selective Perception

An important aspect of communication is based upon *selective perception.* We can never hear or see everything in our environment at any one time. If we did, we would be bombarded by

**TABLE 3-1  Communication Capabilities: Pre-Kindergarten through Adolescence**

| | Code Behaviors | Adaptation to Culture | Functional Communication |
|---|---|---|---|
| Age 3–5 | Uses nonverbal behavior appropriate to situation | Responds differentially to verbal communication regarding gender signals, degrees of emotion, degrees of threat | Integrates verbal and nonverbal strategies |
| | Responds appropriately to facial expressions | Uses silence as a communicative strategy | Responds to persuasive probes |
| | Uses most linguistic rules accurately | Identifies self in communication roles | Uses opinion to support claims |
| | Produces most phonemes accurately | Uses dialect in productive and receptive language | Is somewhat adaptive to listener (for example, speaks differently with younger children than with adults); uses conversational skills that are spontaneous, are mutually interactive, and follow conventionalized patterns |
| | | | Engages in dramatic or symbolic play alone, with peers, or with toys |
| | | | Tries on roles to see what it would be like to be someone else |
| Age 5–9 | Provides nonverbal feedback in conversation with prompting | Produces bidialectal utterances, if the base dialect is nonstandard | Perceives incongruous facial expressions in social interactions |
| | Uses complex syntactic structures | Responds in the classroom in ways appropriate to dialect of own language community | Controls facial expression to mask feelings |
| | Produces all phonemes accurately | Demonstrates leadership roles and competition if culturally appropriate | Demonstrates ability to empathize |
| | Recognizes semantic nuance as well as denotation | Responds to status and power relationships in the communication situation | Distinguishes another's point of view when prompted |
| | | | Makes abstract (in addition to concrete) associations |

| Age | | | |
|---|---|---|---|
| | | | Reads and supplies verbal feedback |
| | | | Uses interpersonal communication roles to further personal goals |
| | | | Describes, explains, and makes inferences regarding the unexpressed thoughts and feelings of others |
| | | | Creates more unified dramatic improvisations |
| | | | Classifies objects on a "part-whole" basis |
| | | | Formulates hypotheses and explanations about concrete matters |
| Age 9–12 | Responds appropriately to nonverbal messages about personal space | Elaborates responses to questions | Uses a variety of arguments in persuasion and plays a variety of persuasive roles (for example, hard sell, soft sell) |
| | Expresses complex syntactic structures in writing as well as in speaking | Answers questions from a variety of perspectives | Plays games with carefully prescribed rules and regulations |
| | | Retells a story rather than relating only parts of it | Represents imagined objects symbolically |
| | | Identifies differences of social dialect and perceives the significance of these differences | |
| Age 12–18 | Evaluates emotional states from verbal and nonverbal communication | Uses a variety of communication roles and styles in the peer culture or own language community | Analyzes persuasive messages in relationship to source. |
| | Uses body language to express sexual role | Reads social class differences from the nonverbal and verbal communication of others | Evaluates a message critically |
| | | | Plays a variety of communication roles |

(Continued)

**TABLE 3-1** (Continued)

| Code Behaviors | Adaptation to Culture | Functional Communication |
|---|---|---|
| Age 12–18 (cont.) | | Responds to the needs of a listener in order to make a message comprehensible |
| | | Provides feedback and adjusts messages to the feedback of others |
| | | Predicts the potential effectiveness of messages |
| | | Provides alternative encodings |
| | | Constructs numerous possibilities and propositions |
| | | Conceptualizes own thought and thoughts of others |
| | | Reasons abstract concepts |
| | | Understands class-inclusion relations |

stimuli that we could not process. Thus, our sensory mechanisms act as perceptual filters through which we select messages from our environment on the basis of our frame of reference. Sometimes we select on the basis of our beliefs and attitudes, prompting the observation that we "hear what we want to hear." Sometimes we listen only to what we readily understand or to those subjects in which we are already interested. One finding is that we tend to identify with speakers whom we like and trust (those who have high credibility for us). For example, if a speaker whom we like says something we do not like, we will tend to distort the message to bring it into line with our favorable impressions of the speaker. In this process, known as reducing dissonance, we selectively perceive information to bring it into line with what we believe.

As messages in our environment become more complex, we become adept at refocusing on or retuning in to a message stimulus. Some factors that influence this focusing process are internal; that is, they rely on mental set, tension level, self-concept, and our sensory capacities (the amount of information we can process at any one time). The teacher can more easily influence the external than the internal factors, by controlling the intensity, novelty, repetitiousness, or duration of a stimulus. For example, we tend to pay attention to stimuli that are larger or more vivid, those that differ and change, those that are repeated, and those that last longer.

Processes of selective perception and attention form the bases for information processing, which in turn forms the basis for all learning. As young children process information, they classify it into concepts or categories. There are classifications for dogs, mothers, fathers, babies, and so on. At first, as was mentioned earlier, the child misclassifies by overgeneralizing, but gradually learns to make the finer distinctions.

In a sense, all learning (and all communication) involves the altering of our perceptions and existing categories as information is processed; new information is always processed through existing perceptual frameworks. For example, a child on an Indian reservation was asked by the teacher to draw a map of the United States and to show the boundaries of the reservation. At first the child drew the reservation to cover half the size of the United States. Through the process of learning and exposure to new information, the child gradually altered these concepts over a period of months and eventually produced a more accurate map.

## SPECIAL PROBLEMS

Many kinds of difficulties can impede the child's communication development. Space permits us to discuss only a few of these problems, those that are most frequently encountered in the classroom.

### Organic Problems

Obviously, a child who is born deaf will have a difficult time developing speech and other communicative abilities. Carmichael and Greenberg (1980), studying mother-child dyads in which half of the children aged three to six were deaf, found that hearing children had a higher percentage of spontaneous communication, asked more questions, and used more behavior requests than their deaf counterparts. Teachers must understand that, since the deaf child has not heard speech and has probably been taught to speak through procedures such as lipreading, that child will find articulation of certain sounds and vocal intonations difficult, and these sounds will differ from those of normal-hearing children.

Children with damage to the structures that produce speech will also have difficulties. Any problem that produces difficulties with breathing, phonation (giving voice to the air stream), resonation (the process of producing speech sounds), or articulation (joint actions of the tongue, lips, soft and hard palates, and gum ridge behind the upper teeth) will produce speech difficulties. Thus, the child with certain types of cerebral palsy or a cleft palate may possess the auditory, cognitive, and intellectual development necessary for communication, but may not be able to produce intelligible sounds. Such children should receive special help from qualified speech pathologists but (as we will discuss in the next chapter), if mainstreamed into a classroom, should be integrated into classroom communication. Students can be taught patience and tolerance in listening and in speaking with others with handicaps.

## Learning Disabilities

In 1977 the federal government, through Public Law 94-142, defined specific learning disability as "a disorder in one or more of the basic psychological processes involved in understanding or in using language, spoken or written, which may manifest itself in an imperfect ability to listen, think, speak, read, write, spell, or to do mathematical calculations. The term includes such conditions as perceptual handicaps, brain injury, minimal brain dysfunction, dyslexia, and developmental aphasia. The term does not include children who have learning problems that are primarily the result of visual, hearing, or motor handicaps, of mental retardation, or of environmental, cultural or economic disadvantage." Thus, learning-disabled children, who by definition have basic intelligence intact, may be unable to process language for communication. The learning-disabled child may have disorders of vocabulary or syntax that present serious decoding problems, for example:

> Mrs. Charters was presenting a lesson in number skills. She gave each child a piece of paper, a pencil, and a ruler. In order to make straight lines on which to write, the teacher said, "Use your rulers to draw a straight line." Karen picked up her ruler and attempted to use it as a pencil [Bangs, 1968, p. 12].

Speech articulation may also be poorly developed if the child cannot discriminate among sounds or cannot produce sounds because of poor coordination of neuromuscular mechanisms. The child may not be able to discriminate such vocal cues as intonation and stress, and will therefore not decode important nonverbal aspects of a message. Some learning-disabled children also have severe disorders of reading, speaking, or handwriting.

One of the most difficult problems in communication occurs in children with auditory perceptual problems:

> When the teacher speaks, the child with an intact alerting and attention system shifts quickly from his inner thinking to what the teacher has said. This seems to be almost an instantaneous shift. But because the child with a disordered mechanism may be unable to make such a rapid shift, he cannot attend to the teacher's comments. He may be said to have internal noise which is affecting his reception of the message [Bangs, 1968, p. 36].

Children with auditory perceptual problems are not hard of hearing — that is, there is no damage to the hearing mechanism, but rather a dysfunction of the part of the brain that processes auditory signals. Such children may be very sensitive to sounds in the environment and may perceive them to be louder than they are; or they may not be able to sort out sounds easily and may have difficulty following conversation in a noisy room. In addition, such children may have difficulties with memory, and particularly with recalling sequences of ideas; or they may have poor oral sentence structure because they cannot remember the sequence of words that make up a sentence. Bangs (1968) cites such an example:

> David was presented with a picture of two cars that had crashed into each other at an intersection. He was asked to tell a story about the scene. There was a pause and then his answer, "Two green lights" [p. 35].

Lieb-Brilhart (1982) summarized the research on nonverbal communication and learning disabilities, noting the debilitating impact of the inability to discriminate and respond appropriately to the social cues of others. Bader (1975) described learning-disabled children as often anxious, trying too hard to say the right thing, often speaking too loudly, getting too close to you when they talk, interrupting frequently, being impulsive, and often naive. Bader and others have emphasized that the psychological impact of these communication problems is often more severe than the academic failures. Such children often benefit from empathy training and role playing with direct instruction in the nonverbal and verbal cues that relate to emotions. While the nondisabled child usually learns these cues naturally through interaction, the disabled child often needs help in reading and interpreting such cues.

It is important for the classroom teacher to realize that the learning-disabled child is usually frustrated by the inability to learn things that other children learn quite easily. Usually these children develop negative self-concepts quite early in life and, because they are intelligent (often of superior intelligence), have developed clever mechanisms for avoiding learning situations and social interactions. Teachers often accuse them of being lazy or of not trying when they would like desperately to learn. In addition to the fact that many of them are hyperactive and easily overstimulated, factors that in and of themselves make these children difficult to manage, they have difficulty in learning rules of play, turn taking, and classroom routines. The teacher, in consultation with the special education specialist, needs to discover the ways in which each of these children learns best, and to set up structured routines and opportunities for individualizing instruction. But most of all, the teacher must learn to praise and reinforce the child when learning does occur.

## Communication Apprehension

Another serious developmental problem in communication is communication apprehension, sometimes labeled reticence, unwillingness to communicate, shyness, and so on. Communication apprehension can involve a fear not only of public speaking, but also of informal and conversational speaking; therefore, it is a much broader problem than stage fright, which is limited to public performance. The highly apprehensive person avoids communicating and disclosing inner feelings as much as possible. McCroskey (1977a) defines communication apprehension as "an anxiety syndrome associated with either real or anticipated communication with another person or persons" (p. 28).

Although a great amount of recent research deals with communication apprehension, there is not a wealth of definitive information that can be used by teachers to help students become less apprehensive. However, research indicates that "between 10 and 20 percent of all college students and adults suffer from extreme communication apprehension, and the percentages may be somewhat higher in secondary and elementary schools" (Hurt, Scott, and McCroskey, 1978, p. 148).

While communication apprehension is not related to intelligence, there is evidence that high apprehensives do worse in college than low apprehensives, especially in test-taking situations (McCroskey, 1977a). In addition, Phillips (1977) found that reticent college students reported the following problems:

- inability to open conversation with strangers or to make small talk
- inability to extend conversations or to initiate friendships
- inability to follow the thread of discussion or to make pertinent remarks in discussions
- inability to answer questions asked in a normal classroom or job situation
- incompetence at answering questions that arise on the job or in the classroom, not through lack of knowledge but due to an inability to phrase or time answers
- inability to deliver a complete message even though it is planned and organized
- general ineptitude in communication situations characterized by avoidance of participation [p. 37]

Some of the indicators of communication apprehension that classroom teachers might observe are: low or cowering voice, avoidance of competitive play, sitting at the back of the room or in the zone of least interaction, refusal to communicate in class, poor eye contact, and high anxiety level. Hurt and Preiss (1978) found that middle school students who were highly apprehensive had negative attitudes toward school and were not considered desirable communication choices by their peers. The research shows that high communication apprehensives achieve less and like school less than low communication apprehensives (McCroskey, 1977a).

While the exact causes of communication apprehension are not clear, some evidence indicates that its origins lie in the early home environment. If a child is not encouraged to communicate, or if communication is punished, the child may not learn to enjoy interaction. Some highly apprehensive students may have histories of child abuse, feelings of low self-esteem, or experiences with critical incidents in which they were forced to perform before others at an early age.

McCroskey (1977b), in his description of factors that might relate to the development of communication apprehension, includes:

*Heredity.*  There is some evidence to suggest that variations in verbal activity and degrees of social introversion can be attributed to genetic factors.

*Reinforcement.*  Some children are reinforced for verbal behavior, while others are not.

*Birth order.*  Only and first-born children tend to receive more attention and reinforcement from their parents and probably more communication than later-born children.

*Communication Values.*  Some home environments place a higher premium on verbal behavior than others do.

*Communication Skill Deficiency.*   Children with language or speech deficiencies may miss out on opportunities for communication, since they are behind in development.

McCroskey (1977a) also points out that many highly communication apprehensive teachers choose to teach in the lower grades, where they are more comfortable, rather than teach at higher levels, where they must interact with older students.

What can the teacher do about the communication apprehensive child in the classroom? McCroskey suggests some ways in which the teacher can avoid hurting the communication apprehensive child:

> The teacher can eliminate grading on "participation"; he or she can provide options for assignments other than formal presentations; the teacher can permit voluntary seating choices so that the communication apprehensive student can be comfortable in the classroom; he or she can avoid calling on communication apprehensive students and forcing involuntary participation; and, most important, the teacher can attempt to structure the course so that students can obtain all necessary information without having to seek extra communication contact with either the teacher or peers [1977a, p. 33].

Phillips (1977) eschews the medical or therapeutic approach to reticence and follows an instructional approach that might be adapted by teachers well trained in rhetoric and oral communication. In essence, he emphasizes speech that is goal oriented and that considers the listener's viewpoint, an approach that follows rhetorical models. The essence of the rhetorical process (which reticent and nonreticent students would benefit from using) includes the following sequence:

1.  discovery of a situation in which some goal can be achieved through the use of speech
2.  identification of the person or persons who are to be modified by the speech
3.  specification of the modifications desired and selection of ideas that will help bring about the changes
4.  analysis of both situations and persons to discover constraints and restraints on speech behavior
5.  adaptation of the ideas the speaker wishes to communicate to the particular audience and situation, and arrangement of them in order
6.  selection of words in which to convey the ideas, and connection of them according to commonly accepted forms
7.  articulation of the words, modulating delivery to suit conditions
8.  observation of the response of the others and assessment of success in order to have information on which to base another attempt [p. 39]

As we understand more about reticence, it is important that teachers learn to identify children with this debilitating problem and work with specialists to help them in the classroom.

# THE TEACHER'S ROLE IN COMMUNICATION DEVELOPMENT

All teachers should be educated to understand how children develop communication competence, and should view the classroom as a place where effective communication can be learned and developed. The following are suggestions that the teacher can follow to enhance the child's communication development:

*The teacher should serve as a model for communication learning.* Shuy (1981), in a very insightful article, cautions against the traditional view of the teacher as a model for linguistic development. As we have noted earlier, most of the structures and rules of the languages are already in place when the child comes to school; furthermore, "once peer models are established, teacher and parent models will diminish" (p. 171). Shuy further states that "the numbers of influences on communication are so great that learning to speak in one context such as the school is a small drop in a very large bucket of the lives of all speakers" (p. 170). He calls for teacher modeling using language to get things done (or a functional communication approach, such as the one discussed earlier in this chapter). Such functions as opening and closing discourse, keeping attention, and seeking clarification are communication functions performed by the teacher that might serve as models for students. Teachers not only can model, but also can directly teach communication functions in a variety of situations that occur in the classroom.

For example, children can be reminded as they share experiences to "think of the other person": "Since you have seen Trafalger Square, but others have not, can you compare it with anything they might have seen in the United States?" In a high school history class, students might disagree on whether there is a need for the Equal Rights Amendment. Students are asked to restate the viewpoint of the other person before they state their own, to make sure that they understand before they disagree. These and numerous other examples illustrate that teachers of all subjects can grasp opportunities to improve communication.

*The teacher should adapt teaching/learning strategies to the cognitive and communication developmental stages identified in given children.* A teacher who understands the various developmental stages can begin to observe children more closely and to listen to them more intently for clues to their abilities. The intervention role becomes one of helping them to move to next-higher levels of development.

Although children learn syntactical rules naturally through interactions with others, they still may be making errors such as *feets* for *feet* or *threwed* for *threw* through generalization of syntactical rules. The teacher might develop games for fun in which exceptions to the syntactical rules are noted. For example, "What are some words that indicate past actions where *ed* is not added?"

This chapter has also described developmental problems of such children as the learning disabled and communication apprehensive. The learning-disabled child who cannot process auditory information may need many visual cues to learn, and will certainly need short, clear instructions. The child who is communication apprehensive should not be forced to speak in front of the class, but may be more comfortable speaking to a small group while sitting down. Children who are not yet sophisticated in giving persuasive arguments to get what they want might be encouraged to listen to ways people got what they wanted and the kinds of arguments they used. The teacher should observe carefully how each child uses language for communication and find ways of helping each to progress.

*The teacher should become sensitive to nonverbal cues in order to understand and communicate better with students.* Bodily movement, facial expression, voice, use of space, touch, etc., are potent means of communication for the teacher and the student.

An obvious way to change space is to have students move the furniture so as to work in small groups and so as to face one another when they interact. In the next chapter we discuss cultural differences among students and the ways in which nonverbal communication might differ among cultural groups. For example, in some cultures telling a student to "look at me when I talk to you" is a violation of a cultural norm that dictates looking down to show respect to someone.

Understanding that learning-disabled children may have difficulties in receiving and decoding nonverbal cues is important to understanding why they do not react to your annoyance until you are extremely angry. Does the teacher look at students, stand near them when they are working to offer support, and otherwise use cues that communicate trust and warmth? Does the teacher encourage students to use nonverbal communication (gestures, pictures, facial expressions) to describe ideas to all students? Does the teacher use these aspects of nonverbal communication to make ideas concrete? Statements such as "You seem sad today, Mary" or "Your smile tells me that you are happy today, Sue" help children to realize that we do communicate nonverbally and that it is all right to respond to the cues that people communicate.

*The teacher should develop classroom activities that foster functional communication competence.* Wood (1977), in two booklets for teachers, describes exercises such as the following for developing such competence in fourth- to sixth-grade students:

### MY BIKE

*Primary Function:*   Controlling

*Objective:*   Adapting alternative ways of refusing particular participants and exploring the consequences.

*Materials:*   Chalkboard; pencil and paper for each student.

*Procedures:*   Give the students a situation and ask how they would refuse someone's request. For example, they could describe ways they would refuse someone's request to use their bicycle. Compose a large class list of various ways of refusing. After students list all of the possibilities, provide them with a list of individuals and ask them to choose and write on a piece of paper a refusal strategy which they think will work best with each person on the list. For example:

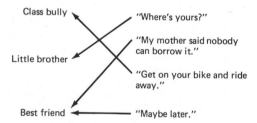

*Questions and Follow-Up:*

1.   How many different ways to refuse were mentioned on the class list?
2.   Of these, which ones were used for the class bully? The little brother? Best friend? Were there more ways to refuse one person than another? Why would that be?
3.   What do you think the other person would say back? Why would he or she say that? [P. 24.]

*Know your school system's method of referrals to specialists and seek their help.* Seek out the speech teacher in your school and nearby universities, the speech pathologist, the learning-disabilities resource teacher, the psychologist, and others who deal with problems related to children's communication. If they are not up-to-date on the literature related to communication development and such problems as communication apprehension, share your sources with them. Have them assist you in spotting children who may need help and in adapting classroom activities to special needs.

*Encourage children to speak and listen, and reinforce them for interacting appropriately.* Use the classroom as a place where children can learn about and practice oral communication skills regardless of the subject matter you are teaching. Help children to "screen out" speech and language differences and to listen for *messages* and *meanings* from one another. For example, a child in class who is difficult to understand because of an articulation problem can be taught through the teacher's behavior that "we are listening for the meaning no matter how long it takes." If a child stutters, do not finish sentences for that child but wait for the communication to be completed. The teacher should encourage through comments, such as "Let's listen to what John has to say," and through nonverbal attentive cues that help the child to speak and the class to listen. The teacher should never permit laughter or derision because of the way a child speaks. In fact, a discussion of why each of us speaks the way we do, how our dialects differ, why some of us may have problems speaking, and so on, often sensitizes children to listen to one another. Of course, it goes without saying (we hope) that teachers must never downgrade students because of reticence, speech defects, dialectal differences or the *way* they communicate. Realizing that speech and communication skills proceed developmentally helps to encourage students to interact and focus on meanings and messages rather than on speech patterns.

We believe that teachers of every subject have a responsibility to help students develop their communication skills. Science, math, and social-studies teachers should help students to listen to one another, to describe ideas in concrete terms so that others understand them, and to adapt to the experiences of other listeners. They may need help from the language-arts or speech teacher, but the whole faculty is responsible for the child's communication development.

*Listen to and empathize with children.* Teachers often have pat responses that they give to students in specific situations. Without looking up from their desks they may say, "John, take your seat; I'm busy right now." "Mary, stop daydreaming and get to work." While these responses may be appropriate at times, teachers need to "look before they leap," that is, they need to look and listen before they respond. When the teacher can pick up verbal and nonverbal cues and acknowledge a child's feelings, disasters are often averted:

> While washing the blackboards, Mario, age ten, managed to get a few drops of water on Jane. She grabbed the eraser, soaked it in water, and shoved it into his face. Mario went berserk. He wanted to hurt her. The teacher held him back, saying, "You are so angry, it's not safe for Jane to be near you. Jane, please move to another side of the class." Mario responded, "I'm going to beat the living daylights out of her." Teacher replied, "I can see how angry you are, and I can also hear your threats. Figure out another way to settle your grievances. We have too much violence as it is." Mario looked at his teacher with surprise. His anger subsided [Ginott, 1972, pp. 162–163].

Teachers must attempt to acknowledge the feelings and problems of children and to help them open up to communication. Some teachers have used diaries in which each child writes down feelings about class and self and gives these to the teacher. They are never graded, but the teacher responds in private to the child with such comments as "I see that you are feeling better about math this week. That's good." Or "I'm so sorry that your dog died, Harry. Perhaps that is why it has been difficult for you to concentrate." Children usually want to communicate, but want to feel that the teacher will really listen and will try to understand.

While it is true that children come to school in most cases having learned the basic elements and rules of using language, they have a long way to go in developing the appropriate use of that language in social contexts. It is the role of the school to help children develop effective communication skills. Since the teaching/learning process is essentially a communication process, the classroom is the obvious place to begin.

# SUMMARY

In this chapter we have focused on the processes through which children develop communication skills and their relationship to classroom communication. We emphasized that the human brain is apparently programmed for speech and that children will go through a normal course of speech and language development if there are opportunities for interaction with other human beings. Teachers should not make judgments concerning intelligence, creativity, or communication competence on the basis of dialect. By the time children enter school, they have usually mastered most of the sounds of the language, have developed extensive vocabularies, and have learned most of the linguistic rules. Children cannot yet give dictionary-type definitions of words, and are still mastering more complex sentence categories for choosing words and structuring language. Thought and language generally develop together, with children gradually learning to adapt messages to the viewpoints of listeners.

Children learn nonverbal communication along with the verbal; kinesics (bodily movement), proxemics, and vocal characteristics are important aspects of nonverbal development. These eventually become very potent cues in communication, and will tend to be perceived as expressive of "true" feelings. Human beings develop functional communication and interact through behaviors in five categories: controlling, feeling, informing, ritualizing, and imagining. Children tend to learn appropriate strategies for interaction naturally, but intervention by the school can help them achieve more complex behaviors, such as those required for persuasion.

Children learn communication skills through operant conditioning, imitation, modeling, self-motivated practice, and rule induction. The process of selective perception is the basis for information processing and all learning.

Special problems in communication development may be organic, including problems with the speech and hearing mechanism; or they may stem from learning disabilities, which may cause problems with vocabulary, syntax, articulation, listening, memory, and social perception. Another serious problem is communication apprehension, an anxiety syndrome associated with communication, which can be helped through avoidance of certain teaching pressures and through a rhetorical model.

The teacher's role in fostering communication development includes modeling appropriate communication strategies and using the classroom as a communication environment.

## Discussion Questions

1. Investigate the literature on right and left brain differences. To what extent and in what ways do you feel that education should be directed to the development of abilities in both hemispheres?

2. Investigate research on the impact of parent-child interactions on speech and communication development. What behaviors should parents adopt to enhance their children's communication development?

3. Listen to students in your class who speak with dialects different from your own. What differences do you notice in phonology, syntax, and word usage? What factors account for the development of these differences?

4. Listen to a young child speaking with an adult or with another child. To what extent is the child exhibiting egocentric speech? To what extent and in what ways is the child communicating nonverbally?

5. Have each member of the class keep a communication diary for one week. Then share your findings by classifying communication behaviors into the five functions of controlling, feeling, informing, ritualizing, and imagining. Which functions are performed most frequently?

6. Considering the relationship of selective perception to communication and learning, to what extent can we ever objectively perceive and process information that is entirely new?

7. Consider a classroom in which there are children with organic or functional communication problems along with children with normal development. How would you, as a teacher, create a communication environment that is productive for all of the children?

# References

Allen, R. R., and Kenneth L. Brown, eds. *Developing Communication Competence in Children: A Report of the Speech Communication Association's National Project on Speech Communication Competence.* Skokie, Ill.: National Textbook Co., 1976.

Allen, Vernon L. "The Role of Nonverbal Behavior in Children's Communication." In *Children's Oral Communication Skills,* W. Patrick Dickson, ed. New York: Academic Press, Inc., 1981, pp. 337–356.

Asher, Steven R., and A. Wigfield. "Training Referential Communication Skills." In *Children's Oral Communication Skills,* W. Patrick Dickson, ed. New York: Academic Press, Inc., 1981, pp. 105–126.

Bader, B. W., with Iowa Association for Children with Learning Disabilities. *Social Perception and Learning Disabilities.* Des Moines, Ia.: Moon Lithographing and Engraving, 1975.

Bangs, Tina E. *Language and Learning Disorders of the Pre-Academic Child.* New York: Appleton-Century-Crofts, 1968.

Berko, Jean. "The Child's Learning of English Morphology." *Word,* Vol. 14 (1958): 150–177.

Carmichael, Heather, and Mark T. Greenberg. "A Comparison Study of Functional Communication in Deaf vs. Hearing Mother-Child Dyads: Descriptive Analysis and Intervention." Paper presented at the University of Southern California Annual International Interdisciplinary Conference on Piagetian Theory and the Helping Professions, Los Angeles, Cal., February 1980. ERIC Document #191216.

Carroll, John B. "Language and Cognition: Current Perspectives from Linguistics and Psychology." In *Language Differences: Do They Interfere?* James L. Laffey and Roger Shuy, eds. Newark, Del.: International Reading Association, 1973.

Delia, Jesse G., Susan L. Kline, and Brant R. Burleson. "The Development of Persuasive Communication Strategies in Kindergartners through Twelfth-Graders." *Communication Monographs,* Vol. 46, No. 4 (November 1979): 241–256.

Dickson, W. Patrick. "Referential Communication Activities in Research and in the Curriculum: A Metaanalysis." In *Children's Oral Communication Skills,* W. Patrick Dickson, ed. New York: Academic Press, Inc., 1981, pp. 189–204.

Ginott, Haim. *Teacher and Child.* New York: The Macmillan Company, 1972.

Gruber, Howard E., and J. Jacques Voneche, eds. *The Essential Piaget.* London: Routledge & Kegan Paul Ltd., 1977.

Higgins, E. Tory, Rocco Fondacaro, and C. Douglas McCann. "Rules and Roles: The Communication Game and Speaker-Listener Process." In *Children's Oral Communication Skills,* W. Patrick Dickson, ed. New York: Academic Press, Inc., 1981, pp. 289–312.

Hopper, Robert, and Rita C. Naremore. *Children's Speech: A Practical Introduction to Communication Development,* 2nd ed. New York: Harper & Row, Publishers, 1978.

Hurt, H. Thomas, and Raymond Preiss. "Silence Isn't Necessarily Golden: Communication Apprehension, Desired Social Choice, and Academic Success Among Middle-School Students." *Human Communication Research,* Vol. 4, No. 4 (Summer 1978): 315–328.

Hurt, H. Thomas, Michael D. Scott, and James C. McCroskey. *Communication in the Classroom.* Reading, Mass.: Addison-Wesley Publishing Company, Inc., 1978.

Knapp, Mark L. *Nonverbal Communication in Human Interaction,* 2nd ed. New York: Holt, Rinehart and Winston, Inc. 1978.

Lane, Harlan L. *The Wild Boy of Aveyron.* Cambridge: Harvard University Press, 1976.

Lieb-Brilhart, Barbara. "Nonverbal Communication of Children with Learning Disabilities." Unpublished paper presented at the Annual Meeting of the American Educational Research Association, 1982.

McCroskey, James C. "Classroom Consequences of Communication Apprehension." *Communication Education,* Vol. 26, No. 1 (January 1977): 27–33 (a).

McCroskey, James C. *Quiet Children and the Classroom Teacher.* Annandale, Va.: Speech Communication Association under the auspices of the ERIC Clearinghouse on Reading and Communication Skills, 1977 (b).

Phillips, Gerald M. "Rhetoritherapy Versus the Medical Model: Dealing with Reticence." *Communication Education,* Vol. 26, No. 1 (January 1977): 34–43.

Pines, Maya. "The Civilizing of Genie." *Psychology Today,* Vol. 15, No. 9 (September 1981): 28–32.

Robinson, E. S. "The Child's Understanding of Inadequate Messages and Communication Failure: A Problem of Ignorance or Egocentrism." In *Children's Oral Communication Skills,* W. Patrick Dickson, ed. New York: Academic Press, Inc., 1981, pp. 167–188.

Shuy, Roger. "Learning to Talk Like Teachers." *Language Arts,* Vol. 58, No. 2 (February 1981): 168–174.

Shuy, Roger W., and Peg Griffin. "What Do They Do at School *Any* Day: Studying Functional Language." In *Children's Oral Communication Skills,* W. Patrick Dickson, ed. New York: Academic Press, Inc., 1981, pp. 271–285.

Vygotsky, Lev Semenovich. *Thought and Language.* Cambridge, Mass.: The M. I. T. Press, 1962.

Wood, Barbara S. *Children and Communication: Verbal and Nonverbal Language Development.* Englewood Cliffs, N.J.: Prentice-Hall, Inc., 1976.

Wood, Barbara S. *Children and Communication: Verbal and Nonverbal Language Development,* 2nd ed. Englewood Cliffs, N.J.: Prentice-Hall, Inc., 1981.

Wood, Barbara S., ed. *Development of Functional Communication Competencies: Pre-K-Grade 6.* Urbana, Illinois: Speech Communication Association under the auspices of the ERIC Clearinghouse on Reading and Communication Skills, 1977.

# For Further Reading

Birdwhistell, Ray. *Kinesics and Context: Essays in Body Motion Communication.* Philadelphia: University of Pennsylvania Press, 1970.

Brown, Roger. *A First Language: The Early Stages.* Cambridge, Mass.: Harvard University Press, 1977.

Cazden, Courtney B., Vera P. John, and Dell Hymes, eds. *Functions of Language in the Classroom.* New York: Teachers College Press, Columbia University, 1972.

Ervin-Tripp, Susan, and Claudia Mitchell-Kernan, eds. *Child Discourse.* New York: Academic Press, Inc., 1977.

Halliday, M. A. K. *Learning How to Mean: Explorations in the Development of Language.* New York: American Elsevier Publishing Company, Inc., 1975.

# Communication
# and Diversity
# in the Classroom

*focus*     STUDENT DIVERSITY AND ITS INFLUENCE ON CLASSROOM
            COMMUNICATION

            BENEFITS OF DIVERSITY

            PROBLEMS IN PROMOTING DIVERSITY

            ASPECTS OF DIVERSITY THAT INFLUENCE COMMUNICATION
            Cultural Differences
            Learning Styles
            Family Characteristics
            Sex Differences
            Communicator Styles of Students
            Handicapping Conditions

            GUIDELINES FOR COPING WITH DIVERSITY

Some time ago a student teacher was teaching a unit in problem-solving discussion in a speech class in a Midwestern high school. Her students, all white, were children of military personnel, mostly officers. Although many of them had lived on overseas bases, their school experiences had been with students very much like themselves. The discussion problem presented by the student teacher centered on the rights of a group of black activists to demonstrate before city hall. The students "solved" the problem in ten minutes. Their solution—to jail the blacks—was an easy consensus. No conflict ensued and no varying opinions were introduced.

Such homogeneity of thought and opinion can thwart growth. Heterogeneity appears to be valuable for offering students new possibilities and various ways of perceiving the world. This notion of student diversity has been viewed as an important factor in the American educational system. This chapter focuses on benefits of diversity, problems in promoting diversity, aspects of diversity that influence communication, and guidelines for coping with diversity.

# BENEFITS OF DIVERSITY

Historically, the United States built its democracy on the notion of cultural pluralism and deliberately set out to build institutions that could accommodate diverse ethnic, racial, and religious groups. In education, the notion of equity has fostered such actions as desegregation of pupils grouped by race or ethnicity, instruction to students for whom English is a second language, equality of options for females and males, and provision of resources for the handicapped.

Various educators have noted the benefits of diversity in the classroom. Yeakey (1979) describes diversity of educational environments as allowing for an examination of what goes on in school as part of the larger context of the rest of the child's life; this increases the likelihood that children will find several environments in which they can experiment and successfully function. Jarvis (1978) notes that accepting and valuing diversity in people permits us to be sensitive to differences in any dimension, such as age, religion, ethnic group, values, and so on. He further emphasizes that learning about diversity can go on right in the classroom, and not just by learning about people in other parts of the world:

> Diversity in people exists every time you put two persons together. . . . Our students can learn a great deal about the diversity in people by discovering the diversity among themselves. . . . By expressing what we think, feel, or believe about any topic, idea or item, whatsoever, and by hearing others express what they think, feel, or believe, we inevitably learn more about what we are and others are [p. 14].

# PROBLEMS IN PROMOTING DIVERSITY

While the concept of pluralism is viewed as desirable in our educational practices, it is not always easy for teachers to cope with on a day-to-day basis.

One problem is that despite the desire for cultural pluralism, the dominant culture tends to prevail. The schools transmit values and role models of the culture through language, literature, history, music and art, ethical beliefs, cultural rituals, and interpersonal relations. In most cases the values and perceptions of the dominant culture are transmitted in the schools. For example, the dominant culture in the United States stresses competitiveness and individualism, while many other cultures emphasize cooperation. Schools are closed for Christmas even when large majorities of non-Christian students are present. Despite the constitutional law separating church and state, the issue of school prayer continues to be an emotional one, since many people view the mission of the schools as one of transmitting religious values.

Despite legislation designed to protect rights of minorities and to foster cultural pluralism, educators' attitudes will continue to determine what is taught in the classrooms. Social studies textbooks, materials used to teach reading, and other educational resources may have improved in recent years in presenting examples of accomplishments of minorities and women. However, whether children absorb this pluralistic view is often determined by the local educational system. For example, in many districts across the country, conflicts ensue about whether to include science materials that teach creationism along with evolution; about the content of sex education courses; and about the rights of the handicapped.

Even when a district seeks to foster pluralism and to protect the rights of the minorities, individual teachers may continue to reflect their own values, which have an impact on teaching. For example, a physical education teacher was heard to remark to a group of parents: "Don't worry about Title IX [which promotes sex equity]; we don't let our girls play football; they sit on the bench and watch the boys play." In the end, what the teacher *selects* for emphasis in the content, how the teacher *feels* about diversity and sex roles, and what the teacher *communicates* will determine whether pluralistic values prevail. Pratte (1981) states that "what is needed is a concentrated and systematic approach to pluralism in the classroom, one that will lead to a rejection of 'cultural elitism' and to an increased acceptance of diverse forms and values" (p. 1).

Another problem is that educational systems tend to thrust teachers into classrooms that have diverse populations with little training or understanding of learner differences and needs. Frequently, teachers are ill equipped to communicate with learners different from themselves or to help diverse learners capitalize upon the values inherent in their interactions with one another.

The remainder of this chapter seeks to help teachers understand those differences among learners that have an impact upon communication and learning. Sensitivity to these factors should improve classroom communication.

# ASPECTS OF DIVERSITY THAT INFLUENCE COMMUNICATION

When teachers understand the sources of differences in students, they communicate more effectively with them. Teachers who are sensitive to differences in the ways their students perceive the world, learn, and communicate can adapt their teaching to these varying experiences. Primary factors of diversity that we will focus on are *cultural differences, learning styles, family characteristics, sex differences, communication styles,* and *handicapping conditions.* As we examine these factors of diversity, it will become apparent that they are interrelated and can be separated for discussion purposes only.

## Cultural Differences

Increasing numbers of studies disclose that every culture has strengths and potential for achievement. However, cultural differences may produce differences in learning styles and in the ways students communicate. In Figure 4-1 Ramírez and Castañeda (1974, p. 60) present their view of the influence of life-styles and value systems from a cultural group on cognitive style.

This view is that child-rearing practices, which include systems of rewards and punishments, cultural goals and expectations, and so on, influence the ways individuals learn and communicate, which in turn influence their thinking or cognitive styles. Gay (1978) likewise notes that the learning styles of various ethnic groups are "inseparably linked to cultural perceptions and values regulating interpersonal relations" (p. 49). She describes two distinctive cognitive patterns that have emerged from research on ethnic learning styles: the *analytic style,* which is stimulus centered in its orientation to reality, requires sustained

FIGURE 4-1 Cultural Influences on Cognitive and Communication Style

attention, is detail specific, is impersonal, and utilizes an elaborated syntactic code; and the *relational style,* which is self-centered in its orientation, requires global characteristics and a descriptive mode of abstracting information from stimuli, determines word meanings by situational contexts, and utilizes a restricted syntactic code. The analytic style appears to be persistent among Anglo and Jewish Americans, while the relational style appears to be exhibited by many Mexican Americans, black Americans, some American Indians, and Asian Americans. Gardner (1980) describes Hispanic children as field sensitive, which includes being imaginative in describing social situations. Such children may have difficulty in school settings that emphasize analytic cognitive styles and that are task centered, rather than "people" centered. Field sensitivity may be related to the intense family ties that influence the incentive styles of Hispanic students. These are reflected in the Hispanic students' ability to cooperate and to be highly motivated by social reinforcement.

Morris (1978), in summarizing research on black Americans' culture and cognitive style, notes that for many black people the church is the hub of social life and provides an extended family with significant adults who provide material and human resources to families. Many black children appear to be more feeling oriented, more people oriented, and more proficient than white children at nonverbal communication (Hale, 1978; Morris, 1978). Morris further notes that white children have many opportunities to manipulate objects and to be object oriented; thus, classrooms are also object oriented in their emphasis on educational hardware such as books, listening stations, and learning kits. Akbar (1978) notes that African American children are viewed as being deviant from the Euro-American, with the latter being the "norm." This view has often contributed to the educational failure of the black child.

The importance of the influence of culturally induced child-rearing practices on cognitive development is underscored by the work of John-Steiner and Smith (1979) in southwestern Pueblo communities. They distinguish between cognitive development that takes place in a primary socialization setting, such as the family, and that which takes place in the more formal school settings. They describe early learning of Pueblo children, which occurs in the context of observing their elders and closely monitoring their activities; this freedom to choose their mentors and to observe and practice skills for long periods of time, with little pressure to perform well within a certain length of time, is in direct contrast to cognitive development activities in the school.

This chapter cannot outline the cultural characteristics of each ethnic group in the United States. However, the teacher can attempt to identify those groups present in the classroom and learn about cognitive and communication styles characteristic of that group. Gay (1978) has identified the following communication variables "identifiable as being culturally determined, as constituting ethnic communication styles, and as being influential in shaping interactions among members of different ethnic groups" (p. 52). These variables are:

attitudes

social organization (status of people within the culture)

patterns of thought

role prescription (how people are supposed to behave)

language

use and organization of space

vocabulary

time conceptualizations

nonverbal expressions

These variables "combine to regulate behaviors and perceptions relative to messages and meanings of communicative acts" (p. 52). Gay points out that these categories offer us a way of analyzing points of conflict between different ethnic communication styles.

Bennett (1979) describes five areas of behavior that form the basis for participation and communication in the culturally diverse classroom, and that may form the basis for conflict between the teacher's world view and the students'.

1. *Cooperation and Competition.*  Since most academic activities in this country are based upon competition and individual achievement, Anglo middle-class children often learn best working on their own. However, in other cultures, such as the black world view, competition and individual excellence may be emphasized in play while cooperation is emphasized in work situations. "What is nearly always interpreted by teachers as cheating, copying, or frivolous socializing may in fact be the child's natural inclination to seek help from a peer (borrowing a pencil or talking after a test has begun)" [p. 266].

2. *The Speaker-Listener Relationship.*  Most white middle-class children have learned to be passive recipients of teacher talk, with teachers doing over 75% of the talking and question asking. Many black children have learned that question-answer sequences reflect hostility. Also, they tend to communicate by involving the whole self with simultaneous responses of thought, feeling, and movement. It is difficult for them to sit in silence and to remove emotions and feelings from thinking.

3. *Written Versus Oral/Aural Tradition.*  Mainstream white culture emphasizes visual learning through the written word. However, many blacks and Latino students have grown up in oral traditions where music and the spoken word were at the heart of their experiences. Such students may learn best when the teacher reads aloud materials that are presented in writing.

4. *The Uses of Words: Communication Versus Manipulation.*  White culture usually emphasizes word accuracy, while black culture may emphasize delivery as a power device. Contrary to white expectations, blacks often gain power through their adeptness

with words and their ability to use a variety of verbal techniques. Street culture is an oral culture that may depend on colorful and creative uses of language.

5. ***Standard English.***   The emphasis on mainstream English (the standard) tends to repress and ignore the language that black children and others have learned from birth. White children may move ahead of black children in reading if reading materials ignore the black child's spoken language. Viewing dialects as substandard and ignoring their importance in learning can seriously hamper progress for minority children.

The area of nonverbal communication is extremely important in classroom communication. "For instance, while direct eye contact in one ethnic group is equated with attentiveness, in another it may be a sign of disrespect and defiance" (Gay, 1978, pp. 53–54). The teacher who insists that a particular Hispanic child "look at me when I talk to you" may be causing the child conflict between cultural norms and the desire to obey the teacher.

Teachers can exhibit attitudes toward cultural differences and foster them in their students to enable them to understand that their communication behaviors are largely determined by their cultural experiences; that each has some different attitudes toward language, and some different vocabularies and word usages; and that each has different criteria for assigning meaning to communication behaviors. They can also convey to their students the specific components of the essential communication differences among ethnic groups (Gay, 1978, p. 56).

## Learning Styles

We have already described the impact of the culture on an individual's style of thinking and learning. Gregoro (1979) describes learning style as consisting of "distinctive behaviors which serve as indicators of how a person learns from and adapts to his environment" (p. 234). Teachers can learn much about children's learning styles as they interact with them over a period of time. Since there are no specific tests for all aspects of learning style, teachers' observations, along with parents' reports, will be the primary factor in identifying how individual children seem to learn best. Fischer and Fischer (1979) have identified the following styles or aspects of individual learning that come from direct observation:

**The Incremental Learner.**   This student learns in a step-by-step fashion, systematically adding pieces to gain larger understanding. Such a student might benefit from programmed learning approaches.

**The Intuitive Learner.**   This student learns by sudden insight and generalization gained through unsystematic gathering of data. Quality of thinking exceeds the verbal ability to describe the process of reaching conclusions. The student may make many wild guesses and errors.

**The Sensory Specialist.**   The student relies primarily on one sense, such as the visual or auditory sense, to form ideas. Multisensory approaches do not work with these children, since they rely primarily upon one sense for gathering information; for example,

> Sheri, when studying her spelling looks at the word carefully, then shuts her eyes to visualize it. . . . By contrast, Steven must write the word at least eight times and seems to learn to spell kinesthetically. Kevin must spell the word aloud because he learns how to spell orally/aurally [p. 248].

**The Sensory Generalist.**   Such a student uses many of the senses to gather information. Sight, sound, touch, smell, and so on, may be used to relate ideas to prior knowledge or to learn new information. In some cases (for example, in many hyperactive children) we find the oversensitive learner, who finds it difficult to sort out or block out irrelevant stimuli. Such a child may need to be removed to a less stimulating environment, such as a study carrel, or may learn best in a one-to-one learning situation.

**The Emotionally Involved.**   Some students need a classroom that carries an intense emotional tone. Fischer and Fischer have identified two types of these classrooms. The first provides a vivid atmosphere that employs poetry, drama descriptions, and high teacher involvement in the content. The second provides active, open discussions where disagreements are common and strong positions are stated and defended; students who thrive in this atmosphere like rivalry and critical interaction.

**The Emotionally Neutral.**   This student works best in a task-oriented, low-key classroom where interpersonal conflicts are subdued. Interestingly, children who themselves may be very emotionally intense may work best in the low-key classroom. It has been frequently noted that some children, those who are disruptive in emotionally charged classrooms, cannot handle the boundaries of social interactions within the learning environment. Humor and joking may be their signal to become class clowns, and interpersonal conflict may cause them to overreact or become verbally or physically aggressive.

**The Explicitly Structured.**   Such a student learns best when goals are clear and unambiguous and limits are carefully stated. For example:

> Mike typically asks the teacher exactly what is expected of him, what sources he should use, what form his report should take, how long it should be, and similar questions. Once given clear and specific answers, he proceeds to do a conscientious job. In learning situations where he must define his goals, select his sources and decide on a method of presenting his findings, Mike is unhappy and insecure. He constantly seeks guidance from peers and from adults [pp. 249– 250].

**The Open-Ended Structured.**   Students who learn best in a fairly open-ended learning environment resist tight structure because they may see connections between what they are learning and many other facets of life.

> Steve, who is of the same age and intelligence as Mike, thrives in the less defined, more open-ended classroom. In fact, where the tasks and directions are explicit, Steve always tries to change or loosen them. He seeks more elbow room for his own ideas and enjoys the challenge presented in the open structure. He comes up with novel ways of presenting reports, does less well when he must follow a prepared form or predetermined sequence of activities [p. 250].

**The Damaged Learner.**   Fischer and Fischer describe a large category of students who are "physically normal yet damaged in self-concept, social competency, aesthetic sensitivity, or intellect in such a way that they develop negative learning styles" (p. 250). Because the disability is imposed on the other identified learning styles, these students are different from other learners and may avoid or reject learning. Such learners need specialized help, either in the mainstreamed classroom or in self-contained learning environments.

**The Eclectic Learner.**   Such students can adapt learning styles for the benefit of others. They succeed in school by adapting from classroom to classroom or from teacher to teacher without making demands for teachers to adjust their ways of teaching.

Students may, of course, demonstrate more than one learning style and may alter these over time. It is important to separate learning style from the notion of intelligence. "The incremental learner may be just as intelligent as the intuitive one; the emotionally involved learner just as bright as the emotionally neutral one" (Fischer and Fischer, 1979, p. 254).

Teachers tend to vary in their teaching styles, and it is a mistake to think that teachers are "stuck" in a particular approach to teaching; they must learn to vary their styles to fit the needs of learners. As Brophy and Evertson (1976) have pointed out, the most flexible teachers, those who implement a "large number of diagnostic, managerial, and therapeutic skills, tailoring behavior . . . to the specific needs of the moment" (p. 139), are the most effective.

When we view teaching as communication, we become more sensitive to the perceptions and viewpoints of those with whom we interact. Through repeated interactions with students, we become aware of their learning styles and try to structure the messages of the learning environment to meet them.

Ellis (1979) helped teachers in a school to expand their teaching strategies through models that helped them practice strategies for (1) teaching concepts from simple to the complex; (2) providing structure or negotiating it with students; (3) selecting topics and materials for study or permitting students to select part or all of them; (4) fostering the development of empathy; (5) encouraging participation in group discussion and activities; (6) helping students formulate and test hypotheses; and (7) enabling students to engage in creative problem solving and testing of alternatives. In addition, teachers learned to serve as facilitators and classifiers of student discussions rather than as the primary sources of information. While many of these skills are neglected in traditional teacher education programs, they are often taught in the context of instructional communication courses as part of the repertoire of every teacher.

## Family Characteristics

Although family structures in America have undergone significant change in the past two or three decades, teachers and textbook publishers often behave as though the norm is that of a two-parent family in which the mother works only in the home and where children are all blood relatives. The evidence is quite to the contrary.

Brown (1980) cites statistics for 1980 indicating that 18% of American schoolchildren live with a lone parent and 48% will live for a considerable amount of time with one parent before they reach the age of eighteen. Single-parent homes occur through divorce, death of a spouse, and birth of children of unmarried mothers or fathers. Evidence reveals that children from one-parent homes have a greater incidence of tardiness, discipline problems, suspensions, and expulsions than children from two-parent homes (Brown, 1980, p. 537). However, it would be very dangerous for teachers to generalize these problems and to view the single-parent home in a negative light. Many families are in various stages of adjustment to death or divorce, and there is great variability in the ways families react. Wallerstein and Kelly

(1980), in a study of sixty families five years after divorce, found 34% of the children resilient and thriving, 29% reacting reasonably well, and 37% depressed and looking backward to the predivorce state. Much of the difference could be attributed to the relationships that children had with both parents and the stability of the relationship established by each with the child.

Children whose families are experiencing divorce may communicate (usually unintentionally) their distress in the classroom. Allers (1980) identified the following signs that such a child might exhibit: absentmindedness (partially complete work, asking teachers to repeat directions, and so on), nervousness, weariness, moodiness, withdrawal, declining grades, acting up (picking on classmates, talking out, destroying materials, and so on), physical complaints, or no change. Those in the last category may be feeling guilty or frustrated even though there are no outward signs of stress.

Among the ways in which teachers can help, Allers (1980) and others suggest:

**Discussion.**  Teachers can open discussions to allow children to compare their situations with those of others who are experiencing or have experienced similar traumas. Discussing such situations as visitations and holiday celebrations may help all of the children in the class, including those from two-parent homes, to understand a variety of solutions to problems.

**Teaching the Words to Express Feelings.**  Often children cannot understand what they are feeling or do not have the words to enable them to express it. Using literature, drama, role playing, and conversation that helps children identify their feelings will encourage their communication with peers and adults.

**Involving Parents.**  Conferences can often help parents become aware of their children's feelings and can encourage their own communication with the children.

Many other factors contribute to diversity with respect to family experiences. For example, many children have been adopted or are living in foster families. Some children may not know that they are adopted, while others may know although the information is not available to the teacher. Teachers must develop sensitivity to feelings of adoptive parents and children.

Children who are adopted may find it difficult to become involved in class projects that trace the family history or require them to compare their blood types with those of their parents. In a conference with an insensitive teacher, an adoptive parent was asked whether she knew anything about the child's "real parents." Acceptance of the adoptee's parents as the child's real parents should be communicated both to the adopted child and to children living with biological parents. In an effort to promote diversity, teachers might model their behavior on that of one parent, who taught her adopted children at a very young age that a person's parents may be the people who "grew" the child in the woman's tummy or may be people who received the child from someone else who grew the baby. While some teachers may not wish to be that descriptive, they might communicate to all children the possible variations in the ways that families grow and develop. The teacher's attitude that allows for diversity will have an impact on children's acceptance of one another.

There are many other factors to which the teacher must be sensitive with respect to family differences. One child may be an only child, while another may come from a large extended family where several generations are represented. One child may be the oldest in a large family and may have experienced a great deal of responsibility for younger siblings, while another may be the youngest and may have had the benefit of a great deal of teaching from older siblings. Zajonc (1976) points out that an only child has few opportunities to be a teacher; this is in contrast to children with siblings, who can teach games, explain new words, and divulge what they may get away with.

Some children may never have left the house in which they were born, while others may be parts of migrant families that have experienced living in many different parts of the country. All of these children have had different experiences; all have experienced different patterns of communication within the family setting. The teacher can capitalize on this diversity by helping children to talk about their differences, using their experiences to help them communicate, thus enhancing learning within the various subject areas. Most of all, the teacher can sensitize children to differences in viewpoints and experiences, and can help them to accept a wide range of people who are different from themselves.

## Sex Differences

To what extent do males and females differ in the ways in which they learn and in which they communicate? Are there differences that the teacher should focus on in the process of teaching? In a thorough review of hundreds of studies on sex differences, Maccoby and Jacklin (1974) concluded that "the sexes are psychologically much alike in many respects" (p. 373). Although some of the differences in behavior (such as superior verbal ability for girls and accelerated math learning for boys in adolescence) may have a biological basis, there is a great deal of conflicting evidence about such differences. In addition, separating the impact of early cultural expectation from actual biological differences is difficult.

An overwhelming body of evidence demonstrates that sex differences in communication are the result of stereotyping, that is, of adult expectations about the ways in which males and females in our society should behave. Kagan (1964) confirmed that children tend to associate male behavior with aggression, dominance, and independence and female behavior with passivity, nurturance, and emotionality. In reviewing the cumulative research on sex differences in speech patterns (that is, in syntactic and phonetic usage, word choice, or conversational style), Thorne (1978) found that there were few real differences, but that research showed a high degree of stereotyping of male and female speech patterns.

Through filming infants and children, Birdwhistell (1970) concluded that the body language (posture, pelvic tilt, and so on) associated with gender is established by the second year of life; however, such behavior is very likely the result of early sex identity and expectations rather than "innate" biological characteristics. Wood (1981) supports this notion by stating that "further study of the body language of gender communication may reveal a shift in children's communication from traditional gender cues to a more modern set of cues" (p. 183).

To support the idea that cultural stereotyping affects the communication of males and females, Edelsky (1977) studied the extent to which there is agreement in adults and children about how men and women talk. She found a definite stereotyping about language and sex in our culture — that is, adults show agreement on many of the particulars concerning the stereotype. Children show a gradual progression in their acquisition of the adult norms from first to sixth grades. Older children have even more stereotyping of judgments about sex and language than do adults. First graders used topic more than form to identify sex in various sentences. For example, the phrase "Oh, dear" in the statement "Oh, dear, the TV set broke" was identified as male "because my dad watches TV" or as female "because my mom watches TV when she's ironing." But at the third-grade level, children were in a transition period between strategies focusing on form or topic:

EXPERIMENTER:  Who says "Won't you pretty please hand me the hammer?"
CHILD:  The lady.
EXPERIMENTER:  Why?
CHILD:  'Cause of "pretty please."
EXPERIMENTER:  How about "Won't you pretty please hand me the baseball uniform"?
CHILD:  Maybe a boy.
EXPERIMENTER:  Why?
CHILD:  'Cause of "baseball uniform" [p. 235].

Edelsky found that adults associated profanity with males and expressions like "divine" and "Oh, dear" with females. However, there is often discrepancy between performance and belief, as demonstrated when one of her male subjects said that men would not use "Oh, dear" because it was passive; but later, when unable to think of a response to another question, he said, "Oh, dear, I'm just going to run the tape down."

Montgomery and Norton (1981) reviewed literature that suggested that males are more dominant than females in communication, while women appear to be more attentive than men; males appear to be more relaxed than females in their communicator styles, while females appear to be more animated (as indicated by eye contact, gestures, facial expressions, and body movements). Their study found that males report being more precise and females report being more animated in their communication behaviors.

However, Karre (1976) has emphasized that differences in style may relate to sex-typed roles. Boys learn that "controlling and manipulating their environments and people around them is the expected role" (p. 45) and that they are expected to be competitive, solve problems, and take risks. Girls learn that they are expected to be dependent and passive in their interactions with others as well as more sociable, conforming, and accommodating to the needs of others. Karre believes that these differences in communication are learned early through cultural expectations and are later reinforced by the media, where commercials depict females as homebound or blithering idiots who cannot make decisions about simple products in the supermarket. Using Brockriede's descriptions (Darnell and Brockriede, 1976), Karre described two theories — sex differences in communication that are culturally learned, and the notion of the Rhetorically Sensitive Person as a goal — that teachers might use for all students. At one end of the continuum is the Noble Self, a person who tends to control rather than share choices, to engage in monologue rather than dialogue, and to "rape or seduce" rather than love. At the other end of the continuum are the Rhetorical Reflectors, who tend to play a passive role in communication, operating on the perceived wishes of others and accommodating themselves to the choices of others. In the midrange is the Rhetorically Sensitive Person, whom Brockriede views as a believer in shared choice, dialogue, and loving behavior; in other words, the "ideal" communicator who wants neither to control the communication transaction nor to play either a passive role or the victim of a controller. This person is "genuine, aims at accurate empathic understanding, offers the other person unconditional positive regard, embodies presentness, works for a spirit of mutual equality, and helps establish a supportive psychological climate for himself/herself and for others" (Karre, p. 45).

Unfortunately, through the reinforcing of cultural stereotypes, many males communicate the Noble Self, while many females play the role of Rhetorical Reflector. In a similar vein Bate (1976) reported that women students are more uncomfortable than male students in asserting themselves in various interpersonal situations, and that women report more fear in speaking before groups. However, men may be rewarded for dogmatic or authoritative responses in conflict situations; unfortunately, they may worry about being "real men" if they express warmth and reveal personal emotions. The goal for the teacher is to help students become men and women who communicate as Rhetorically Sensitive People.

How do the school and the teacher's behavior perpetuate culturally derived differences? Recent studies confirm that teachers treat boys and girls differently in the classroom. Teachers' messages reflect their culturally induced stereotypes about sex differences. Major findings about teachers' communication with the sexes are:

1. Teachers spend more time interacting with boys than with girls (Brophy and Good, 1974; Wirtenberg, Klein, Richardson, and Thomas, 1981).
2. High-achieving boys receive more teacher approval and active instruction, while low-achieving boys are likely to receive more criticism. High-achieving girls receive less praise than both low- and high-achieving boys (Parsons, Futterman, Kaczala, and Meece, 1979).
3. Boys receive more discipline than girls (Jackson and Lahaderne, 1967), and there is a difference in disciplinary actions. Boys are more likely to be reprimanded in a harsh and public manner and to receive heavier penalties than girls. Teachers are also more likely to respond when boys are aggressive than when girls are, and to use more loud reprimands when scolding boys (Serbin, O'Leary, Kent, and Tonick, 1973).
4. Boys receive a larger number of negative communications, but more teacher questions seem to be directed at boys, and their ideas are used more often (Wirtenberg, Klein, Richardson, and Thomas, 1981).

In relation to the ways schools reinforce the stereotype, Gillis (1981) reports:

Educators often organize the materials and equipment traditionally associated with each of the sexes in separate areas of the classroom or playground. This encourages girls and boys to work and play separately and ensures that few children will attempt to use materials or participate in activities traditionally associated with the opposite sex (Levy and Stacey, 1973; Ricks and Pyke, 1973). In fact, teachers discourage children from engaging in behavior and activities associated with the opposite sex and have less tolerance for boys who do so than for girls who do so (Chasen, 1974; Levitan and Chananie, 1972) [p. 184].

Teachers of speech communication appear to be just as guilty as others of sexist practices in the classroom. Sprague (1975) found that most anthologies of model speeches feature speeches by men. Furthermore, she found that many hypothetical applications of communication skills perpetuate role stereotypes: for example, a man arguing a case in court and a woman making an announcement at a PTA meeting. Audience analysis sections of texts usually emphasize that women are more persuasible and less logical than men, and that sex is an important variable to know because it will make a difference in how you adapt your content to your audience. In written speech critiques by college teachers, Sprague found, women teachers wrote a greater proportion of positive as compared to negative comments than did male teachers. Also, women students received proportionately more positive comments from teachers of both sexes than did male students. Finally, female students receiving B, C, and D grades received proportionately more positive comments than did male students in those same categories.

It is evident, then, that "the language, organization, curriculum and materials of the school are giving children constant messages about what are considered appropriate behaviors, aspirations and valued traits in persons of their sex" (Gillis, 1981, p. 183). Unfortunately, these stereotypes have a negative impact upon many aspects of living, including career choice. In general, women are underrepresented in the higher levels of education; more boys than girls take math, a subject "generally considered a critical filter which has historically excluded women from a wide range of nontraditional occupations such as engineering and physics" (Wirtenberg, Klein, Richardson, and Thomas, 1981, p. 314). The different expectations teachers hold for boys and girls continue the cultural stereotypes that begin in many homes and become powerful socializing agents for students.

How can the teacher overcome sexist behavior in self and students?

The teacher must become more aware of values and attitudes about sex roles that have been inherited from the culture, and must attempt to break the stereotypes in the classroom.

Karre (1976) offers examples of activities that the teacher can use to help students become aware of their stereotypes; for example, in the elementary school:

> Have students make *Gift Lists*. Using Wards, Sears, or any other large catalog, have students choose and cut out a gift for each member of their family. (Clothing should be excluded from possible selections.) When the gift lists and pictures are completed, discuss the following questions: Why did you choose certain gifts for certain people, i.e., toaster for Mom, golf bag for Dad, train for brother, doll for sister? Did you choose the gifts because you thought the person would really use the gift? Because it was something the person could want? Would you reverse the gifts you gave your mother — father — sister — brother? Why or why not? Do our perceptions and concepts of what is right for males and females influence our selection of gifts? [p. 49.]

For older students, the following activities might be appropriate:

> Have students examine their writing and speech for *Sexist Language*. Analysis could take the following directions: How does language limit and shape thought? Discuss the connotations of "old maid," "Dear Sir," "chick," "dude," etc. Discuss the usage of "he," "him," "mankind," "manpower," etc. for the plural of both sexes. Encourage suggestions for less sexism in language, i.e., Dear Gentlepeople, personkind, peoplepower, etc.

> Invite into the classroom *Guests* who provide evidence of alternative career choices, such as female cab drivers, lawyers, veterinarians; male cooks, nursery school teachers and nurses. Also invite guests to share hobbies that break stereotyped expectations for leisure-time activities. Invite men who do needlework. (Sharing Rosey Grier's success in the needlepoint business would be a good preparation.) Invite women who work on cars [pp. 49–50].

Bate (1976) advocates the concept of assertive speaking as a guideline for effective interpersonal communication. In model programs, students try out their own style of speaking to a peer, a person in authority, or one doing a service for them. As both boys and girls practice assertiveness in such situations as initiating an interaction, expressing an opinion, or refusing a request, sex stereotyping tends to diminish.

Other things that teachers can do to minimize sex stereotyping and help students of both sexes achieve their communication potential are:

1. In disciplining students, relate penalties to the behavior and apply them in the same manner for members of both sexes.
2. Become more aware of when you criticize and praise, and attempt to do both in an equitable manner for the sexes.
3. Avoid stereotypes of speech delivery related to sex, and "acknowledge that a wide range of styles of presentation can be effective [and should] avoid shackling girls by a narrow concept of what is ladylike" (Sprague, 1975, p. 45).
4. Integrate seating arrangements, lines, teams, and instructional groups to provide a maximum interaction between the sexes. Evidence shows that behavior problems improve rather than deteriorate when such integration occurs (National Advisory Council, 1981).
5. Assign helping roles in such a way as to minimize sex stereotyping. Boys can be the class secretary, set the table for a party, and sew costumes for a play, just as girls can help carry chairs, distribute books, and hammer nails for a play set.

## Communicator Styles of Students

We attempt to emphasize throughout this book that communication is the basis for the teaching/learning process. We have examined several factors that are sources of student diversity in the classroom. All of these — cultural environment, learning styles, family characteristics, and sex differences (real or perceived) — will affect the ways students learn to communicate. Each human being develops a communicator style that is unique, and each student and teacher will bring a unique style to the teaching/learning process.

Communicator style, which is a relatively recent subject for research, is important for the teacher who is attempting to understand the sources of diversity in the classroom. Communicator style has been defined by Norton (1977) as "the way one verbally and paraverbally interacts to signal how literal meaning should be taken, interpreted, filtered or understood" (p. 527). In other words, we are concerned with the way individuals behave through words and nonverbal actions in response to meanings. Norton has identified the following variables that describe communicator style:

*Dominant.* The dominant communicator talks frequently, takes charge in a social situation, comes on strong, and controls informal conversations.

*Dramatic.* The dramatic communicator manipulates exaggerations, fantasies, stories, metaphors, rhythm, voice, and other stylistic devices to highlight or understate content.

*Contentious.* The contentious communicator is argumentative.

*Animated.* The animated communicator provides frequent and sustained eye contact, uses many facial expressions, and gestures often.

*Impression Leaving.*   The impression leaving communicator tends to be remembered because of the stimuli which are projected. What is said and the way it is said is emphasized.

*Relaxed.*   The relaxed communicator is calm and collected, not nervous under pressure, and does not show nervous mannerisms.

*Attentive.*   The attentive communicator really likes to listen to the other, shows interest in what the other is saying, and deliberately reacts in such a way that the other knows he or she is being listened to.

*Open.*   The open communicator readily reveals personal things about the self, easily expressed feelings and emotions, and tends to be unsecretive, unreserved, and somewhat frank.

*Friendly.*   The friendly communicator is encouraging to people, acknowledges other's contributions, openly expresses admiration and tends to be tactful.

*Precise.*   The precise communicator tries to be strictly accurate when arguing, prefers well-defined arguments, and likes proof or documentation when arguing.

*Voice.*   Voice is a style component which focuses upon how recognizable a person sounds in terms of loudness.

*Communicatc image.*   A person with a good communicator image finds it easy to talk with strangers, to small groups of people, and with members of the opposite sex [pp. 528–529].

Using Norton's style categories, Stohl (1981) examined the relationship between preschool children's communicator styles and their perceived attractiveness by their teachers and peers. She found that the higher the children were rated on each style, the more attractive they were to teachers and peers. In comparison with those rated by peers as the least attractive children, the moderately and highly attractive children had better communicator images and were more impression leaving, open, dramatic, contentious, and animated. Stohl concluded:

> Taking charge of the social situation communicatively makes children more noticeable to their peers and, hence, possibly more attractive. Even the contentious style which tends to have negative connotations for most adults is a strong covariate of peer attractiveness [p. 371].

However, children who were perceived as more attractive to teachers had a style of communication that was more friendly, attentive, and relaxed. While the "attentive style is attractive for adults . . . it is not relevant for children's rating of attractiveness" (p. 373). Stohl also found that older children were perceived as having different style characteristics from younger children: "As children get older, they are perceived to communicate in a more open, relaxed, friendly, and attentive style" (p. 374). In other words, they more closely approximated adults' perceptions of desirable communication characteristics.

Teachers undoubtedly will find children in their classes who are in different phases of development with respect to communicator styles. However, children, as they get older, will demonstrate communication profiles that are unique and reflective of their personalities.

Also relevant to communicator style is the notion of communication apprehension discussed in Chapter 3. Consistent with Stohl's findings are those of McCroskey and Daly (1976), who found that teachers have negative perceptions of quiet children (those having high communication apprehension). Daly and Friedrich (1981) attempted to discover factors in the early lives of college students that appeared to be related to the development of communication apprehension. They discovered that, in addition to the amount of positive reinforcement and encouragement received at home, the school was an important factor in whether students became apprehensive. College students who were apprehensive about communicating tended to perceive a greater amount of correction received for mistakes in school than did their less apprehensive classmates. In other words, negative messages about communication and learning in the early grades probably play a role in students' development of communicator style, particularly in those aspects related to motivation and enjoyment in communicating.

## Handicapping Conditions

An additional factor of student diversity emerges from handicapping conditions in children and the recent emphasis on mainstreaming, in which handicapped children are placed in the regular classroom. It was recently recognized that fewer than half of all handicapped children were receiving an appropriate education through traditional special education programs (Miller and Miller, 1978 – 79). As a result, Congress in 1975 enacted Public Law 94-142, the Education of All Handicapped Children Act, which guarantees each handicapped child the right to a free public education in the "least restrictive environment." This means that for some students, especially those with mild handicaps, the regular classroom must provide the least restrictive environment, while other students require help in more specialized programs.

The National Association for Retarded Citizens (NARC) considers mainstreaming to be a philosophy or priniciple of educational service delivery that "allows maximal temporal, social and instructional interaction among mentally retarded and nonretarded students in the normal course of the school day" (Coursen, 1981, p. 3). This description stresses the idea of mainstreaming as being for all children, since it increases the interaction among diverse groups. Proponents of mainstreaming emphasize that belief in the process is critical to its success; also, while specific skills are important, "a belief that all children are entitled to appropriate quality education" is necessary to the success of mainstreaming (Coursen, 1981, p. 35).

Indications are that increasing the interactions between handicapped and nonhandicapped children will benefit both groups. Thompson (1980), in reviewing the research on the handicapped, found: (1) handicapped adults tend to be perceived as inferior; (2) nonhandicapped adults and children tend to avoid interactions with the handicapped and to exhibit cues of discomfort when communicating with them; (3) handicapped children (as early as preschool age) are likely to be rejected by their peers; (4) decreased contact experienced by handicapped children and adults may result in fewer opportunities to develop interpersonal and interactive skills; (5) a handicap may have negative effects on a child's self-image and self-esteem.

Using network analysis to measure interaction patterns, Thompson found that handicapped mainstreamed children engaged in more mixed contact and were more likely to play with nonhandicapped children at home than those not mainstreamed. Likewise, McHale and Boone (1980) demonstrated that "play between autistic children and children from regular classes under carefully directed circumstances is a practical and effective way for teachers to enhance the social skills of both autistic and nonhandicapped children" (p. 53). Johnson and Johnson (1981) showed that friendships between handicapped and nonhandicapped students can be enhanced in the mainstreamed classroom when cooperative, rather than individualistic, instructional procedures are used.

Sapon-Shevin (1979) lists five features of a well-mainstreamed classroom; these have implications for classroom communication:

1.  *Intentionally Heterogeneous Classrooms.*  Teachers can develop programs that *use* rather than ignore individual differences through such techniques as multiage or "family" groupings.

2.  *Peer Tutoring and Cooperative Instruction.*  Students with strengths in specific subjects can help those with weaknesses, thereby helping students to view differences positively.

3.  *Multi-level, Flexible Curriculum.*  In addition to using a variety of sensory modalities to help students learn, teachers can plan units in which students are working on the same objective, but at their appropriate levels.

4.  *Interdisciplinary Programming.*  Rather than pull students out for special services, special teachers can team teach with regular teachers, sharing responsibility for the learning of "normal" and "exceptional" students.

5.  *Preparation and Education of Children.*  Children in mainstreamed classrooms should be educated concerning all kinds of differences — sexual, racial, ethnic, physical, and mental. "Positive precepts concerning the value and respectability of every human being must be instilled at every phase" [p. 374].

In bringing about an appropriate environment for mainstreaming, the support of the school principal is vital: to communicate support for the program, facilitate communication between regular and special education teachers, lead staff development programs, and understand anxieties that teachers often feel in working with special students (Coursen, 1981). Dodd (1980) notes that classroom teachers often do not support mainstreaming because of their fears of working with handicapped individuals. They have not been prepared to deal with disability or their own feelings about it. A sensitive principal may help teachers to "open up" about their fears and to discuss them with one another.

Teachers frequently report that they do not feel qualified to manage classrooms in which there are exceptional learners. An exceptional learner has been defined as "an individual who because of uniqueness in sensory, physical, neurological, temperamental, or intellectual capacity and/or in the nature or range of previous experience, requires an adaptation of the regular school program in order to maximize his or her functioning level" (Hewitt and Forness, 1977, p. 75).

Hewitt and Watson (1979) report that of the 12% of the nation's school-age children who fall into the exceptional learner category, the largest percentage (approximately 63% of these children) is made up of the mildly mentally retarded, the learning disabled, and the behavior disordered. Understanding the problems involved in communicating with these three groups of children should help management of the mainstreamed classroom.

**1. Mildly Retarded.**  Such children usually show attentional deficits and have difficulties in discriminating relevant from irrelevant cues. They often have a tendency to transfer negative rather than positive learning; the more retarded they are, the more limited they are likely to be in their repertoire of experiences. While they are often highly motivated to learn, they may be overly susceptible to social praise and tend to rely on others to solve their problems. Hewitt and Watson (1979) emphasize the necessity for the teacher to use a variety of cue dimensions such as color, form, size, and texture in teaching these children. In addition, teachers should stress accuracy and avoid trial-and-error approaches, use overlearning (practice beyond initial mastery of material), and distribute this practice over a period of time. Training these students to be independent, with continuous reduction of cues provided by adults, is vital. In communicating with the mildly retarded child, the teacher should ask for repetition of steps out loud. The teacher's task is also to help children become less social in certain situations and to rely more on their own judgments than on the judgments of others.

**2. Learning Disabled.**  The term "learning disability" has emerged to describe a large group of children who have difficulties learning in the traditional school system.

> Among children designated as learning-disabled, many seem to have trouble selecting — from among the mass of sensory stimulation impinging on them — that stimulus which is relevant to the task at hand. Others may well perceive stimuli in an atypical fashion, and still others seem to code information in an ineffective or inefficient way. Some of these children seem impulsive, some hyperactive, some distractible, and some undermotivated. There are those who have detectable abnormalities in brain functions and others who have secondarily acquired low self-esteem, expectations of failure, high anxiety in the face of learning tasks, or such behavior problems as aggression or withdrawal [Ross, 1976, p. 2].

In addition to the problems of the learning-disabled child described in Chapter 2, the teacher should remember that in the mainstreamed classroom, learning-disabled children may exhibit behavior problems because of their difficulties in social behavior. Bryan and Bryan (1978) cite evidence that parents, strangers, peers, and teachers tend to view the social behavior of learning-disabled children negatively. The learning-disabled child's difficulties in social behaviors appear to stem from social perception difficulties or the inability to identify and recognize the meaning and significance of the behavior of others (Johnson and Myklebust, 1967). For example, Wiig and Harris (1974) demonstrated that learning-disabled children had more difficulty than a nondisabled group in identifying the emotions of anger, fear, embarrassment, and joy.

Mounting evidence indicates that social-perception difficulties in learning-disabled children appear to stem from problems in decoding and encoding nonverbal cues in communication (Bryan, 1977; Bryan, Sherman, and Fisher, 1980). Parents and teachers report that they frequently must become very angry at learning-disabled children before they recognize the anger. Since such children sometimes miss cues of sarcasm, humor, and other subtleties, their behavior is often inappropriate.

Unfortunately, teachers may react differently to learning-disabled children than to nondisabled children on the basis of their nonverbal behavior. Lyon (1977) studied twelve boys in a self-contained classroom for the handicapped and found that those boys rated low by the teacher on a social-personal attribute scale received a greater amount of negative nonverbal behaviors (frowns, shakes of the head, glares, touching to restrain them, and so on) than those rated higher. Bryan and Perlmutter (1979) found that adult females viewing videotapes of learning-disabled and nondisabled children rated the disabled more negatively on the basis of their nonverbal behaviors.

Because of their hyperactivity, many learning-disabled students may be put on drugs such as amphetamines to help increase attention span. The hyperactive child's problems may be manifested in "short attention span, restlessness, hyperactivity due to fleeting and wandering attention, poor interpersonal relations with peers related to inability to focus attention on subtle social cues, and the relative inability to understand verbal instructions and follow them, particularly instructions of teachers" (Sprague and Gadow, 1976, p. 115). These authors present evidence that drugs definitely alter classroom behavior and learning performance for many hyperactive children. It is important, however, that the teacher be involved in the drug therapy by performing diagnostic functions and reporting on the effects of the drug. "The teacher is the physician's clinical laboratory for the child's response to treatment" (p. 122).

In general, learning-disabled children need to experience success in learning; to imitate the social behaviors of nondisabled children; and to be taught in ways that will enable them to process and remember information, since they frequently cannot process too many directions at once. They may need instructions repeated or presented in various sensory modalities, may benefit most from one-to-one help in the classroom, and may need concepts interpreted for them, particularly those involving social interaction with which others of their age need little help. Such children also respond well to a structured environment, where rewards and consequences are clearly related to behaviors that are within the control of the child; they can tolerate little change and do not deal well with the unexpected. A change of classroom teachers, new children in the class, visitors, or holidays may overstimulate the hyperactive, learning-disabled child to such a point that focusing attention becomes impossible.

**3. The Behavior Disordered.** The child with an emotional disturbance or behavior disorder may or may not be learning disabled; conversely, the learning-disabled child may or may not demonstrate behavior disorders. Since the groups overlap, "what we may be moving toward is *good* education for children with learning and behavior problems rather than very specifically conceived educational approaches for the mildly retarded, or for the learning disabled, or for the behavior-disordered" (Hewitt and Watson, 1979, p. 314).

Several approaches in managing the behavior-disordered child are described by Hewitt and Watson (1979). These include drugs for hyperactivity just as in the case of the learning-disabled child and the "life space interview," a technique in which the teacher confronts the child with "the here and now events associated with a problem, and provides support and direction for avoiding the problem in the future" (p. 316). Most widely used in managing the behavior-disordered child are behavior modification approaches such as those described in Chapter 2 of this text. Most of these approaches rely on the teacher to set contingencies or to administer consequences. However, Hewitt and Watson describe approaches where exceptional learners serve as regulators of their own behaviors. Four strategies are used in self-regulation:

1. **Self-Assessment.**  Learners examine their behavior and decide if expectations have been met.

2. **Self-Recording.**  The learner objectively records the frequency of one or more behaviors.

3. **Self-Determination of Reinforcement.**  The learner selects from available reinforcers what was earned, based on performance of one or more behaviors.

4. **Self-Administration of Reinforcement.**  The learner dispenses the reinforcement which may or may not be self-determined, based on performance.

Using a tally card or rating scale, students have successfully used self-recording procedures to reduce behaviors such as talking, hitting, and whining. Hewitt and Watson point out that effective approaches with exceptional learners tend to be effective with nonexceptional learners. Likewise, if the teacher learns to communicate with handicapped children, *all* children are likely to benefit. They state:

> Rather than different in kind, the methods of special education are, in general, different in degree: more repetition, more stimulus input, more emphasis on preacademic skills already mastered by nonexceptional children, more one-to-one teacher-child contact, more emphasis on relationship building, more individualization of curriculum, more specificity in the use of rewards and punishments, more systematic record keeping, and more total environmental concerns [p. 332].

## GUIDELINES FOR COPING WITH DIVERSITY

By now it should be evident that every classroom houses a diverse population of students, some being more diverse than others. The more students interact with others who are different in culture, learning styles, sex, communication style, family characteristics, and physical ability, the more skilled they will become in human relations. The school has the role of fostering human relations based upon sound communication. In recognition of this, some state and local education agencies have developed curricula for multicultural, nonsexist education. One of the best examples is that produced by the Iowa State Department of Public Instruction in 1980. Among the basic assumptions underlying the Iowa program are the following that have implications for fostering productive communication in the classroom:

1. There are many different cultural elements in our society and these differences are not likely to vanish. Events cause them to emerge in each new generation. This cultural diversity is a strength and one of the cornerstones upon which America was built.
2. It is good that persons have as much freedom as possible in choosing the career or life-style compatible with their interests and abilities.
3. The level of prejudice one holds toward another group is indirectly proportional to the amount of meaningful interaction one has with the members of the group.
4. If one can learn to hate and mistrust others, then one can learn to like, trust, and appreciate others for what they are. As a result of selected instructional materials,

teaching practices, and curriculum content, student attitudes and behavior can be changed. However, this will not happen unless it is carefully planned.

5. Prejudice and discrimination are rooted in ignorance. The more facts one knows about the culture, history, and achievements of another group, the less apt one is to show prejudice toward members of that group. Persons inexperienced in intergroup relations frequently alienate members of other groups with whom they actually want to be friendly by inadvertently expressing themselves in the language of prejudice.

   - Testimonials: "I like your people," "You are as good as I am," "Some of my best friends are . . ." "She really did well for a woman."
   - Slips of the tongue: "That's darn white of you," "I jewed him down," "I worked like a nigger."
   - Ethnic jokes: The person who is a member of the group toward which the joke is aimed cannot be sure if the storyteller accepts or rejects the stereotypes laughed at. This is even more true when the jokes are aimed at a group which has been and still is the victim of prejudice and discrimination.
   - Caricatures of racial groups: From time to time, public programs have exaggerated or burlesqued supposed characteristics of racial groups for effect.

6. Intergroup understanding is impeded by ignoring individual and group differences and treating all persons as if they were alike. It is also impeded by the opposite approach which is treating people of other groups as if they were totally different. All human beings, whether they be male or female, black or white, Jew or Christian, have the same basic needs and are more alike than they are different. However, there are very real differences in customs, values, and beliefs which have been passed from one generation to another within cultures. Both similarities and differences must be recognized and efforts must be made to understand the reasons for the differences if better intergroup understanding is to result.

   - The "treat everybody alike" method approach ignores real differences in custom and beliefs that are rooted in the culture of individuals.
   - The "treat everybody alike" method ignores the fact that a woman or a minority person may bring to the situation an emotional outlook brought about by bitter and unpleasant experiences.
   - The "treat everybody alike" principle assumes that there are no cultural differences worth acknowledging and preserving in the life of members of other groups.
   - The "treat everybody as if they are totally different" approach ignores the very basic qualities all human beings have in common.

7. A multicultural, nonsexist education program is more apt to succeed if the members of the various groups are represented in the planning, implementation, and evaluation process. This is hard to do in school districts which have no minority population, but even in these districts it might be possible to utilize a resource person in an advisory capacity. There is no excuse for any district not to involve both women and men; while in the "one race schools" efforts should be made to involve members of various ethnic, religious, and socioeconomic groups [pp. 5–6].

The Iowa program lists a set of student objectives that may be adapted to any community or to various factors of diversity in a given classroom. Those objectives and the preamble deserve to be excerpted here, since they are built primarily upon principles of effective communication.

The ultimate objective of the multicultural, nonsexist education program is to help students achieve maximum understanding, respect, and appreciation of themselves and others. This means that students must be provided with specific activities that are planned carefully and given proper scope and sequence. Teaching guides should be aimed at achieving specific student objectives. The following are some suggested objectives for a multicultural, nonsexist education program:

- A positive, realistic self-concept in every student regardless of race or sex. The students should be able to talk about themselves comfortably in the classroom. They would realize the things they like and dislike about themselves. Of the things they do not like, they should distinguish between those they cannot change (must learn to accept) and those where improvement is possible.
- Student ability to listen.
- Student awareness of the ways that human beings are alike and ways in which they differ (e.g., race, sex, culture) that give them an individual and group identity. The student should be able to list similarities as well as differences when shown pictures of various races of human beings.
- Student awareness of the various racial, cultural, and ethnic groups which make up America, as well as the realization that diversity enriches life and is a fundamental cornerstone upon which America was built.
- A student awareness of the history, the contributions, the cultures, and the values of various subgroups in American society (races, sexes, ethnic groups . . . ). The student should be able to list the major contributions various ethnic groups have made to American culture.
- Student awareness of the history and the contributions of women, as well as men, in developing this country.
- Students' awareness of their basic values and the extent to which their actions are consistent with those values.
- A basic student realization of the life styles, roles, and careers open to both men and women in our society.
- Student ability to cooperate with other students in group problem solving activities. Where possible, this should be within race and sex integrated groups.
- Student familiarity with writings, music, art, and the unique customs of various ethnic and racial groups and of women as well as men.
- Student empathy for the desires, feelings, needs, and problems of others including the unique problems of a specific group that has been discriminated against in the United States. It should be a group to which the student does not belong . . . [p. 17].
- Student ability to role play social situations involving personal or intergroup conflict.
- Student ability to recognize ethnocentrism in descriptions of other cultures or groups.
- Student ability to do a comparative analysis of the experiences of European and minority ethnic groups [p. 18].

# SUMMARY

In this chapter, diversity was viewed as a positive force in the classroom, one that could be used to foster productive communication among students. Problems in promoting diversity occur because the dominant culture tends to prevail in schools and because teachers are thrust into classrooms with little training or understanding of learner differences or needs. Often they cannot communicate with learners different from themselves.

Primary sources of diversity were described in the areas of cultural differences, learning styles, family characteristics, sex differences, communication styles, and handicapping conditions. These factors become interrelated as they operate in the classroom.

Cultural differences emerge in child-rearing practices and are reflected in the ways individuals learn and communicate. Research on ethnic learning styles shows that some cultures emphasize an analytic style that is more stimulus centered and impersonal, while others emphasize a relational style, which is more self-centered and people-centered. Gay (1978) has identified nine variables that are culturally determined and that influence interactions among members of different ethnic groups.

Children exhibit various learning styles, for which the teacher must demonstrate a variety of instructional approaches. Nine learning styles identified by Fischer and Fischer (1979) were described: the incremental learner, the intuitive learner, the sensory specialist, the sensory generalist, the emotionally involved, the emotionally neutral, the explicitly structured, the open-ended structured, the damaged learner, and the eclectic learner.

Family characteristics are becoming more important in the classroom with the rise of single-parent homes, especially through divorce. While children from one-parent homes tend to exhibit more problems in school than those from two-parent homes, the teacher must recognize that families are in various stages of adjustment. Teachers can help by promoting discussion of feelings, teaching the words to express feelings, and involving parents. Teachers must also become sensitive to student differences stemming from adoption, birth order, family size, and mobility.

The sexes tend to be psychologically alike, according to research studies; however, home and family tend to stereotype the differences between them. Cultural stereotyping about language and communication affects interaction and exaggerates the differences between the sexes. The teacher should promote the notion of the Rhetorically Sensitive Person who believes in shared choice, dialogue, and loving behavior; such a person wants neither to control the communication transaction nor to play a passive role. Research indicates that teachers interact differently with boys and with girls, and that these differences foster sex stereotypes. Teachers can minimize stereotyping through classroom exercises, assertive speaking, and more equitable treatment of boys and girls.

Communicator style was described through Norton's twelve variables: dominant, dramatic, contentious, animated, impression leaving, relaxed, attentive, open, friendly, precise, voice, and communicator image. Children with certain styles were seen more positively by teachers.

Handicapping conditions were discussed in the context of the mainstreamed classroom, where all students can benefit from diversity. Research was presented to demonstrate that increasing interactions between handicapped and nonhandicapped children will benefit both groups. Factors of a well-mainstreamed classroom, along with the needed support of the principal, were discussed, as were problems of learning and communication for the mildly retarded, the learning disabled, and the behavior disordered — the three categories of disabled children likely to be found in the mainstreamed classroom.

The teacher can cope with diversity by becoming committed to the values of multicultural, nonsexist instruction such as those found in the assumptions and objectives of the Iowa program.

# Discussion Questions

1. If possible, observe two classrooms that differ in the degree of homogeneity of students — that is, one containing students with varying cultural backgrounds, learning styles, family backgrounds, and so on, the other students who are more alike in these factors. Compare the two classroom environments with respect to teacher-student interactions and student-student interactions. Are certain kinds of learning possible in one classroom and not the other? To what extent does the teacher in the diversely populated classroom use opportunities for enhancing learning and communication?

2. What are the implications of various learning styles for teacher-student interaction? For example, in what ways would teachers structure messages differently for incremental learners or for those seeking explicit rather than open-ended structure?

3. What kinds of classroom communication activities might help students when one of them is experiencing divorce or death of a family member?

4. Observe as many classrooms as possible. To what extent do teachers foster sexism in communication?

5. Formulate a plan for teacher-student communication in a mainstreamed classroom. What are some strategies that might be used to enhance communication among students?

# References

Akbar, Na'im. "Cultural Expressions of the African American Child." 1978. ERIC Document #179633.

Allers, Robert D. "Helping Children Understand Divorce." *Today's Education,* Vol. 69 (November – December 1980): 26–29.

Bate, Barbara. "Assertive Speaking: An Approach to Communication Education for the Future." *Communication Education,* Vol. 25 (January 1976): 53–59.

Bennett, Christine. "Teaching Students as They Would Be Taught: The Importance of Cultural Perspective." *Educational Leadership,* Vol. 36 (January 1979): 259–268.

Birdwhistell, Ray. *Kinesics and Context: Essays in Body Motion Communication.* Philadelphia: University of Pennsylvania Press, 1970.

Brophy, Jere E., and Carolyn M. Evertson. *Learning from Teaching: A Developmental Perspective.* Boston: Allyn and Bacon, Inc., 1976.

Brophy, Jere E., and Thomas Good. *Teacher-Student Relationships: Causes and Consequences.* New York: Holt, Rinehart and Winston, Inc., 1974.

Brown, B. Frank. "The School Needs of Children from One-Parent Families." *Phi Delta Kappan,* Vol. 61, No. 8 (April 1980): 537–540.

Bryan, J. H., and Barry Perlmutter. "Immediate Impressions of LD Children by Female Adults." *Learning Disability Quarterly,* Vol. 2 (1979): 80–88.

Bryan, J. H., R. E. Sherman, and A. Fisher. "Learning Disabled Boys' Nonverbal Behaviors within a Dyadic Interview." *Learning Disability Quarterly,* Vol. 3 (1980): 65–71.

Bryan, T. H. "Learning Disabled Children's Comprehension of Nonverbal Communication." *Journal of Learning Disabilities,* Vol. 10 (1977): 36–61.

Bryan, T. H., and J. H. Bryan. *Understanding Learning Disabilities,* 2nd ed. Sherman Oaks, Cal.: Alfred Publishing Co., Inc., 1978.

Chasen, B. "Sex Role Stereotyping and Prekindergarten Teachers." *Elementary School Journal,* Vol. 4 (1974): 220–235.

Coursen, David. *Administration of Mainstreaming.* Prepared by ERIC Clearinghouse on Educational Management. Published by Foundation for Educational Administration, 1575 Old Bayshore Highway, Burlingame, Cal. 94010, 1981.

Daly, John A., and Gustav Friedrich. "The Development of Communication Apprehension: A Retrospective Analysis of Contributary Correlates." *Communication Quarterly,* Vol. 29, No. 4 (Fall 1981): 243–255.

Darnell, Donald, and Wayne Brockriede. *Persons Communicating.* New York: Holt, Rinehart and Winston, Inc., 1976.

Dodd, Julie. "Mainstreaming." *English Journal,* Vol. 69 (April 1980): 51–55.

Edelsky, Carole. "Acquisition of an Aspect of Communicative Competence: Learning What It Means to Talk Like a Lady." In *Child Discourse,* Susan Ervin-Tripp and Claudia Mitchell-Kernan, eds. New York: Academic Press, Inc., 1977, pp. 225–258.

Ellis, Susan S. "Models of Teaching: A Solution to the Teaching Style/Learning Style Dilemma." *Educational Leadership,* Vol. 36 (January 1979): 274–277.

Fischer, B., and L. Fischer. "Styles in Teaching and Learning." *Educational Leadership,* Vol. 36 (January 1979): 245–251.

Gardner, Ruth C. "Learning Styles: What Every Teacher Should Know." Paper presented at Rocky Mountain Regional Conference of International Reading Association, Boise, Idaho, November, 1980. ERIC Document #198059.

Gay, Geneva. "Viewing the Pluralistic Classroom as a Cultural Microcosm." *Educational Research Quarterly,* Vol. 2, No. 4 (Winter 1978): 45–59.

Gillis, M. K. "Sex Stereotypes: Evidence that School Can Make a Difference." *Educational Horizons,* Vol. 59 (Summer 1981): 182–186.

Gregoro, Anthony F. "Editorial: Learning/Teaching Styles: Potent Forces Behind Them." *Educational Leadership,* Vol. 36 (January 1979): 234–236.

Hale, Janice. "Exploratory Reflections on Childrearing in Afro-American Families." 1978. ERIC Document #185143.

Hewitt, Frank M., and Steven R. Forness. *Education of Exceptional Learners.* Boston: Allyn and Bacon, Inc., 1977.

Hewitt, Frank M., and Philip C. Watson. "Classroom Management and the Exceptional Learner." In *Classroom Management: The Seventy-eighth Yearbook of the National Society for the Study of Education,* Daniel L. Duke, ed. Chicago: University of Chicago Press, 1979, pp. 301–332.

Jackson, P., and H. Lahaderne. "Inequalities of Teacher-Pupil Contacts." *Psychology in Schools,* Vol. 4 (1967): 204–210.

Jarvis, Gilbert A. "The Role of Foreign Language Study in the Late Twentieth Century." *Bulletin of the Pennsylvania State Modern Language Association,* Vol. 57 (Fall 1978): 9–17.

Johnson, D., and H. Myklebust. *Learning Disabilities: Educational Principles and Practices.* New York: Grune & Stratton, Inc., 1967.

Johnson, Roger T., and David W. Johnson. "Building Friendships Between Handicapped and Nonhandicapped Students: Effects of Cooperative and Individualistic Instruction." *American Educational Research Journal,* Vol. 18, No. 4 (Winter 1981): 415–423.

John-Steiner, Vera, and Larry Smith. *What Do We Know about Teaching and Learning in Urban Schools?* Volume 8: *The Educational Promise of Cultural Pluralism.* Washington, D.C.: National Institute of Education, Department of Education, 1979. ERIC Document #185163.

Kagan, Jerome. "Acquisition and Significance of Sex-Typing and Sex Role Identity." In *Review of Child Development Research, I,* M. Hoffman and L. Hoffman, eds. New York: Russell Sage Foundation, 1964, pp. 137–167.

Karre, Idahlynne. "Stereotyped Sex Roles and Self Concept: Strategies for Liberating the Sexes." *Communication Education,* Vol. 25 (January 1976): 43–52.

Levitan, T., and J. Chananie. "Response of Female Primary Teachers to Sex-Typed Behavior in Male and Female Children." *Child Development,* Vol. 43 (1972): 1309–1316.

Levy, B., and J. Stacey. "Sexism in the Elementary Schools: A Backward and Forward Look." *Phi Delta Kappan,* Vol. 55, No. 2 (October 1973): 105–109.

Lyon, S. "Teacher Nonverbal Behavior Related to Perceived Pupil Social-Personal Attributes." *Journal of Learning Disabilities,* Vol. 10 (1977): 173–177.

Maccoby, Eleanor E., and Carol N. Jacklin. *The Psychology of Sex Differences.* Stanford, Cal.: Stanford University Press, 1974.

McCroskey, J. C., and J. A. Daly. "Teachers' Expectations of the Communication Apprehensive Child in the Elementary School." *Human Communication Research,* Vol. 3 (Fall 1976): 67–72.

McHale, Susan M., and Wanda Boone. "Play between Autistic and Nonhandicapped Children." *The Pointer,* Vol. 24 (Spring 1980): 28–32.

Miller, Darvin L., and Marilee A. Miller. "The Handicapped Child's Civil Right as It Relates to the 'Least Restrictive Environment' and Appropriate Mainstreaming." *Indiana Law Journal,* Vol. 54, No. 1 (1978–79): 1–28.

Montgomery, Barbara M., and Robert W. Norton. "Sex Differences and Similarities in Communicator Style." *Communication Monographs,* Vol. 48, No. 2 (June 1981): 121–132.

Morris, Lee, ed. "Extracting Learning Styles from Social/Cultural Diversity: A Study of Five American Minorities." Office of Education, Washington, D.C.: Teacher Corps, 1978. ERIC Document #158952.

National Advisory Council on Women's Educational Programs. *Title IX: The Half Full, Half Empty Glass.* Washington, D.C.: Government Printing Office, Fall 1981.

Norton, R. W. "Teacher Effectiveness as a Function of Communicator Style." In *Communication Yearbook I,* An Annual Review published by the International Communication Association. New Brunswick, N.J.: Transaction Books, Rutgers, The State University, 1977, pp. 523–541.

Parsons, J., R. Futterman, C. Kaczala, and J. Meece. "Attributions and Academic Choice: Origins and Change." In *National Institute of Education Annual Report.* Washington, D.C.: National Institute of Education, 1979.

Pratte, Richard. "Guest Editorial." *Theory into Practice,* Vol. 22 (Winter 1981): 1.

Ramírez, Manuel III, and Alfredo Castañeda. *Cultural Democracy, Biocognitive Development, and Education.* New York: Academic Press, Inc., 1974.

Ricks, F., and S. Pyke. "Teacher Perceptions and Attitudes Which Foster or Maintain Sex Role Differences." *Interchange,* Vol. 1 (1973): 26–33.

Ross, Alan O. *Psychological Aspects of Learning Disabilities and Reading Disorders.* New York: McGraw-Hill, Inc., 1976.

Sapon-Shevin, Mara. "Mainstreaming: Implementing the Spirit of the Law." *Journal of Negro Education,* Vol. 48, No. 3 (Summer 1979): 364–381.

Serbin, L., D. O'Leary, R. Kent, and I. Tonick. "A Comparison of Teacher Response to the Preacademic and Problem Behavior of Boys and Girls." *Child Development,* Vol. 44 (1973): 796–804.

Sprague, Jo. "The Reduction of Sexism in Speech Communication Education." *The Speech Teacher,* Vol. 24, No. 1 (January 1975): 37–45.

Sprague, Robert L., and Kenneth D. Gadow. "The Role of the Teacher in Drug Treatment." *School Review,* Vol. 85, No. 1 (November 1976): 109–140.

Stohl, Cynthia. "Perceptions of Social Attractiveness and Communicator Style: A Developmental Study of Preschool Children." *Communication Education,* Vol. 30, No. 4 (October 1981): 367–376.

Thompson, Teresa L. "Communication between Handicapped and Nonhandicapped Children: A Network Analysis of a Mainstreaming Program." Unpublished paper presented at Annual Meeting of the Speech Communication Association, November, 1980.

Thorne, Barrie. "Gender . . . How Is It Best Conceptualized?" Unpublished paper delivered at the Annual Meeting of the American Sociological Association, Michigan State University, 1978.

Wallerstein, Judith S., and Joan B. Kelly. "California's Children of Divorce." *Psychology Today,* Vol. 13 (January 1980): 67–76.

Wiig, E., and S. P. Harris. "Perception and Interpretation of Nonverbally Expressed Emotions by Adolescents with Learning Disabilities." *Perceptual and Motor Skills,* Vol. 38 (1974): 239–245.

Wirtenberg, Jeana, Susan Klein, Barbara Richardson, and Veronica Thomas. "Sex Equity in American Education." *Educational Leadership,* Vol. 39, No. 4 (January 1981): 311–319.

Wood, Barbara S. *Children and Communication: Verbal and Nonverbal Language Development,* 2nd ed. Englewood Cliffs, N.J.: Prentice-Hall, Inc., 1981.

Yeakey, Carol Camp. "Ethnicity as a Dimension of Human Diversity: Implications for School Processes and Policies." In *Human Diversity and Pedagogy,* Edmund Gordon et al., eds. Princeton, N.J.: Educational Testing Service, 1979, pp. 194–242. ERIC Document #177066.

Zajonc, R. B. "Family Configuration and Intelligence." *Science,* Vol. 192 (April 16, 1976): 227–236.

# For Further Reading

Affleck, James. *Teaching the Mildly Handicapped in the Regular Classroom.* 1980. LC 4661.A38 NIEE.

Copper, Grace C. "Everyone Does Not Think Alike." *English Journal,* Vol. 69, No. 4 (April 1980): 45–50.

"Cultural Pluralism: Can It Work?" *Theory into Practice,* Vol. 22, No. 1 (Winter 1981).

Curtis, Mary E., and Robert Glaser. "Changing Conceptions of Intelligence." In *Review of Research in Education,* David C. Berliner, ed. Vol. 9 (1981): 111–143.

Dweck, Carol, William Davidson, Sharon Nelson, and Bradley Enna. "Sex Differences in Learned Helplessness: II. The Contingencies of Evaluative Feedback in the Classroom," and "III. An Experimental Analysis." *Developmental Psychology,* Vol. 14, No. 3 (1978): 268–276.

Friedman, Paul G. "Special Needs of Handicapped, Reticent, Gifted, Bilingual, and Female Students." In *Education in the 80's: Speech Communication,* Gustav W. Friedrich, ed. Washington, D.C.: National Education Association, 1981, 131–143.

*Multicultural Nonsexist Education in Iowa Schools: Language Arts.* State of Iowa, Department of Public Instruction, Educational Equity Section, June, 1980.

Shiman, David. "Confronting Prejudice in the Schools." *USA Today.* Vol. 109, No. 2428 (June 1981): 41–43.

# Communication and Attitudes in the Classroom

*focus*  INFLUENCE OF TEACHER ATTITUDES ON CLASSROOM
COMMUNICATION

HOW TEACHERS COMMUNICATE ATTITUDES
Teacher Expectancy
Attribution Theory
Self-Fulfilling Prophecy
Interactions of Expectancies, Attribution Theory, and Self-Fulfilling
Prophecy

HOW TEACHERS CAN CHANGE THEIR PREDICTIVE BEHAVIOR
Change Teachers' Expectancies
Change Children's Attributional Styles
Use Feedback and Praise Designed to Teach
Involve All Children in Classroom Interaction
Show Respect for All Pupils
Listen to All Children Regardless of Achievement Level

HOW TEACHERS PROJECT THEIR IMAGES
Communicator Style
Credibility
Attraction
Power
Self-Concept

CHANGING TEACHER IMAGE

When Haim Ginott (1972) was a young teacher, he wrote:

> I have come to a frightening conclusion. I am the decisive element in the classroom. It is my
> personal approach that creates the climate. It is my daily mood that makes the weather. As a
> teacher I possess tremendous power to make a child's life miserable or joyous. I can be a tool of
> torture or an instrument of inspiration. I can humiliate or humor, hurt or heal. In all situations it is
> my response that decides whether a crisis will be escalated or de-escalated, and a child
> humanized or dehumanized [pp. 15–16].

Numerous studies provide evidence that the teacher's communication has an impact upon the child's self-concept, potential for growth, and actual achievement (Kash and Borich, 1978). One study (Branan, 1972) reported that college students, when asked to describe their most negative experiences, listed interpersonal situations, most of which involved interactions with teachers. Most frequent in their elementary and high school experiences were such negative incidents as humiliation before the class, embarrassment, and unfair evaluation. A survey of public schools found that 77% of the teacher interactions with their students were negative and only 23% positive (Madson, Madson, Sandargas, Hammond, and Edgar, 1970).

This chapter explores the ways in which teachers communicate attitudes, both positive and negative, and the factors that influence students' perceptions of the teachers. The concepts described here, it is hoped, will help you to become aware of the potential for enhancing or inhibiting student growth through communication.

## HOW TEACHERS COMMUNICATE ATTITUDES

Teachers' own experiences and value systems as well as their self-concepts determine how they are likely to behave toward students in the classroom. Three concepts help to describe the ways in which attitudes are communicated: *expectancy, attribution theory,* and *self-fulfilling prophecy.* These concepts embody behaviors that are interactive; together they help to explain the impact of the teachers' messages on student behaviors.

### Teacher Expectancy

In 1968 Rosenthal and Jacobson published *Pygmalion in the Classroom,* which reported their study conducted in the Oak Hill School of San Francisco during 1964. Children in kindergarten through fifth grade were given a phony test that the teachers were told was designed to identify the "late bloomers," or those students who were ready to make a spurt in academic and intellectual development. Actually, the "bloomers," who were identified to the teachers, were a random sample that included 20% of the Oak Hill students. Real tests of ability were given to all stuents at the beginning and end of the school year. Results showed that the "late bloomers" made significant improvement in academic development in comparison with the other students. The changes were attributed to teachers' expectations, which were higher for the "late bloomers" and which apparently caused the teachers to treat them differently.

The Oak Hill results stimulated hundreds of articles on teacher expectancy, many of which emphasized the virtues of positive thinking by teachers. However, several researchers failed to replicate the results of the Rosenthal-Jacobsen experiment, and others criticized its methodology (Braun, 1976). While expecting a student to do well is not enough to produce increased achievement, evidence reveals that teacher expectancy affects classroom communication and the potential for student achievement (Kash and Borich, 1978).

**Sources of Teacher Expectancy.**   What are some of the sources of teacher expectancies? What factors tend to influence the attitudes of teachers toward individual students?

*Characteristics Related to Sex Roles.*   Traits that fit the stereotype of feminine, such as affectionateness, love of children, tenderness, and so on, tend not to be perceived by teachers as indicative of high-achieving students (Benz, Pfeiffer, and Newman, 1981). Good, Sikes, and Brophy (1973) found that low-achieving males in sixteen junior high school classrooms received inferior treatment, while high-achieving males received more favorable and more frequent contact with teachers. Palardy (1969) found that in first-grade classes where teachers did not think boys could achieve as well as girls, the boys had a lower level of achievement. Chapter 4 of this text provides other information related to the differential treatment of students on the basis of sex.

*Perceptions of Physical Attractiveness.*   Rich (1975) found that children perceived as attractive by teachers received more desirable personality ratings than unattractive children; however, a misbehavior was deemed less undesirable if attributed to an unattractive rather than an attractive child. A study by Clifford and Walster (1973) demonstrated that elementary school teachers expected students who were perceived in photographs as being attractive to have higher I.Q.'s and better social relationships than those whom they perceived as unattractive. There is no doubt that teachers tend to expect more from students whom they perceive as attractive than from those whom they perceive as unattractive.

*Characteristics Related to Race.*   Teachers may unconsciously hold stereotypes about children from different ethnic groups; these perceptions have the potential for being communicated and accepted by children as expectations of one another. The U.S. Commission on Civil Rights (1973) found that teachers tended to exhibit more empathic behavior toward Anglos than they did toward Mexican American children. Rubovits and Maehr (1973) found that teachers treated white children more positively than black children. Beady and Hansell (1981) found that black teachers and white teachers in black elementary schools had different expectations for the college success of their students. Black teachers, more than white, expected black students to be successful in college. However, white teachers' expectations did not differ for black students and white students, and black teachers and white teachers did not differ in their evaluations of elementary school achievement, effort, or expectations of high school success. Perhaps this is an indication that integrated schools produce teachers who formulate expectations of students that are not based on race. The U.S. Commission on Civil Rights Report (1973, p. 21) also found that teachers tended to exhibit more praise and encouragement toward Anglos than they did toward Mexican Americans. Unfortunately, teachers' stereotypes about children from different groups tend to be communicated and accepted by children as expectations of one another.

*Characteristics Related to Socioeconomic Status.*   According to evidence, some teachers tend to hold expectations of their pupils based on socioeconomic status. Rist (1970), in a long-term observation of a black kindergarten teacher and her thirty black pupils, found that seating assignments coincided with social class of the students. The teacher grouped the students at three tables according to what she perceived as their ability to learn. Table 1 children, from families with higher incomes and education levels, were better and more neatly dressed than were children from Tables 2 and 3. During the year, the teacher interacted more frequently with those from Table 1 and described children at Tables 2 and 3 as not knowing what was going on in the classroom. The startling observation was that even though some children from Tables 2 and 3 scored higher on an end-of-year I.Q. test than some at Table 1, they retained the "ability" grouping in first grade that was assigned to them in kindergarten. Thus, expectations for their success were established very early. Likewise, Mazer (1971), using photographs and descriptions of students' socioeconomic status, asked teachers to estimate student performances; findings indicated that socioeconomic status of the pupil was even more important than sex or race in determining the teachers' predictions. Kash and Borich (1978) state:

> Because our schools do in fact reflect middle-class values and goals, teachers who feel that middle-class pupils have more academic potential than lower-class children are no doubt dealing with a perceived reality. But however accurate or inaccurate it may be, this perception generates teacher behavior; and it is the *behavior* that must be examined for its effect on the self-concept development of all potential learners. Behavior which the teacher considers "innocent" or well-intentioned may be devastating to the child seeking identity [p. 109].

Other sources of teacher expectancy have not yet been fully supported by research — for example, such student characteristics as the reputation of older siblings (Seaver, 1973), personality characteristics associated with student names (Harari and McDavid, 1973), and degree of quietness (with quiet children being perceived more negatively, according to McCroskey, 1977). All affect the expectations that teachers have for their students.

**Effects of Teacher Expectancies on Students.**   What are the effects of teacher expectancies on students? Documentation indicates that when teachers hold differing expectancies of their students, they tend to communicate with them in ways consistent with these expectancies.

Teachers tend to call on students perceived as high achievers more frequently than they call on students perceived as low achievers (Good and Brophy, 1972; Finn, 1972; Rist, 1970), the result, perhaps, of not wanting to embarrass a student who is likely to give the wrong answer or of feeling a sense of failure as a teacher if students give wrong answers. Unfortunately, most students learn that if the teacher thinks that they will perform poorly, they are not called on; when they are not called on, performance becomes even poorer.

Teachers tend to provide more feedback to the responses of high achievers than to low achievers (Brophy and Good, 1970). Teachers tend not to react to the low achievers' responses with corrective or evaluative feedback, a process very important in learning. The U.S. Commission on Civil Rights report (1973) described the following classroom event:

> One Chicano sat toward the back in a corner and volunteered several answers. At one point the teacher did not even acknowledge, much less reinforce his answer. At another time he volunteered an answer which was perfectly suitable. Yet the teacher stated: "Well, yes, uh huh, but can anyone else put it in different terms?" The teacher than called on an Anglo boy who gave the same basic response with very little paraphrasing. The teacher then beamed and exclaimed: "Yes, that's it exactly" [pp. 40–41].

This example describes how a teacher's expectations for students of a given ethnic group influence expectations for achievement, which, in turn, influence response patterns in the classroom.

Teachers tend to work in closer proximity to students who are high achievers than to those who are low achievers. Adams and Biddle (1970) found after videotaping sixteen classrooms that students most likely to participate in classroom interactions were seated in a T-shaped area, with the top of the T at the center front of the room and the stem extending down the middle. The most participation came from students in the first three seats in the stem. Likewise, Rist's study (1970), previously described, discovered that students of perceived high ability were placed together at one table and teachers spent more time working with them than with those of perceived lower ability. In general, there is evidence that "a front-center seat facilitates achievement, positive attitudes and participation . . . for those somewhat predisposed to speak in class" (Weinstein, 1979, p. 580).

Teachers tend to use praise more often with high achievers than with low achievers. Brophy and Good (1974) found that children perceived as high achievers received the most teacher praise. Brown, Payne, Lankewich, and Cornell (1970) found that in "mixed" classrooms, teachers of one race facing pupils of another used more praise in classroom interaction than in classrooms where teachers instructed students of the same race. However, Rubovits and Maehr (1973) reported that in an integrated classroom black children received more criticism and less praise from their white teachers than did the white children. These seemingly conflicting results possibly are linked to the expectations that individual teachers hold for students of their own and different races.

Teachers tend to allow high achievers more time to answer a question than they do low achievers (Brophy and Good, 1970). It is possible that when the high achiever hesitates with an answer, the teacher expects that the time is being used to formulate a worthwhile response. When the low achiever hesitates, the teacher may be anticipating the wrong answer. Teachers apparently unconsciously communicate to students what kinds of answers they expect from them.

Teachers tend to model fewer respectful behaviors toward low achievers than toward high achievers; students tend to "incorporate" these tendencies into their own interactions with their peers. When Rist (1970) observed a kindergarten classroom, he found that by the end of the year children identified by the teachers as high achievers reacted toward the low achievers in ways similar to those of the teacher. Stipek (1981) found, for children in kindergarten through third grade, that ratings of their classmates reflected teachers' ratings of the academic status of the child being rated.

Teacher expectations for pupils tend to influence pupil self-concepts. Stipek and Hoffman (1980) found that high-achieving boys in the first and third grades had higher expectations for success on a task than low-achieving boys; differing performance expectations were attributed to the children's internalization of performance feedback. Although Stipek (1981) found that kindergarten and first-grade children's ratings of their own ability were related neither to the teacher's rating of their achievement status nor to ratings they received from peers, this changed in the second and third grades. These older children's self-ratings reflected both their academic status in the classroom, as determined by their teacher, and their classmates' ratings of their competence. Thus, teacher expectancies in the early years, when self-concepts are forming, are likely to lay the groundwork for the student's entire academic career. The conclusion of Brophy and Good (1970) that teachers demanded better performance from those children for whom they had higher expectations and tended to accept poor performance from students for whom they held low expectations are potent indicators of how children are likely to develop concepts of their own abilities. Figure 5–1 illustrates how teacher expectations derived from various sources influence the teacher "output," or behaviors toward pupils. These behaviors affect the pupils' self-expectations, which, in turn, affect their behaviors. The behaviors are perceived by teachers as supporting their expectancies.

**FIGURE 5-1  The Behavioral Cycle between Teacher Input and Learner Output**

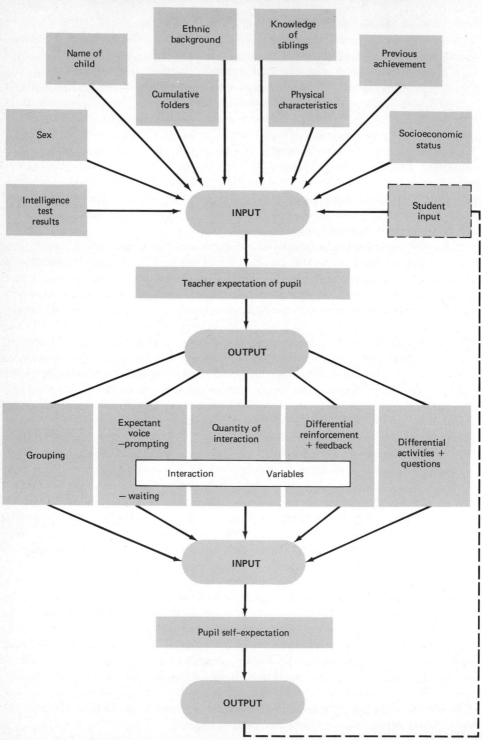

## Attribution Theory

As just explained, teachers formulate expectancies and make predictions for their students in the classroom; they then behave in ways that are congruent with those expectations. Students, as they interact, tend to accept and adjust to the messages of the teacher. As this process occurs, teachers unconsciously develop reasons that validate their expectancies and their differential treatment of students in the classroom. This process of justifying behaviors is explained by attribution theory.

Attributions have been described by Weiner (1979) along three dimensions: *locus of causality*; *stability of causes*; and *controllability*.

**1. Locus of Causality.**   This concept was first described by Heider (1958), who reported that the reasons people give to explain behaviors and events emphasize internal factors (those arising within the individual) or external factors (those arising from environmental factors). For example, ability and effort would be causes arising from inside the individual, while difficulty of the task and luck would be causes arising from external factors. Weiner, Russell, and Lerman (1979) later found, following feedback on tests, that people who attribute their success to external factors report feelings of gratitude and surprise, while those who emphasize internal factors report confidence and satisfaction. Those students who fail and attribute their failure to internal factors report feeling guilt, self-blame, and regret; failing students who blame external factors report anger and surprise. For children in first, third, and fifth grades, Frieze and Snyder (1980) found that testing outcomes are attributed mainly to internal factors such as effort and ability; this self-blame for testing outcomes is viewed by the researchers as developing "within the school environment with teachers and other students being major contributors to it" (p. 194). Affective responses concerning causality of success or failure apparently continue into adulthood. Forsyth and McMillan (1981) found that college students who attributed their success on an examination to internal personal factors felt more relaxed, competent, calm, adequate, and good compared with students who attributed this success to external factors. In addition, students who externalized failure reported more positive levels of affect than failing students who internalized the failure. Attributions about success or failure apparently help students to insulate themselves from the negative implications of the performance or to take advantage of the positive implications (Forsyth and McMillan). If students fail after expending high effort on a test, they tend to feel more inadequate and dissatisfied than they do if they expend little effort (Covington, Spratt, and Omelich, 1980).

In general, researchers have identified "internal" learners, those who tend to ascribe success or failure to their own efforts; and "external" learners, those who tend to ascribe success or failure to events or individuals beyond their control (Thomas, 1979). Some research suggests that internal learners may respond to teacher feedback differently from external learners. For example, internal learners may achieve more when they determine the correctness of their own responses in reading assignments, while external learners may do better when the teacher determines correctness (Pascarella and Pflaum, 1981).

**2. Stability of Causes.**   This factor refers to the "permanence" of the reasons individuals use to explain their success or failure. Studies have indicated that expectancies on the part of students and teachers following feedback are linked to stability (Feather and Simon, 1971;

Weiner, Frieze, Kukla, Reed, Rest, and Rosenbaum, 1971). When students attribute their success to such relatively permanent factors as ability or nature of the task, their expectations for success tend to increase; when they attribute their success to relatively unstable factors such as luck or effort, they tend to have less positive expectancies for future results (Covington and Omelich, 1979; Weiner, Nierenberg, and Goldstein, 1976).

Such attributes as ability, personality, diligence, laziness, and task difficulty are relatively stable causes, while effort, mood, and luck may be highly changeable. In general, stable attributions lead to expectancies for continued success or failure, while unstable attributions lead to expectations for changes in outcomes (Frieze and Snyder, 1980).

**3. Controllability.**   This dimension was added to Weiner's model when it was found that locus and stability were not enough to explain how people react to outcomes. For example, mood and effort are both internal and unstable causes that people attribute to outcomes, but mood is much less under the individual's control than is effort. Forsyth and McMillan (1981) review research indicating that an individual's feeling of loss of control is associated with depression, poor motivation, deterioration of physical health, and stress-related illness. They found that college students who felt that internal, controllable, and stable factors produced their examination scores reported more happiness than all other attributors. They found that "the affective reactions of students who felt their performance was caused by factors they could control — such as personal effort and amount of time devoted to studying — were more positive . . . than the reactions of students who believed they did not control the cause of their outcomes" (p. 400). Frieze and Snyder (1980) found that children tended to give causal explanations that differed across four situations, one of which was a testing situation. Testing situations were viewed by the children (more than catching a frog, playing football, or an art project) as the most internalized and the most under the control of the child. Frieze and Snyder conclude that because a child's early causal belief structure seems to be dependent on maturity and experience with a situation, "a child can be taught to employ a productive, beneficial and realistic causal schemata for any situation, including those encountered in the schools" (p. 195).

The dimension of controllability is related to the phenomenon of "learned helplessness" described by Seligman (1975). This is a phenomenon in which a person learns, over time, that he or she has no control over the outcome of events. In other words, there is little relation between the effort expended and the attainment of a goal. When Benson and Kennelly (1976) in an experiment gave students negative feedback unrelated to their performance, significant performance problems occurred. Thomas (1979) observed that the school behaviors of learning-disabled children appear to fit the learned helplessness model, for even after remediation has been tried, they are low in persistence, are anxious, and are unwilling to attempt tasks at appropriate ability levels. She relates these problems of the learning disabled to findings from the research about learned helplessness, which are summarized as follows:

1.   Individuals who attribute outcome to effort are likely to work harder or longer than those who attribute outcome to ability.
2.   To the extent that individuals attribute failure of a task to ability, they are likely to be less persistent as measured by length of time at a task and number of problems attempted.
3.   To the extent that attributional cues have been part of experimental instructions or suggestions, learned helplessness may or may not transfer to a new task [p. 215].

## Self-Fulfilling Prophecy

In this phenomenon people define themselves in particular ways and then behave in manners congruent with those definitions. The person of low self-concept predicts failure and then behaves in such a way as to bring the prediction to fruition, thereby fulfilling the self-prophecy. Johnson (1961) used the theory of self-fulfilling prophecy to describe how a person becomes a stutterer. He observed that there are normal disfluencies in young children as they are learning to speak, and that adult anxieties about these can cause a child to stutter:

> The problem called stuttering begins, then, when the child's speech is felt, usually by the mother, to be not as smooth or as fluent as it ought to be. There seems as a rule to be a quality of puzzlement mixed with slight apprehension and dread about the mother's feelings. She uses the only name she knows for what she thinks must be the matter with her youngster's speech, and that word is "stuttering." . . . She may not be sure of herself at first in deciding that her child is stuttering, but her use of the word crystallizes her feelings and serves to focus her attention on the hesitations in the speech of her child [p. 138].

While research has never fully supported Johnson's or any single theory as to the cause of stuttering, it is an excellent description of the mechanism of self-fulfilling prophecy. A child is labeled according to someone's evaluation of initial behavior and, once the label has been applied, continues to validate it through further similar behavior. Likewise, Rist's (1970) study of the teacher who placed kindergarten children in ability groups reflecting socioeconomic status demonstrates the same mechanism. Once the teacher had labeled the pupils according to ability, they tended to interact with her in ways that confirmed her expectations; once the "prophecy" was fulfilled, it tended to confirm the original expectation and was, therefore, perpetuated.

## Interactions of Expectancies, Attribution Theory, and Self-Fulfilling Prophecy

These three phenomena are interrelated and maintained in the classroom through the messages communicated between teachers and students. Let us look at two hypothetical examples to see how these phenomena interrelate:

1. The teacher holds a high expectancy for John based upon observations of past performance, physical attributes, and socioeconomic status.
2. On a particular day, John performs well by answering the teacher's question.
3. The teacher attributes John's successful performance to his superior ability (internal and stable attributes).
4. Specific incidents are perceived by the teacher as validating and reinforcing the high expectancy for John; the teacher continues to expect successful performance on future tasks.
5. The teacher treats John differently from other students, who are perceived as low achievers (that is, the teacher pays more attention to him, praises him, encourages him, reinforces him, and so on).
6. John internalizes the teacher's high expectations and the attributions of high ability for his success; he develops a "prophecy" concerning his behavior, which through even greater effort, motivation, and success he continues to fulfill.

7. The continued success confirms the teacher's expectations, and the circular process is repeated.

However, if John should be unsuccessful on a later task, the teacher might attribute the failure to luck ("John probably misunderstood the directions") or to some other external factor such as task difficulty ("The directions that I wrote were unclear"). Thus, John's behavior is made congruent with the expectancies of the teacher and the positive differential treatment of John can proceed. Now let us look at another example:

1. The teacher holds a low expectancy for Mary, based upon observations of past performance, sex role behavior, physical attributes, or socioeconomic status.
2. On a particular day, Mary performs well by achieving a high grade on a test.
3. The teacher attributes this success to luck ("I don't see how she got that answer. Mary is not good at math. It was a lucky guess") or to task difficulty ("It was too easy").
4. Mary's behavior continues to be "explained" so that it is congruent with the teacher's expectations, which continue to presume unsuccessful performance on future tasks.
5. The teacher, through verbal and nonverbal behavior, unconsciously communicates this low expectancy to Mary (interacts less, praises less, criticizes more, does not reinforce correct responses, and so on).
6. Mary internalizes the teacher's low expectancies and eventually believes that the reasons for failure are internal and stable ("I am dumb and will always be dumb"). Helplessness is learned as Mary comes to believe that learning and success are not within her control.
7. Mary behaves in accordance with her developing self-concept in order to fulfill the prophecy of failure that she has internalized from teachers.
8. Mary continues to perform poorly, thereby confirming the teacher's expectancies.
9. The circular process is repeated.

Because of the cycles involving expectancies, attributions, and self-fulfilling prophecies, many students are probably performing below their potentials (Evans and Rosenthal, 1969; Finn, 1972).

## HOW TEACHERS CAN CHANGE THEIR PREDICTIVE BEHAVIOR

The following six methods describe how teachers can attempt to change their own or their students' predictive behavior.

### Change Teachers' Expectancies

Some research studies have experimented with ways of changing teachers' expectancies of pupils (Meichenbaum, Bowers, and Ross, 1969; Palardy, 1969; Rosenthal and Jacobson, 1968). Kash and Borich (1978) report that attempts to change expectancies have been successful when "(1) teachers were given biasing information early in the school year, before they had an opportunity to make their own assessments and observations; (2) teachers were relatively inexperienced; and (3) the validity of the biasing information was reinforced by a trusted school official or expert" (p. 52).

## Change Children's Attributional Styles

Other studies have attempted to change the attributional styles of children. Dweck (1975) worked with twelve children identified as helpless who tended to attribute learning outcomes to external and uncontrollable factors or to the absence of ability. For twenty-five days half of these children received success-only experiences in arithmetic, while the other half received attribution retraining. The training consisted of the experimenter verbally attributing the child's failures to lack of effort and telling them such things as "That means you should have tried harder." The children in the success-only condition continued to display poor perform-ance following failure, but the children who received attribution retraining, which emphasized effort over ability, demonstrated persistence and improved performance following failure. Fowler and Peterson (1981) demonstrated that children could change their attributions to effort with retraining that involved reinforcement through "inner speech." Before a learning trial, subjects listened to a recording of a boy or girl saying, "I got that right. That means I tried hard"; and then, "No, I didn't get that. That means I have to try harder." The subjects were told that these are good things to say to themselves when they succeed or fail in school. Students practiced saying these statements aloud, then in a whisper, and finally silently to themselves. Fowler and Peterson conclude that this approach "may be more effective in getting them to alter their self-reported attributions to effort than having someone else tell them to try harder" (p. 259). Thus, teachers can increase student performance by ensuring that students practice messages that can help them to attribute success or failure to actual efforts.

## Use Feedback and Praise Designed to Teach

Teachers should avoid empty praise and should ask themselves such questions as: What is good about this picture or story that the child has created? Why is this answer correct or incorrect? Both high and low achievers need reasons if their performances are to be expanded.

## Involve All Children in Classroom Interaction

Each child has strengths and unique experiences that can be tapped in the course of instruction. The teacher must strike a balance between forcing disclosure of personal experiences against that child's will and helping the child to use experiences that contribute to classroom learning. "John, you have been in California. How does that climate compare with ours?" might be a question asked of the low-achieving child whose family has been mobile. "Mary, I understand that you fish often. What do the different fish like to eat?" might be asked to help the teacher and students break down sex-role stereotypes and to involve the student in learning.

The teacher may want to consider a variety of seating arrangements for classroom activities. Having students sit in different places in the classroom may increase their interactions with the teacher and with each other.

## Show Respect for All Pupils

Derision or uncomplimentary remarks have no place in a classroom. "Didn't your mother teach you manners?" "Don't you ever change your clothes?" have been heard in the classroom and can contribute little toward productive self-fulfilling prophecies. Ginott (1972) describes an incident of disrespectful and damaging teacher behavior:

> An art teacher showed two drawings to his students. He asked them to tell which one they liked best. Henry, age twelve, took his time to answer. The teacher said: "We don't have all day. Make up your mind, if you have any." Henry blushed while his classmates giggled [p. 59].

He provides an additional example:

> Felix, age nine, complained to his teacher that a boy from the sixth grade had hit him over the head with a book.
>
> TEACHER: He just came over and hit you! Just like that! You didn't do anything. You were just an innocent bystander, and he was a perfect stranger.
> FELIX (in tears): Yes.
> TEACHER: I don't believe you. You must have done something. I know you. When it comes to provoking, you are an expert.
> FELIX: I didn't do anything. I just stood in the hall, minding my own business.
> TEACHER: I'm in the hall every day. No one ever attacks me. How come you always attract trouble? You'd better watch out or one of these days you'll be in very hot water.
>
> Felix put his head on the desk and cried, while his teacher turned to the business of the day [p. 63].

Ginott recommends that the teacher in such a case mirror the child's feelings with statements such as "It must have hurt awfully," "You must have felt furious." Statements that show respect and understanding will contribute to more positive prophecies for success on the part of the child.

## Listen to All Children Regardless of Achievement Level

Rogers (1969), in recalling his school days, reports the following:

> A child would ask the teacher a question and the teacher would give a perfectly good answer to a completely different question. A feeling of pain and distress would always strike me. My reaction was, "But you didn't hear him." I felt a sort of childish despair at the lack of communication which was (and is) so common [p. 222].

Ginott (1972) recommends that a message in response to a child's plight, complaint, or request have the following qualities:

It accurately acknowledges the child's statement or state of mind.

It does not deny his perception.

It does not dispute his feelings.

It does not disown his wishes.

It does not deride his taste.

It does not denigrate his opinions.

It does not denigrate his character.

It does not degrade his person.

It does not argue with his experience [p. 97].

# HOW TEACHERS PROJECT THEIR IMAGES

We have discussed the ways in which teachers communicate attitudes based upon their expectations of their students. However, it is important to realize that as instruction proceeds (and before it ever begins) students develop perceptions and expectations of their teachers. The perceptions students hold of their teacher can be called the teacher's image. No one knows exactly what information is used by students to form images of their teachers; however, it is known that certain teacher behaviors tend to create a more favorable classroom environment than others. In this section, we will briefly discuss some of the aspects of a teacher's image that influence students: communicator style, credibility, attraction, power, and self-concept.

## Communicator Style

As described in the last chapter, communicator style refers to the general way in which a person is perceived to communicate along twelve dimensions observed by Norton (1977): dominant, dramatic, contentious, animated, impression leaving, relaxed, attentive, open, friendly, precise, voice, and communicator image. Norton (1980) analyzed student ratings of college communication instructors and concluded:

> An ineffective teacher is not very lively or animated, does not signal enough attentiveness or friendliness, and does not have a very precise style. In addition, the ineffective teacher is not very relaxed and does not use a dramatic style [p. 8].

While most of the research on communicator style has been conducted at the college level, the elements of a positive profile described by Norton (1980) appear to be very applicable for elementary and secondary school teachers. The following elements, as adapted from descriptions provided by Norton, appear to be part of the effective teacher's communicator style.

*Friendly.*   Signals that the other person is worthy of recognition, affirmation, and identity. It implies that teachers and students are involved in a partnership in learning, and emphasizes interaction rather than "teaching at" the student.

*Precise.*   Moves the student toward the knowledge of the teacher through clear explanations. Signals that the teacher is comfortable with the content. Involves anticipating student problems with content and moving to surmount those difficulties.

*Attentive.*   Signals that students are being understood and listened to. Signals interaction rather than "one-to-many" communication, and is characterized by alertness to student cues.

*Lively/Animated.*   Signals that the teacher is highly expressive verbally and nonverbally, especially with gestures, facial expressions, and eye behavior. Encompasses "enthusiasm," which appears to be the best predictor of an effective teacher across studies. Uses gestures and facial and eye expressions to emphasize the literal message or to add redundancy to it.

*Relaxed.*   Signals that the teacher is calm in his or her communicative behavior. The person is free from nervous mannerisms and is perceived as confident and in control. It reflects a person who is comfortable with the teaching process.

*Dramatic.*   Entails overstating, understating, or altering the literal meaning for heightened effect. Relates to the animated style in helping emphasize crucial points in an explication. It is characterized by stories, anecdotes, metaphors, sarcasm, irony, puns, and jokes.

These aspects of style do not occur in isolation, but are interactive to form the image of the teacher. An important part of communicator style is the notion of *immediacy,* which has been defined by Andersen, Norton, and Nussbaum (1981) as "those communication behaviors manifested and perceived when a person maintains closer physical distance, uses direct body orientation, is relaxed, uses purposeful body movement, gestures, engages in positive head nods, smiles, uses eye contact, and is vocally expressive" (p. 378). As one would expect, students see the effective teachers as those exhibiting immediacy and a positive communicator style.

An earlier study by Beck (1967) provided results that validate the applicability of communicator style profiles for the elementary and secondary school levels. In Beck's study, 2,108 sixth-grade pupils rated 75 teachers on teacher merit. Factor-analytical procedures produced the following strongly perceived dimensions of teacher merit:

- a warm, friendly, and supportive personality that is judged in terms of teacher approachability, irritability, and personal popularity
- the ability to communicate in a clear and lucid manner
- teacher behavior leading to either positive or negative motivation of the pupil
- effective disciplining behavior that leads to proper conduct on the part of the pupil
- a flexibility that results in the introduction of novel perspective and the utilization of mechanical and audiovisual aids to instruction [p. 128].

While more research must be done on the effects of communication style and on the ways teachers can change their styles, it is important for teachers to understand that the ways they communicate will have an impact on their students' perceptions of them.

## Credibility

Although a broad body of research on credibility in the communication process is available, very few of the concepts have been applied to classroom interactions. However, it is useful for the teacher to understand this potent aspect of the communication process that creates the teacher's image. By *credibility* we mean *the image of the speaker as perceived by the listeners.* The perceived reputation and expertise of a person, as well as education, physical appearance, knowledge of a topic, speech delivery, and so on, may contribute to credibility. Four aspects of credibility appear to be most relevant to the teaching/learning process: trustworthiness, prestige, competence, and dynamism.

**Trustworthiness.**   This is the concept of the perceptions of the individual's integrity, honesty, and sincerity. Once a person is found to be dishonest, as in the case of Richard Nixon for many television viewers during the Watergate incidents, it is very difficult to reestablish credibility. Some years ago one of the authors was teaching a public-speaking class. A freshman, seeking to persuade his classmates that train crossings in the United States needed to be made safer, held up a dirty, blood-soaked ballet slipper. He began his speech by telling of an incident where a girl was killed because of faulty signals at a crossing and then went on to tell how she was a ballet dancer. He knew because she was his sister. He moved his classmates and instructor to tears and was indeed very persuasive. However, after class, when a classmate offered sympathy on the death of his sister, the speaker laughed and said, "Hey, that was only for effect — I never had a sister." Word spread quickly among the students, who were angry that they had been used for a phony emotional appeal. Thereafter the student was booed when he went to the podium, and students did not believe what he had to say. He was no longer trustworthy in their eyes and had forfeited his credibility.

Children can usually spot insincerity rather quickly. Praise that is meaningless or words that are too sugary usually turn students off. Related to this notion is the loss of trust when a teacher makes idle threats in disciplining a class. In addition, if the teacher's nonverbal behavior, such as vocal emphasis and facial and bodily expressions, is contradictory to the verbal message, trustworthiness can be reduced. Thus, if a teacher says, "That was a good job," but his or her voice or bodily action says something else, students may believe the nonverbal cues.

**Prestige.**   Early studies of speaker credibility indicated that listeners were persuaded largely on the basis of the prestige of the speaker (Haiman, 1949; Harms, 1961). For the most part, the results of these studies are still valid. Today's students, however, as they get older and more educated, may judge teachers' credibility more by their behavior — such as their speech delivery — than by their authority or prestige. Bettinghaus (1961) demonstrated that when listeners' attitudes toward the speaker become more favorable, their attitudes toward the speech topic shift in the direction of the speaker's assertion. He also found that delivery was very important in listeners' perceptions of a speaker. Part of prestige may be communicated through dress. For example, Thompson (1961) found that college students rated a female speaker higher and learned more from her when she was fashionably dressed than when she was shabbily dressed. However, this finding is not as true today, given the wide array of acceptable dress codes for teachers. Nevertheless, students are not likely to accept instruction unless they perceive the teacher as a person of high status or prestige.

**Competence.**   Closely related to prestige is the speaker's competence as an aspect of credibility. This concept refers to the wisdom, authority, and expertise demonstrated by the speaker. Teachers who are habitually unprepared or who do not understand their subject matter are quickly viewed as incompetent by students. On the other hand, the teacher who never says, "I don't know," and instead fakes an answer to a question, also runs the risk of being perceived as incompetent.

**Dynamism.**   Roberts and Becker (1976) found that effective industrial-arts teachers were those rated high in dynamism, delivery, time spent with students, positive reinforcement of students, and positive attitudes toward students. Thus, dynamism is a complex aspect of credibility and is interrelated with many of the elements discussed under teacher style. The quality is communicated not so much by what is said, but by how the teacher says it through verbal and nonverbal means. The speaker who generates goodwill with listeners and projects energy, enthusiasm, and sincerity is usually perceived as dynamic. Most politicians use speech coaches and media experts in attempts to achieve dynamism. Teachers perceived as dynamic are probably those who empathize well with students, who like to teach, and who bring a sense of the vivid and dramatic into the classroom.

## Attraction

An aspect of the teacher's image that appears to be important, despite little research to validate its specific aspects, is the notion of attraction between teachers and students. McCroskey and McCain (1974) defined three dimensions of interpersonal attraction: social or liking, task or respect, and physical or appearance.

**Social Attraction.**   This dimension is characterized by a friendly relationship or the degree to which students feel that they would like to spend time with the teacher. This feeling is likely to be fostered by the elements of communication style that we have discussed. Teachers who interact frequently with pupils both in and out of class usually are perceived as socially attractive. Teachers who can find common interests and experiences with their students and who have favorable communication styles are likely to be perceived as attractive.

**Task.**   The second dimension of attraction refers to the degree to which the student desires to establish a work relationship with the teacher. Teachers who can communicate to their students a desire to work with them and to help them achieve are likely to be perceived as attractive. It is not unusual for elementary school children to work hard and attempt to do their best for a teacher whom they admire. As children grow older, they begin to evaluate how much their teachers work and how much they are rewarded for the work they do.

**Physical Attraction.**   This third dimension is even more complex. A great deal of research supports the notion that teachers' perceptions of pupils are based upon physical characteristics (see, for example, Kash and Borich, 1978, pp. 65–76). However, much less is known about the teacher's physical self in presenting an image for students. According to Knapp (1978), research supports the idea that "appearance and dress are part of the total nonverbal stimuli which influence interpersonal responses—and under some conditions they are the primary determiners of such responses" (p. 186). A study by Rollman and Madison (1980) found that students ascribed different personality characteristics to teachers based upon their styles of dress. Results further indicated that if a teacher comes to class dressed in jeans and a casual shirt, all other things being equal, the teacher will increase the probability of being perceived as friendly, flexible, and sympathetic, while at the same time decreasing the chances of being perceived as knowledgeable, organized, and well prepared. If the teacher should come dressed more formally, the opposite is likely to occur. The researchers concluded that no one style of dress can be recommended for all teachers, since perceptions of dress interact with too many other variables.

The more people get to know one another, the less important is physical attractiveness in the relationship. In classroom communication, it is likely that the more students perceive their teachers to be competent and caring, the more they perceive them high in social, task, and physical attraction.

## Power

The teacher assigns grades, disciplines students, and selects classroom activities in which students must participate. The power of the teacher is "legitimate," and most students recognize it to be so. However, Strom (1973) has identified some strategies that are misuses of power in the classroom: when teachers attempt to appear omnipotent, omniscient, or infallible; when teachers act as though they know something about students' files or about hearsay concerning students; or when teachers attempt to get students to submit through threats (the "big lie") that they cannot carry out — for example, "John, if you don't sit still, I will tie you to the chair."

Graubard and Rosenberg (1974) report many techniques that have helped to reduce the power struggles between teachers and students. In one project, students were trained in communication skills that helped them to negotiate. The training consisted of:

- helping students to state their own position or desires
- requesting feedback from the other person involved in the transaction
- recognizing and stating the difference between the two positions
- suggesting solutions of the problems by stating which options were more desirable [p. 9].

Graubard and Rosenberg describe the following situation using that approach:

You want to go somewhere, but your parents will not let you go. The options are then identified. They may be: (1) tell them to go to hell; (2) go anyway; (3) ask them why they object or refuse; (4) ask them to take you and pick you up; (5) express disappointment and try for another time; (6) make them feel guilty; (7) sneak out. The consequences might be: (1) getting slapped across the room; (2) earning the privilege of going out; (3) getting grounded; (4) getting a reasonable explanation; (5) parents changing mind; (6) staying home and feeling depressed; (7) parents calling police.

Once the desired consequence is determined by the student, the matching option is simulated by peers, with one child playing the role of the learner and another playing the role of an authority figure [p. 99].

Such techniques, if teachers could apply them in the classroom, would serve to help students in decision making and might diminish the image of the teacher as all knowing and all powerful. The object of the teacher's power should be skillful guidance and management of the classroom; it is misused when coercion and manipulation prevail.

## Self-Concept

The teacher's self-concept is a very important aspect of the teacher's image that affects classroom communication. Kash and Borich (1978) describe the following findings from research on self-concept:

1. Self-confident teachers generally exhibit classroom behaviors and provide supportive environments that foster positive pupil self-concepts.
2. Teachers identified as effective helpers exhibit consistent and decisive classroom behavior and "positive," "realistic" self-concepts.
3. Preservice teachers typically go through stages of concern: first, they are primarily concerned with self and self-protection; later, they shift from self-concern to concern for the task of teaching and, finally, to concern for pupils.
4. Teachers with positive self-concepts whose concerns for pupils are greater than their concerns for self will use the classroom environment to foster positive self-concepts of pupils [pp. 47–48].

An example given by Kash and Borich describes the impact of teacher self-concept on students:

> Suppose that a teacher's basic psychological state is one of mistrust. We would hypothesize that this teacher is fearful and suspicious in the classroom and in his or her relationships with pupils, parents, and colleagues. But how is this fear manifested in classroom behavior? Assuming that the mistrust stemmed from early experiences with parental significant others, we would expect a fear of all authority figures. To cope with this fear, the teacher might identify with all authority figures and authoritarian roles, adopting and imitating negative and controlling behaviors while at the same time seeking approval from those in command. Or, the teacher might continue to identify with children, the "victims" of authority, unable or unwilling to assume or perform any authoritarian behavior [p. 48].

Persons with self-confidence and positive feelings about their professional tasks have less need for an image of infallibility, for one-upmanship, and for manipulative ploys than persons with insecure and negative feelings about the professional task. Feelings about the self are communicated in the classroom through both verbal and nonverbal behaviors. A teacher's walk, posture, eye contact with students, use of gestures, and so on are indicative of how the teacher feels about the self.

## CHANGING TEACHER IMAGE

In the early part of this century, teachers were told how to dress and behave during and after school hours. They were not permitted to smoke or drink in public and in some cases were not permitted to marry—all of this to create a proper image for those who had a special influence on the young. Times have changed, and teachers have wide latitude in projecting their unique images in the classroom. They can send messages that communicate that they are the "tough guy," the "sensitive human being," the "everybody's buddy," the "sex symbol," or the "mother-father" (Hurt, Scott, and McCroskey, 1979, pp. 127–29). Each of these and others that you have encountered have both strengths and weaknesses that may enhance or create barriers to effective classroom communication. Developing an appropriate style is not a simple matter. However, if the teacher demonstrates the elements of an effective communication style, establishes high credibility as a communicator, uses power judiciously, and has a strong self-concept, the appropriate image for effective learning will likely be established.

How can a teacher improve the behaviors that contribute to image? To date no single method has been supported by research. However, all teachers need feedback on their images if changes are to occur. Asking a trusted colleague to observe you critically for aspects of style is one way to begin. Providing students with opportunities for evaluations of teacher behavior is another. Norton (1980), for example, used the following items in his study of style in college communication courses. Perhaps they could be adapted by elementary and secondary teachers to provide the basis for student feedback on aspects of teacher image:

My instructor:

communicates in a very lively/animated way

has an effective style of presentation

communicates in a very friendly way

is careful and precise when answering questions

communicates in a very evasive way

communicates in a very dominant way

communicates in a very serious way

leaves a very strong impression in communicating

communicates in a very humble way

communicates in a very dramatic way

is a very good communicator

communicates in a very attentive way

communicates in a very argumentative way [p. 2].

# SUMMARY

Evidence indicates that the teacher's communication has an impact upon the child's self-concept and potential for achievement. Teachers' attitudes are communicated through the expectancies they hold for pupils' classroom behaviors. Teachers form their expectancies on the basis of perceived sex-role behavior, physical attractiveness, cultural characteristics, and socioeconomic status. Teachers tend to behave in ways that are congruent with their expectancies. They communicate differently with high and low achievers in ways that confirm these expectancies. Attribution theory explains the ways in which teachers act to confirm their expectations and the ways in which students eventually accept and adjust to the messages of the teacher. Three dimensions of attribution form the basis for justifying classroom behaviors: locus of causality, stability of causes, and controllability. Self-fulfilling prophecy is a concept that interacts with expectancy and attribution to explain how teachers and students interact over time. Through this phenomenon, students learn to predict success or failure and to behave accordingly, thereby "confirming" their teachers' expectations. Research has demonstrated that teachers and students can change their expectations and attributions. Classroom interactions can be modified through feedback, appropriate use of praise, respect for student feelings, and empathic listening.

The perceptions that students have of the teacher also have an impact upon communication. Aspects of the teacher's image in the classroom occur through communicator style, perceptions of credibility, attraction, use of power, and self-concept. Teachers must be conscious of the ways in which these factors of image contribute to classroom interactions and student learning.

# Discussion Questions

1. Discuss the sources of teacher expectancy described in this chapter. Are there any other sources that you have observed in your own school days or in recent visits to schools? Do expectancies differ in various regions of the country? In private and public schools? In the homogeneous and heterogeneous classroom?
2. Observe teachers in elementary and secondary classrooms. In what ways do their expectancies seem to influence their interactions with students?
3. Discuss how various class members react when they receive the results of their tests in this course. How does attribution theory explain their reactions? How does the teacher's behavior affect student reactions?
4. Write a short essay describing the image you wish to project in the classroom with respect to communication style, credibility, attractiveness, power, and self-concept. What kinds of messages will help you achieve the desired image with your students?

# References

Adams, R. S., and B. J. Biddle. *Realities of Teaching: Explorations with Videotape.* New York: Holt, Rinehart and Winston, Inc., 1970.

Andersen, Janis F., R. W. Norton, and J. F. Nussbaum. "Three Investigations Exploring Relationships between Perceived Teacher Communicator Behaviors and Student Learning." *Communication Education,* Vol. 30 (October 1981): 377–92.

Beady, Charles H., Jr., and Stephen Hansell. "Teacher Race and Expectations for Student Achievement." *American Educational Research Journal,* Vol. 18 (Summer 1981): 191–206.

Beck, William R. "Pupils' Perceptions of Teacher Merit: A Factor Analysis of Five Postulated Dimensions." *Journal of Educational Research,* Vol. 61 (November 1967): 127–28.

Benson, J. S., and K. J. Kennelly. "Learned Helplessness: The Results of Uncontrolled Reinforcements or Uncontrolled Aversive Stimuli." *Journal of Personality and Social Psychology,* Vol. 34 (1976): 138–45.

Benz, Carolyn R., I. Pfeiffer, and I. Newman. "Sex Role Expectations of Classroom Teachers, Grades 1–12." *American Educational Research Journal,* Vol. 18 (Fall 1981): 289–302.

Bettinghaus, E. P. "The Operation of Congruity in an Oral Communication Situation." *Speech Monographs,* Vol. 28 (August 1961): 131–42.

Branan, J. "Negative Human Interaction." *Journal of Counseling Psychology,* Vol. 19 (1972): 81–82.

Braun, Carl. "Teacher Expectation: Sociopsychological Dynamics." *Review of Educational Research,* Vol. 46 (Spring 1976): 185–213.

Brophy, J., and T. Good. "Teachers' Communication of Differential Expectations for Children's Classroom Performance: Some Behavioral Data." *Journal of Educational Psychology,* Vol. 71 (1970): 365–74.

Brophy, Jere E., and Thomas Good. *Teacher-Student Relationships: Causes and Consequences.* New York: Holt, Rinehart and Winston, Inc., 1974.

Brown, W., L. Payne, C. Lankewich, and L. Cornell. "Praise, Criticism and Race." *Elementary School Journal,* Vol. 70 (1970): 373–77.

Clifford, M. M., and E. Walster. "The Effect of Physical Attractiveness on Teacher Expectation." *Sociology of Education,* Vol. 46 (1973): 248–58.

Covington, M. V., and C. L. Omelich. "Are Causal Attributions Causal? A Path Analysis of the Cognitive Model of Achievement Motivation." *Journal of Personality and Social Psychology,* Vol. 32 (1979): 1487–504.

Covington, M. V., M. F. Spratt, and C. L. Omelich. "Is Effort Enough or Does Diligence Count Too? Student and Teacher Reactions to Effort Stability in Failure." *Journal of Educational Psychology,* Vol. 72 (1980): 717–29

Dweck, C. S. "The Role of Expectations and Attributions in the Alleviation of Learned Helplessness." *Journal of Personality and Social Psychology,* Vol. 31 (1975): 674–85.

Evans, J., and R. Rosenthal. "Interpersonal Self-Fulfilling Prophecies: Further Extrapolations from the Laboratory to the Classroom." *Proceedings of the 77th Annual Convention of the American Psychological Association,* Vol. 4 (1969): 371–72.

Feather, N. T., and J. G. Simon. "Causal Attributions for Success and Failure in Relation to Expectations of Success Based upon Selective or Manipulative Control." *Journal of Personality,* Vol. 39 (1971): 527–41.

Finn, J. D. "Expectations and the Educational Environment." *Journal of Educational Research,* Vol. 42 (1972): 387–410.

Forsyth, D. R., and J. H. McMillan. "Attributions, Affect and Expectations: A Test of Weiner's Three-Dimensional Model." *Journal of Educational Psychology,* Vol. 73, No. 3 (1981): 393–403.

Fowler, J. W., and P. C. Peterson. "Increasing Reading Persistence and Altering Attributional Style of Learned Helpless Children." *Journal of Educational Psychology,* Vol. 73 (1981): 251–60.

Frieze, I. H., and H. N. Snyder. "Children's Beliefs about the Causes of Success and Failure in School Settings." *Journal of Educational Psychology,* Vol. 72, No. 2 (1980): 186–96.

Ginott, Haim. *Teacher and Child.* New York: The Macmillan Company, 1972.

Good, T., and J. Brophy. "Behavioral Expression of Teacher Attitudes." *Journal of Educational Psychology,* Vol. 63 (1972): 617–24.

Good, T., N. Sikes, and J. Brophy. "Effects of Teacher Sex and Student Sex on Classroom Interaction." *Journal of Educational Psychology,* Vol. 65 (1973): 74–87.

Graubard, P., and H. Rosenberg. *Classrooms That Work.* New York: E. P. Dutton & Co., Inc., 1974.

Haiman, F. "An Experimental Study of the Effects of Ethos in Public Speaking." *Speech Monographs,* Vol. 16 (September 1949): 190–202.

Harari, H., and J. W. McDavid. "Name Stereotypes and Teacher Expectancies." *Journal of Educational Psychology,* Vol. 65 (1973): 222–25.

Harms, L. S. "Listener Judgments of Status Cues in Speech." *Quarterly Journal of Speech,* Vol. 47 (1961): 164–68.

Heider, F. *The Psychology of Interpersonal Relations.* New York: John Wiley & Sons, Inc., 1958.

Hurt, H. Thomas, Michael D. Scott, and James C. McCroskey. *Communication in the Classroom.* Reading, Mass.: Addison-Wesley Publishing Company, Inc., 1979.

Johnson, Wendell. *Stuttering and What You Can Do about It.* Minneapolis: Univesity of Minnesota Press, 1961.

Kash, Marilyn M., and Gary D. Borich. *Teacher Behavior and Pupil Self-Concept.* Reading, Mass.: Addison-Wesley Publishing Company, Inc., 1978.

Knapp, Mark L. *Nonverbal Communication in Human Interaction,* 2nd ed. New York: Holt, Rinehart and Winston, Inc., 1978.

Madson, C. H., C. K. Madson, R. A. Sandargas, W. R. Hammond, and D. E. Edgar. "Classroom RAID (Rules, Approval, Ignore, Disapproval): A Cooperative Approach for Professionals and Volunteers." Unpublished manuscript, University of Florida, 1970.

Mazer, G. E. "Effects of Social-Class Stereotyping on Teacher Expectation." *Psychology in the Schools,* Vol. 8 (1971): 373–78.

McCroskey, James C. *Quiet Children and the Classroom Teacher.* Annandale, Va.: Speech Communication Assoc. under the auspices of the ERIC Clearinghouse on Reading and Communication Skills, 1977.

McCroskey, James C., and T. A. McCain. "The Measurement of Interpersonal Attraction." *Speech Monographs,* Vol. 41 (1974): 261–66.

Meichenbaum, D. H., K. Bowers, and R. Ross. "A Behavioral Analysis of Teacher Expectancy Effect." *Journal of Personality and Social Psychology,* Vol. 13 (1969): 306–16.

Norton, R. W. "Teacher Effectiveness as a Function of Communicator Style." In *Communication Yearbook I,* An Annual Review published by the International Communication Association. New Brunswick, N.J.: Transaction Books, Rutgers, The State University, 1977, pp. 523–541.

Norton, R. "Style Profile of the Ineffective Teacher." Unpublished paper, Purdue University, 1980.

Palardy, J. M. "What Teachers Believe—What Children Achieve." *Elementary School Journal,* Vol. 69 (1969): 370–74.

Pascarella, Ernest T., and Susanna W. Pflaum. "The Interaction of Children's Attribution and Level of Control over Error Correction in Reading Instruction." *Journal of Educational Psychology,* Vol. 73 (1981): 533–40.

Rich, Jordan. "Effects of Children's Physical Attractiveness on Teachers' Evaluations." *Journal of Educational Psychology,* Vol. 67, No. 5 (1975): 599–609.

Rist, R. C. "Student Social Class and Teachers' Expectations: The Self-Fulfilling Prophecy in Ghetto Education." *Harvard Educational Review,* Vol. 40 (1970): 411–51.

Roberts, Churchill L., and Samuel L. Becker. "Communication and Teaching Effectiveness in Industrial Education." *American Educational Research Journal,* Vol. 13 (Summer 1976): 180–97.

Rogers, Carl R. *Freedom to Learn.* Columbus, Oh.: Charles E. Merrill Publishing Co., 1969.

Rollman, Steven A., and James Madison. "Some Effects of Teachers' Styles of Dress." Unpublished paper presented at the Southern Speech Communication Association Convention, Birmingham, Ala., 1980.

Rosenthal, Robert, and Lenore Jacobson. *Pygmalion in the Classroom: Teacher Expectations and Pupils' Intellectual Development.* New York: Holt, Rinehart and Winston, Inc. 1968.

Rubovits, P. C., and M. L. Maehr. "Pygmalion Black and White." *Journal of Personality and Social Psychology,* Vol. 25 (1973): 210–18.

Seaver, W. G. "Effects of Naturally Induced Teacher Expectancies." *Journal of Personality and Social Psychology,* Vol. 28 (1973): 333–42.

Seligman, M.E.P. *Helplessness: On Depression, Development, and Death.* San Francisco: W. H. Freeman and Co., Publishers, 1975.

Stipek, Deborah J. "Children's Perceptions of Their Own and Their Classmates' Ability." *Journal of Educational Psychology,* Vol. 73, No. 3 (1981): 404–10.

Stipek, Deborah, and J. Hoffman. "Children's Achievement-Related Expectancies as a Function of Academic Performance Histories and Sex." *Journal of Educational Psychology,* Vol. 72 (1980): 861–65.

Strom, R. "Reversing Coercive Strategies." In *Education for Affective Achievement,* R. Strom and P. Torrance, eds. Skokie, Ill.: Rand McNally & Company, 1973, pp. 281–90.

Thomas, Adele. "Learned Helplessness and Expectancy Factors: Implications for Research in Learning Disabilities." *Review of Educational Research,* Vol. 49 (Spring 1979): 208–21.

Thompson, K. "Dress as Related to the Effectiveness and the Assessment of the Effectiveness of a Performance and the Relation of the Authoritarian Personality to the Evaluation of the Performer." Unpublished master's thesis, Pennsylvania State University, 1961.

U.S. Commission on Civil Rights. "Teachers and Students: Differences in Teacher Interaction with Mexican-American and Anglo Students." *Mexican-American Education Study* (March 1973). ERIC Document #073881.

Weiner, B. "A Theory of Motivation for Some Classroom Experiences." *Journal of Educational Psychology,* Vol. 71 (1979): 3–25.

Weiner, B., I. H. Frieze, A. Kukla, R. Reed, S. Rest, and R. Rosenbaum. *Perceiving the Causes of Success and Failure.* Morristown, N.J.: General Learning Press, 1971.

Weiner, B., R. Nierenberg, and M. Goldstein. "Social Learning (Locus of Control) versus Attributional (Causal Stability) Interpretation of Expectancy of Success." *Journal of Personality,* Vol. 44 (1976): 52–68.

Weiner, B., D. Russell, and D. Lerman. "The Cognition-Emotion Process in Achievement-Related Contexts." *Journal of Personality and Social Psychology,* Vol. 37 (1979): 1211–20.

Weinstein, Carol S. "The Physical Environment of the School: A Review of the Research." *Review of Educational Research,* Vol. 49 (Fall 1979), 577–610.

# Further Reading

Good, T., and J. Brophy. *Looking in Classrooms.* New York: Harper & Row, Publishers, 1973.

McCroskey, James C., and Rod W. McVetta. "Classroom Seating Arrangements: Instructional Communication Theory versus Student Preferences." *Communication Education,* Vol. 27 (1978): 99–111.

McLaughlin, Margaret I., and Keith V. Erickson. "A Multidimensional Scaling Analysis of the 'Ideal Interpersonal Communication Instructor.'" *Communication Education,* Vol. 30 (1981): 393–98.

Norton, R. "Foundations of a Communicator Style Construct," *Human Communication Research,* Vol. 4, No. 2 (Winter 1978): 98–112.

Smith, Howard A. "Nonverbal Communication in Teaching." *Review of Educational Research,* Vol. 49 (Fall 1979): 631–72.

# part 2

# APPLICATIONS

Using communication in the classroom to facilitate learning is extremely important to the instructional process. In writing Part 2 of this book we have made some assumptions: To apply communication effectively to the classroom context, the teacher has a content basis, a reason to communicate that content, objectives to accomplish, an instructional strategy or strategies, and a means to measure what has been accomplished. The intent of this section is not only to provide some of the most-used methods in the instructional setting but to discuss them from a communication perspective. Designing instruction — that is, making decisions as to which methods are best or most appropriate for the classroom — is beyond the purpose of this text. Many excellent instructional design texts already exist to aid the teacher in this area.

In this part we explain the importance of effective communication interaction in the classroom; describe teacher communication competencies and structuring, soliciting, and reacting behaviors. We provide an in-depth view of the lecture and discussion as a means of communicating in the classroom; and explain gaming, simulation, and role playing as communication strategies that are effective for involving students in the learning process. Communication and individualized learning are emphasized. In addition, we discuss the development of self-instructional programs, personalized systems of learning, learning contracts, and the notion of instructional resources.

Part 2 brings together the technology of the computer, student responders, videotape recordings, and communication in a unique blend of the innovations in education and the communication that is required by the teacher to use them. Finally, we examine the assessment of communication in the instructional process as well as feedback, and also describe systematic observation as a means for teachers to see themselves as communicators. Feedback as a means for communicating and assessing the instructional process, whether teacher to student, student to teacher, or parents to teacher, is illustrated and discussed here.

# Communicating: Indirect Teaching Behaviors

chapter **6**

---

*focus*    IDENTIFICATION OF INDIRECT TEACHING BEHAVIORS

IDENTIFICATION OF TEACHING COMPETENCIES

TEACHER BEHAVIOR VARIABLES
Structuring
Soliciting (Question-Answer Process)
Reacting

Not all teachers have the same communication characteristics or behaviors. In fact, if you think about your school experiences, you will probably realize that the good teachers do not behave with much similarity. Rather, each stands out as an individual. Each has certain identifying characteristics, skills, methods, values, and techniques. Thus, good teaching, like good communication, is a personal thing. Indirect teaching behaviors are those that every teacher possesses in one degree or another. According to Amidon and Flanders (1967), indirect teacher behaviors are those that maximize the students' freedom to respond, while direct teacher behaviors reduce the students' freedom to respond. They further categorize indirect influences: accepting feelings, praising or encouraging, accepting or using students' ideas, and asking questions. Direct influences are categorized as: lecturing, giving directions, and criticizing or justifying authority. Dunkin and Biddle (1974) have indicated that teacher directness and teacher indirectness have been defined as opposites of one another. Gage and Berliner (1979) suggest that they are not opposites but rather are representatives of two different dimensions. Directness is similar to structuring or organizing, while indirectness is similar to warmth or openness. It is, therefore, possible to be structured (direct) and still be accepting of students' feelings (warm). In either case, we are interested in the behaviors of the teacher who creates effective classroom interaction and, ultimately, learning. In this chapter, we identify some of the indirect teaching behaviors that seem to be important to effective classroom teaching and classroom interaction. To put the matter in perspective, however, we must first examine what we know about teacher competencies.

# IDENTIFICATION OF TEACHING COMPETENCIES

Generally, two approaches are used to define good teaching. The first approach — that those who know something can teach it — is based on the concept that good teachers are scholars. It is true that in order to teach, the teacher must know something, but the reverse is not necessarily true — that is, knowing something does not automatically mean being able to teach it. Probably each of us can remember a teacher who seemed to know the subject matter but couldn't get it across. Good teaching involves much more than just knowing.

The second approach to defining good teaching is related to specific competencies a teacher should possess. Basically, this approach rests on the premise that if we know what behaviors and skills superior teachers possess, then we can train teachers to have those behaviors and skills. The problem has been in identifying the specific competencies or skills. Numerous off-the-cuff lists have been published, but they are not in agreement and have little scientific support. However, a scientific study by Amidon and Giammatteo (1967) examined the verbal patterns of teachers, comparing one group that was rated average to another group that was rated superior. The following results are revealing:

Superior teachers tended to *accept feelings* three times as often as did average teachers.

Superior teachers and average teachers used statements of *praise and encouragement* about equally, but superior teachers provided students with reasons for the praise more often than did average teachers.

Superior teachers used over twice as many *student ideas* as did average teachers.

Average teachers tended to ask specific *questions* calling for narrow and predictable responses ("What does two plus two equal?"), while superior teachers used *questions* to clarify ideas.

Superior teachers *lectured* to their classes in a continuous fashion less than did average teachers. However, the total amount of lecture time was about 40% for both groups. Also, the superior teachers were interrupted more often while they were lecturing to respond to student questions than were average teachers.

Superior teachers used half as many *direction-giving* statements as did average teachers.

Superior teachers used half as many *criticism* statements as did average teachers. In addition, direction-giving followed by criticism appeared in the verbal patterns of the average teachers twice as frequently as it did in the verbal patterns of superior teachers.

Superior teachers' students had markedly different *verbal patterns* than did those of average teachers. Student-initiated statements in superior teachers' classes were double those of students in the average teachers' classes.

*Participation by students* accounted for over 52% of class time in classes taught by superior teachers, but for only 40% of class time in classes taught by average teachers.

Superior teachers had half as much *silence and confusion* as did average teachers.

Teaching, as we pointed out in Chapter 1, is more than talking, but a few visits to the classroom will illustrate that a majority of instructional communication is teacher talk: 66% is either teacher or student talk (Flanders, 1970). Further, through talk, teachers present information, praise or criticize students, give directions, ask questions, or accept and help clarify student ideas and feelings. Apparently, these are some of the important communication competencies needed by teachers.

According to Goodlad and Klein (1970), indirect teaching is the most frequently used method of instruction in today's schools:

> At all grade levels, the teacher-to-child pattern of interaction overwhelmingly prevailed. This was one of the most continuously recurring pieces of data. The teachers asked questions and the children responded and usually correctly — that is, with the response approved or acknowledged as correct by the teacher. It is fair to say that teacher-to-child interaction was the mode in all but about 5 percent of the classes [p. 51].

This approach to teaching parallels what many refer to as informal communication or teacher talk.

Another study that focused on teacher interaction competencies described teaching as a continually repeated chain of events. The four links of the chain, according to Bellack, Kliebard, Hyman, and Smith (1966), are:

1.  The teacher provides structuring, briefly formulating the topic or issue to be discussed.
2.  The teacher solicits a response or asks a question of one or more students; then
3.  A student responds or answers the question; and
4.  The teacher reacts to the student's answer.

Bellack, Kliebard, Hyman, and Smith suggest that not all four links must occur to complete the interaction. Structuring and reacting, for example, may not occur each time. However, questioning and responding generally occur, and are considered by many to be the essential components of classroom communication.

## TEACHER BEHAVIOR VARIABLES

Gage and Berliner (1979) suggest that structuring, soliciting, and reacting are the three teacher behavior variables that make up the majority of classroom communication. Although there is some variation among scientific investigations in terms of behaviors identified, there are some seemingly important behaviors common to most. It is these behaviors with which we are concerned. The following is a discussion of the three teacher behavior variables.

### Structuring

According to Bellack, Kliebard, Hyman, and Smith (1966), structuring is a function of the teacher in which the teacher sets the context for behavior by either initiating or stopping interaction, for example, by attempting to focus the attention of students on a particular topic or problem. Structuring is essentially a form of providing direction for student thinking or behavior. In reviewing research, Gage and Berliner (1979) found four dimensions of teacher structuring behavior: (1) rate of teacher initiation, (2) signal giving, (3) organization, and (4) directness.

Communication interactions must be initiated, and the rate of initiation is a factor in structuring. The scant evidence we have from research suggests that either too little or too much initiation is harmful.

A teacher gives signals to indicate to students that something is to begin or end, or that something is important and should be noted by them. This is done by using words that emphasize — for example, "Remember the term *process*. It is critical to the understanding of communication." Pinney (1969) refers to signals that tell students of the importance of something as *verbal markers*; for example, "You need to know this." Using signals such as voice changes or pauses is another means of communicating importance and, thus, is a means of giving structure to what is being taught.

Organization is in itself a signal to students, who are quite perceptive and can detect when a teacher is not well organized. This, of course, will eventually affect credibility and, in turn, learning.

Directness, mentioned at the beginning of the chapter, is a form of structuring that can be used to control or reduce student communication. For example, when teachers lecture or give directions, they limit student interaction.

## Soliciting (Question-Answer Process)

Soliciting — asking for responses from students — is probably one of the most difficult communication skills for teachers to learn. Yet it has been estimated that teachers spend 70 to 80% of their talking time asking questions. Questions are used for a variety of purposes in the classroom: to control behavior, to give instructions, to initiate instructions, to create learning, to evaluate learning, and to stimulate thinking. However, a question is more than a series of words that ends with a question mark: It is a verbal utterance that seeks a response. You might have noticed that about every other utterance of children is a question. This is apparently the entry point by which most of us learn. Unfortunately, effective questioning skills are not innate in most of us, but they can be learned and developed with practice. Questioning is the most basic communication tool in classroom communication.

**Effective Questions.**    The major concern is not the number of questions to ask but the effects the questions have. The three concerns in developing a question are: (1) knowing the types of questions available to be used; (2) asking the questions for a purpose; and (3) phrasing the questions.

Questions can be classified in many ways. Regardless of the system used for classification, the *first* step in developing skills in asking questions requires an ability to identify and understand various types of questions and their uses as well as the types of responses they will produce. Generally, teachers ask two types of questions, both of which basically provide a way of labeling according to what the student is asked. We will be concerned with two primary types of questions (closed and open) and two secondary types (mirror and probe).

*Primary Question — Closed.*    This kind of question requires rather low-level thinking, short factual answers, or other predictable responses, including yes and no. The closed question is restrictive, and, therefore, the responses to it are predictable because they allow for only a very limited number of acceptable or "right" answers. A yes-no question, referred to as bipolar, is an extreme type of closed question, for it allows the student no freedom of expression. Often, closed-type questions are used in drills to test listening or reading comprehension. Some samples are:

1. Which building in Chicago is the tallest?
2. How many sides to a rectangle?
3. What did Kathi do after she found the money?
4. Did the list of words in the text provide enough variety from which to choose?
5. What is the capital of Nebraska?

As you can see, the responses to these questions are quite predictable. However, the closed question can be very useful in teaching: to collect information, to verify ideas and understanding of materials, and to review previously studied material. The closed question also allows high control over a discussion; further, it takes less time to obtain answers and requires less effort from students.

On the other hand, the closed question restricts the information one can obtain and limits the opportunity for the student to volunteer information that in turn might lead to a higher level of thinking. Learning to sequence closed questions can be a valuable teaching strategy if they are used to identify, group, and note relationships, and to lead to questions at higher levels of thinking. The danger in using closed questions is the potential overuse of them.

*Primary Questions — Open.* The open question, a second type of primary question, attempts to generate a response of more than just a few words. There are two subtypes. One is an open-ended question that is extremely vague and general; it merely specifies a topic or asks the student to talk. Some examples are:

1. How did you like the story?
2. What are your feelings about this assignment?
3. Tell me about yourself.
4. What do you like about our country?

The second kind is a more direct open-ended question. It identifies or limits the topic area as well as asking for a more specific reply. Some examples are:

1. How did the grammar rules affect your writing style?
2. What do you think are the major criticisms of the movie?
3. Why do you think house number five was the best?

Regardless of the degree of openness, the open question is extremely useful because it brings out the students' understanding of a situation or concept; it also tends to motivate them to explore a subject more deeply or to experiment more freely than does the closed question. In addition, it gives the teacher an opportunity to listen.

*Secondary Questions — Mirror and Probe.* These types of questions are techniques to encourage students to expand on responses thought to be incomplete. The mirror question is a restatement of what the student has just said. For example, if the student has said, "I find reading about our involvement in space to be quite interesting," a mirror question might be: "So you think our involvement is interesting? Why?" This method provides an effective technique to get more specific information.

The probing question directs the thinking of the student to further explanations of what has been said. In a sense, it is a follow-up question to a superficial or incomplete response and allows for a deeper investigation into the reasons for expansion at a higher level of thinking. The probe does not always start with a why or how, although these are common probes. A probe can be brief vocal sounds or short phrases, such as "I see," "Please continue," "Uh-huh," "Go on," or "Why do you believe that?"

Since the probe is considered to be a secondary (neutral/nondirective) question, it can be introduced at any time in the interaction. The student can interpret it as an indicator of attentiveness and interest, which acts as encouragement to continue speaking. The probe serves two functions: (1) to motivate further communication and (2) to control the interaction by providing direction to the student.

The second concern in asking effective questions is determining the purpose or objective of a question. Questions can serve three broad levels of learning. The first, the cognitive-memory level, involves generally narrow questions limited to low-level thinking; they ask the student to recall facts or definitions or to identify something. Examples of cognitive-memory questions are "In what year did Columbus discover the New World?" or "What is the definition of communication according to our text?" Each of these is merely asking the students to respond with a memorized answer.

The second, the convergent-level question, goes beyond mere recall to association of facts and principles or to explanations. For example, "Explain how the source, receiver, and message could be used to define communication," or "How does communication help to resolve conflict?" Each of these asks the students not only to exhibit what they have learned from their class discussions or reading, but also to go beyond to their own thoughts and ideas.

The third level is the divergent level. A divergent question asks the student to analyze, to apply, or to evaluate. For example, "The story tells of a young man who is torn between fighting for his country and his true desire for peace. Given society's views today, what decision would be in his best interest?" A probe following this question might be: "Why do you think that?" The divergent question, by stimulating interest and providing motivation for exploration and experimentation, is likely to lead to the development of insight, appreciation, and positive attitude. It provides the opportunity for the student to think. In responding, the student may predict, hypothesize, or infer.

Chaudhari (1975) wrote that "bridging the gap between learning and thinking, however, requires a large expenditure of energy, and the process usually has to be incited by questions that go beyond what has been learned" (p. 30). It is common knowledge, according to Chaudhari, that children enjoy learning when they can think creatively. Bruner (1959) suggests that one of the rewards of learning comes when a learner uses the knowledge that has been acquired to further thought. According to Hunt (1961), questions provide one of the best means for producing "cognitive strain" on students so that they begin to invent methods or systems for handling information more effectively and efficiently.

According to Hunkins (1969), the role of questions is still imprecise as it relates to critical and creative thinking. However, a number of studies suggest that if students are asked higher-level questions, they can be led to think more creatively. Thus, teachers need to use convergent and divergent level questions more often.

The third concern in asking an effective question involves phrasing or wording. An effective question not only conveys its function accurately but is also clearly phrased. In other words, the grammatical arrangement of the question can influence its clarity; it also reflects its intent. Questions that use too many words, use illogical word order, or use words that do not stimulate a suitable response must be considered poorly phrased. Thus, the intent of a question may be appropriate, but unless it is stated with a logical word order and in words meaningful for the respondent, the intent may not be communicated. The intent of a question may be clear in the teacher's mind, but unless clearly stated, it may not be understood by the student for whom the question was intended. A question can bring out more than one response, particularly if it is seeking a high level of thought; but if it is not specific enough, the student will end up guessing, requesting clarification, or not responding. For example, "What about the theme of the story?" does not offer any criteria or guides for a meaningful answer. *What about* provides little or no suggestion as to what is expected in an answer.

Certain words can give clues to the respondent as to what is expected in the question. For example, questions that begin with *who, what, where, which,* and *when* are often associated with cognitive-memory types of questions. *How* and *why* are often related to questions used to bring out explanation, and thus offer indications of a convergent-thinking type of question. *What if* can be associated with a divergent question. Using these words, of course, does not guarantee that the question will automatically fall into a particular classification.

Many problems can be encountered when attempting to phrase an effective question, but given the amount of time teachers devote to asking questions, learning to phrase questions as effectively as possible is important. Students who respond to a question by saying that they do not understand it may be indicating that the question has been poorly phrased. This response is often associated with ambiguously worded questions, which are the result of inadequate criteria being specified so that a meaningful response can be formed. The following are examples of ambiguously worded questions:

1. What about the Supreme Court?
2. Tell us about the new book.
3. Something happened?

These questions, with their unclear purposes, do not guide the students to an expected response and are unfair because they fail to communicate their intent. Moyer (1965) found that about 40% of the teachers he observed asked questions that suffered from ambiguity in their phrasing. Questions that are phrased correctly will utilize clear and understandable wording, be grammatically correct, and contain content relevant to the intent of the question. The above questions can be easily rephrased to limit or avoid ambiguity as follows:

1. What is the purpose of our Supreme Court?
2. How did you like our new book?
3. Explain what happened to John in the story.

Another problem in phrasing occurs when a question leads to only a yes-or-no type of response. The problem usually occurs when clue words like *who, what, where, when,* or *which* are not used in the question. Questions producing only a yes-or-no response generally begin with an auxiliary verb such as *are, is, could, would, do,* and so on. Examples of this type of question are:

1. Is all language verbal?
2. Does the story provide us with a solution?
3. Could we say that oil is the main energy source?

To offset these poorly phrased questions and to avoid the yes, no, or I-don't-know responses, the teacher should use follow-up questions that ask the students to explain their responses. The intent of the above questions would be clearer if they were rephrased:

1. What are some other forms of language besides verbal?
2. Explain what you think are the possible solutions to the story.
3. What is the main energy source in this country?

The simple changing of the interrogative terms (i.e., *what* or *explain*) reduces the need for a second question. While this change does not necessarily alter the level of thought required to answer the question, it does make the question clearer.

A third problem in phrasing arises when a question becomes too complex by including too many ideas for the student to consider at one time. Teachers often attempt to clarify a question by including several questions within it, on the premise that the additional requests will make the question more clear for the student. Often, however, the additional requests confuse rather than clarify. An effective question should contain only one thought or idea. Some examples of poorly phrased questions are:

1. Why does the rudder on an airplane go up or down when the plane is taking off, landing, or flying?
2. How, when, and why did the pollution in our city begin?
3. What causes or why is it that air must enter our voice boxes in order for sounds to be produced?

The phrasing of these questions could be improved by simply asking two or more separate questions that are clearer and shorter.

When phrasing questions, remember that poorly phrased questions hinder thought and reduce the quality of a response. The learning process is often negatively affected by questions that inadequately communicate their intent.

**Question-Asking Strategies.**    Teachers' effectiveness as question askers depends not only on how well they develop questions, but also on how they use the questions.

Four strategies should be noted in asking questions. First, ask a reasonable number. Asking too many questions will affect the quality of the responses and the amount of response time used by students. A few well-constructed questions that allow for adequate response time are preferable to a rapid-fire series of questions.

Second, attempt to distribute questions to all students in the class. Sometimes teachers have a tendency to ask questions of only certain students. The effectiveness of teaching can often be judged on the basis of student participation. The quality of the answers and the number of students who actually respond to questions can determine one's effectiveness in questioning. If a few extroverted or favorite students monopolize the answering of questions, the quality of learning might be judged only by what is done by a few. In many instances, those who are responding the most need to respond the least.

Third, attempt to use questions to encourage participation. Whenever possible, ask questions that allow more than one student to respond. If the teacher asks well-constructed questions and allows free student participation, the amount of teacher talk will be decreased and the instruction can become more student centered.

Fourth, use students' responses effectively. This is a critical aspect of successful questioning, for the teacher's use of an answer is as important as the question that elicited the response. The effectiveness of questioning depends on how well the teacher accepts, reinforces, discriminates, and encourages students to build on their initial responses. The wholesale acceptance of any answer by a student can deter the development of thinking skills; punishing a student for an incorrect or incomplete answer can discourage participation, too. This places extreme importance on the teacher's response to answers. The next section focuses on reacting behaviors to students' responses.

## Reacting

Teacher reacting behavior is essentially the response the teacher gives to students' communication. Gage and Berliner (1979) list four types of teacher responses: wait time, positive, negative, and structuring.

**1. Wait Time** is the time a teacher waits after asking a question. It can, also, be the time used by the teacher in responding to a student's comment. Rowe (1976) suggests that teachers wait at least three seconds for a response after they have asked a question. She feels that most teachers react too quickly (within one second) to students' comments. Increasing wait time produces the following beneficial effects (according to Rowe, p. 81):

1. The length of the response increases.
2. The number of unsolicited but appropriate responses increases.
3. Failures to respond decrease.
4. Confidence, as reflected in decrease of inflected (questionlike tones of voice) responses, increases.
5. Incidence of speculative responses increases.
6. Incidence of child-child comparisons of data increases.
7. Incidence of evidence-inference statements increases.
8. The frequency of student questions increases.
9. Incidence of responses from students rated by teachers as relatively slow increases.
10. The variety in type of moves made by students increases.

The increase of wait time, according to Rowe, also gives a conversational quality to classroom interaction.

**2. Positive Reactions** are those that praise students. While research results on the use of praise are somewhat mixed, it is generally accepted that praise increases achievement and motivation. Positive reactions can be simply a smile to indicate approval or a direct response telling the students of approval and acceptance of their behavior. Like most things, too much praise can have detrimental effects.

**3. Negative Reactions** involve disapproval of students' behavior. As mentioned earlier in this chapter, it has been shown that average teachers use twice as much criticism as do superior teachers. While we are not suggesting that criticism be eliminated, we are suggesting that it be done in as supportive a manner as possible. The effective use of criticism is best accomplished when the teacher is flexible and fair in its use. Comments like "You don't understand what you are talking about" or "You are wrong" certainly have their place. But it is much better to react with "Your attempt is interesting, but it seems as if you don't completely understand what you have said," or "This is a difficult question to answer; why don't you try again?" Our point here is that not only what is said to the student, but also how it is said, can make a difference in the teacher-student relationship.

**4. Structuring Reactions**   redirect students' comments by either rewording the response or asking another student to respond to the question. The structuring reaction is especially effective when students' comments are incorrect or incomplete. Reacting to students is one of the most important types of teacher communication, because the impact of a teacher's reaction can lead to more effective learning by improving motivation and the learning climate. In Chapter 11 we discuss further reacting behavior in our discussion of feedback.

# SUMMARY

Good teaching generally means effective classroom communication and can be defined by two approaches: (1) teachers who possess knowledge can teach; knowledge is important to teaching, but good teaching usually involves much more than just knowing. (2) Both superior and average teachers understand the specific competencies needed to be successful in the classroom, but superior teachers seem to be able to use these competencies with more success than do average teachers.

Teacher talk and student talk account for approximately 66% of classroom instructional time. Teacher communication usually takes the form of information presentation, praise or criticism toward students, direction giving, asking questions, and accepting and clarifying student ideas and feelings.

Structuring, soliciting, and reacting behaviors are teacher functions and a part of teacher classroom interaction. Structuring is a form of providing direction for students' thinking or behavior, and encompasses four dimensions of teacher behavior: rate of teacher initiation, signal giving, organization, and directness. Soliciting asks for responses from students. Questioning techniques present a means of getting students to respond in the classroom and concern various types of questions, including closed, open, mirror, and probing, as well as strategies for asking questions. Reacting is the response the teacher gives to students' communication. Four types of teacher responses are explained: wait time and positive, negative, and structuring responses.

# Discussion Questions

1.   How would you describe a competent classroom teacher?
2.   What is meant by indirect teaching skills?
3.   Which qualities or characteristics of indirect teaching do you think are most effective in increasing classroom learning? Why?
4.   Before asking a question, a teacher should consider the various types of questions. Why?
5.   What determines whether a question asked by a teacher is a good one?

# References

Amidon, Edmund J., and Ned Flanders. "Interaction Analysis as a Feedback System." In *Interaction Analysis: Theory, Research, and Application,* Edmund J. Amidon and John B. Hough, eds. Reading, Mass.: Addison-Wesley Publishing Company, Inc., 1967, pp. 121–40.

Amidon, Edmund J., and M. Giammatteo. "The Verbal Behavior of Superior Elementary Teachers." In *Interaction Analysis: Theory, Research, and Application,* Edmund J. Amidon and John B. Hough, eds. Reading, Mass.: Addison-Wesley Publishing Company, Inc., 1967, pp. 186–88.

Bellack, A. A., H. M. Kliebard, R. R. Hyman, and F. L. Smith. *The Language of the Classroom.* New York: Teachers College Press, Columbia University Press, 1966.

Bruner, J. S. "Learning and Thinking." *Harvard Educational Review,* Vol. 29 (1959): 184–92.

Chaudhari, U. S. "Questioning and Creative Thinking: A Research Perspective." *Journal of Creative Behavior,* Vol. 9 (1975): 30–34.

Dunkin, M. J., and B. J. Biddle. *The Study of Teaching.* New York: Holt, Rinehart and Winston, Inc., 1974.

Flanders, Ned A. *Analyzing Teacher Behavior.* Reading, Mass.: Addison-Wesley Publishing Company, Inc., 1970.

Gage, N. L., and David C. Berliner. *Educational Psychology,* 2nd ed. Boston: Houghton Mifflin Company, 1979.

Goodlad, J. I., and M. F. Klein. *Behind the Classroom Door.* Worthington, Oh.: Charles A. Jones, 1970.

Hunkins, F. P. "Analysis and Evaluation Questions: Their Effects upon Critical Thinking." Paper presented at the 1969 AERA Convention, Los Angeles, 1969.

Hunt, J. McV. "Motivation Inherent in Information Processing and Action." (Mimeo.) Urbana, Ill.: University of Illinois, 1961.

Moyer, John. "An Exploratory Study of Questioning in the Instructional Process of Selected Elementary Schools." Unpublished doctoral dissertation, Columbia University, New York, 1965.

Pinney, R. H. "Presentational Behaviors Related to Success in Teaching." Unpublished doctoral dissertation, Stanford University, California, 1969.

Rowe, Mary Budd. "Wait-time and Reward as Instructional Variables: Their Influence on Language, Logic, and Fate Control; Part One — Wait-time." *Journal of Research in Science Teaching,* Vol. 11 (1976): 81–94.

# For Further Reading

Andrews, John. "'Playground Questions,' 'Focal Questions,' and 'Brainstorm Questions': Tools for Improving Discussion Participation." *Teaching Development Newsletter.* University of Calif. at San Diego, 1980.

Andrews, John. "The Verbal Structure of Teacher Questions: Its Impact on Class Discussion." *POD Quarterly,* Vol. 2 (Fall/Winter 1980), 129–63.

Crump, Claudia. *Self-Instruction in the Art of Questioning.* Unpublished booklet, Indiana University, Bloomington, Ind., 1969.

Good, Thomas L., and Jere E. Brophy. *Educational Psychology: A Realistic Approach,* 2nd ed. New York: Holt, Rinehart and Winston, Inc., 1980.

McKeachie, Wilbert J. *Teaching Tips: A Guidebook for the Beginning College Teacher,* 7th ed. Lexington, Mass.: D. C. Heath & Company, 1978.

Payne, Stanley L. *The Art of Asking Questions.* Princeton, N.J.: Princeton University Press, 1951.

Sanders, Norris M. *Classroom Questions: What Kinds?* New York: Harper & Row, Publishers, 1966.

# Communicating: Lecture and Discussion Methods

*chapter* **7**

---

In this chapter we discuss two predominant methods of classroom communication—the lecture and the discussion—that are used in many different ways. Lectures can be short (two to five minutes) or long; monologues or interactions; expositions of one view or of many; and impromptu or prepared in advance. Discussions can be formal, with a set agenda, or informal, with no agenda at all; short in duration or as long as an entire course; teacher involved in all aspects of the discussion or not teacher involved at all (except in the planning stages); and spontaneous or planned. The lecture and discussion methods can be intermixed with one another or they can be separate aspects of a given lesson. Each requires communication competencies on the part of the teacher to ensure successful and efficient learning.

It is important to understand that not all teaching or communication methods are equally effective or appropriate for obtaining all instructional objectives. "Which teaching or communication approach is best?" This question has no answer unless it is related directly to the specific objectives the teacher wishes to achieve, the teacher's communication competencies, and the specific characteristics of the students being taught. Some methods clearly produce better results for some students and teachers than others. McKeachie and Kulik (1975) reviewed numerous studies related to a variety of teaching methods according to the type of educational objective each accomplishes best. Their findings suggest that the lecture is better for learning facts, while the discussion method is better for comprehension, application, analysis, synthesis, and evaluation of information. While the results are not conclusive and are based upon many variables, the lecture appears to be superior when the objective is to have students learn factual information; discussion appears to be superior when the objective is for students to do higher-level thinking and to improve attitudes and motivation toward learning.

Our purpose here is not to demonstrate or prove which method is superior, but to explain each as a means for communicating in the classroom. Even though they can be mixed, we begin with the lecture method and then follow with the discussion method.

## THE LECTURE METHOD[1]

The lecture, which is a popular means of communicating within the classroom, can easily be compared to a speech. Whenever a teacher explains, points out relationships, gives examples, or provides criticism, it generally takes the form of a lecture. As we mentioned earlier, certain instructional objectives, teacher competencies, student abilities, and administrative conditions justify the lecture method over other methods. For those teaching elementary or lower levels, however, lectures in the traditional "college sense" are seldom used. Instead, the teacher at the lower level often provides what is referred to as mini-lectures, or explanations that are brief clarifying, motivating, and/or informing statements. The length of the lecture depends on many factors. At the lower levels it depends on the ability and willingness of students to pay attention, for the attention span of youngsters is generally much shorter than those on the college level. Even at the latter level, the hour-long lecture is generally used only with large classes.

As already pointed out, the results of numerous research studies suggest that the lecture method is as effective as other methods of instruction. Gage and Berliner (1979, p. 447) believe this to be true when (1) the basic purpose of the teacher is to disseminate information; (2) the information is not available elsewhere; (3) the information needs to be made adaptable to differing groups; (4) interest in a subject is to be aroused; (5) the information need be recalled for only a short period of time; or (6) the lecture is used to present an introduction to or instructions for other learning activities. They further state that the lecture is *inappropriate* when (1) objectives other than information acquisition are sought; (2) the information is too complex, abstract, or detailed; (3) learner-active participation is required for achievement of the objectives; (4) analysis, synthesis, or integration of material

[1] Much of the information on lecturing preparation, development, and delivery was adapted from William J. Seiler, E. Scott Baudhuin, and L. David Schuelke, *Communication in Business and Professional Organizations*. Reading, Mass.: Addison-Wesley Publishing Company, Inc., 1982.

is required; or (5) the students are average or below average in ability or educational experiences.

Having decided that the lecture method is appropriate and suitable to the learners and the objectives, it is then time to prepare for it — probably the most important stage in the potential success or failure of the lecture. The development of content and its organization are two of the most critical components, and involve gathering and assimilating materials into some organized and coherent form. In successful lectures the teacher must have command of the information to be presented and know what supporting materials are available, that is, examples and audiovisual materials. The lecture attempts to supply learners with information they themselves cannot readily secure because of the lack of time, expertise, familiarity with the subject, or accessibility. The lecture generally focuses on creating understanding, intensity of interest, acceptance, action, and pleasure. Each of these aspects is student and learning oriented, and thus places a great amount of responsibility on the teacher and the lecture itself. It is extremely important that teachers know their students and their students' abilities and readiness to learn the subject of the lecture. The more teachers know about their students and the surroundings for the presentation, the better are their chances for achieving their objectives. After determining the specific objectives of the lecture, the content of the lecture is ready to be developed.

## Development of Content

Content development is often limited by time constraints and the amount of information available. Keeping this in mind, the teacher (1) determines the main points of the lecture, (2) gathers supporting and clarifying material, (3) arranges the main points, (4) prepares an outline, and (5) develops the introduction and conclusion.

## Main Points

The main points form the major subdivisions and are critical to the accomplishment of the overall objective of the lecture. Let's assume that the objective of a lecture is to have the students learn about the Civil War. To determine the main points, several questions and considerations must be taken into account: "What exactly is it that students are to learn about the Civil War?" The answer should be based upon the objectives that have been established by the teacher. Each objective may become a main point of the lecture or may provide guides as to what the main points of the lecture should be. If, for example, the objective of the teacher is to have students learn the five causes of the Civil War, then each cause may become a main point of the lecture. Once the main points are determined, the next step is to determine supporting and clarifying materials.

## Supporting and Clarifying Material

The amount of supporting and clarifying material depends on the teacher's objective, the students' knowledge and attitudes toward the subject, and the environment in which the lecture is to take place. How the main points are clarified is one of the most important, if not the most important, consideration in preparing and developing the lecture. As in other aspects of teaching, the teacher, in forming supporting and clarifying materials, must be creative as well as knowledgeable about what is available for use. A multitude of possibilities exists in selecting supporting and clarifying materials. The best place to begin is with one's self. For ideas, reflect on past experiences, recall what works best with students, and finally examine what resources are available; many schools have media specialists or library facilities. One of the best resources is other teachers. Remember that the idea behind the lecture is not only to present information, but also to create learning in the most enjoyable and effective way possible. This cannot be done without some hard work. The following describes some of the most widely used forms of supporting and clarifying materials.

*Testimony* is a form of support and clarification that can act as proof or add impact to what is being said. Generally, a teacher's credibility is sufficient for students to accept an idea, but at times using testimony adds to what the teacher is saying and thus makes it more acceptable to the students. It is, of course, the responsibility of the teacher to cite sources of information whenever possible. For example, a teacher recently commenting on the U.S.'s space flights said:

> In class we have been discussing the impact space flights have had on all of us. In a recent aerospace magazine, one of the astronauts was quoted as saying: "The earth from space looks like a small beautifully colored ball that could be picked up and thrown like a baseball." This should indicate to each of us how fragile our lives are.

The detail the teacher used in citing the source of information was ample to add credibility and to make the statement more impressive to the students. Thus, testimony does not always have to be a detailed reference.

*Explanation* is a simple, concise, uncolored statement that clarifies; it is extremely useful when presenting complex information. The more unfamiliar the students are with a subject, the more important is the explanation. The teacher must constantly be evaluating what students understand and don't understand. Definition is an excellent example of an explanation. If students do not understand the terminology being used, they probably will become confused and either learn the wrong thing or not learn at all. Introducing the meaning of a word is particularly important when a term is abstract or complex, that is, has more than one meaning.

Although explanations and definitions are means for making something clearer, they usually are not adequate by themselves but need to be supplemented by comparisons or illustrations. The use of additional supporting and clarifying materials depends on verbal and nonverbal feedback and on intuition based upon the teacher's experience with past students or on how important it is that the students completely understand what is being said.

*Analogy* is the comparison of two things that are similar in certain essential characteristics. Two kinds — figurative and literal — are used to explain or prove the unknown by comparing it to the known. Figurative analogies draw comparisons between things in different classes or orders; for example, a thermostat, a device well known and understood by most, could be used to explain communication feedback. The thermostat reacts to the temperature in the room and sends messages back to the furnace which, in turn, either sends more heat or shuts off. Communication feedback can be compared to the thermostat (more on feedback in Chapter 11). A literal analogy compares members of the same class — that is, one person with another, one concept with another, one object with another, or one system with another.

There are numerous uses for analogies in classroom communication in general and in lecturing specifically. Figurative analogies are used to make ideas clear or vivid, and literal analogies are used to supply evidence to prove points. Both methods are not only effective and creative for proving and clarifying, but are also efficient because they save many words and explanations in making information more understandable and acceptable.

*Illustrations* are detailed narrative examples or instances that usually exemplify concepts, conditions, or circumstances, or relate or demonstrate findings. Illustrations are often expanded examples that are presented in narrative form; they are usually striking and memorable. An illustration can be factual or hypothetical, as long as it is clear to the students which it is. The factual illustration tells what has actually happened while the hypothetical illustration tells what could or probably would happen. For example, to explain ESP (extrasensory perception) a teacher provided the following illustration:

> ESP is communication that is associated with communication outside normal sensory activity. It is a kind of telepathy or an ability to predict into the future. Have you ever sensed that someone you knew was going to have an accident, and then later in the day found that it was true? This is a form of ESP. You have predicted events in the future, and if you are able to do this consistently, you are considered to have ESP.

Illustrations are one of the forms of supporting and clarifying materials most frequently used by the classroom teacher.

*Statistics* are figures that show relationships among phenomena or that summarize and interpret many instances. Statistics enable the teacher to summarize a large amount of data rapidly, aid in analyzing specific occurrences or instances, and help to isolate trends or to predict future events. For example, according to a national survey, public speaking is the number-one fear of most adults in the United States; in addition, about one out of every five persons in the United States suffers from communication anxiety. In this light, one out of five of you probably suffers from some form of communication anxiety.

Statistics are often difficult for students to comprehend; therefore, identifying relationships or comparisons, as represented in the example above, should be used when appropriate. Statistics should be translated into understandable terms, and large numbers should be rounded when possible. Sometimes the best method of presenting statistical information is to project it visually by displays such as graphs, charts, and tables.

*Restatement* is simply the use of different words to say the same thing. It is not mere repetition, which expresses the same idea using the same words, but includes the use of summaries, synonyms, rephrasing, and repetition, and perhaps visual or other sensory reinforcement. Restatement is a form of idea support that may appear to be inconsequential; yet if well planned, it can add additional clarity and meaning to what is being said. The following is an example of the use of restatement:

> Energy in the United States is one of the most important aspects of our life. To put it another way, every American citizen uses about five times as much energy as any other citizen in the world. To understand how important energy is to us, try turning off all your electricity for one day. You will quickly see how it affects our lives.

Thus, restatement is a valuable and useful method of getting an idea or situation across from several perspectives.

While testimony, explanation, analogy, illustration, statistics, and restatement are the most common forms of verbal supporting and clarifying material, *audiovisual aids* are a special form because they combine both verbal and visual modes of presentation. Considerable emphasis has been placed on the use of audiovisual materials as a means of improving instruction and learning in the classroom. With the increased interest in innovations (computers, games, and so on) and in using audiovisual materials (films, overhead projections, film strips, photographs, slides, and so on), a substantial amount of information has accumulated concerning the influence of media materials on the learning process. Most sources agree that audiovisuals contribute to a different kind of experience and can add an additional channel for presenting information to the conventional lecture.

The problem that often confronts the teacher involves designing and utilizing audiovisual materials to insure the best learning. Contributors to scholarly journals and textbooks offer many prescriptive suggestions, and a growing body of literature based on research deals with the influences of audiovisuals on the instructional process.

In his monograph to highlight the problem of designing audiovisual materials, Travers (1964, pp. 1.03 – 1.04) uses the analogy of an engineer designing a bridge. He explains:

> The engineer confronts the same problem in designing a bridge as the person who constructs audio-visual materials. The engineer, working on structural problems, relies on principles of classical mechanics which physicists have produced. Although the engineer may fully realize that the principles of physics may only apply to a limited degree to his problem and that simplifying assumptions may have to be done, there are no substitutes for the principles, and he knows that he must work with them even if his bridge design violates many of the assumptions on which they are based.
>
> Just as the engineer almost certainly designs better bridges by basing his design on well-established scientific principles despite their limited applicability to his problem, so too does it seem reasonable to assume that audio-visual teaching materials will be improved when they too are designed on the basis of sound psychological principles.

Seiler (1972), after an extensive review of the literature, developed the following guidelines for teachers who are interested in improving their use of audiovisual materials in the instructional setting:

1. Audiovisual materials should be concrete and related to the students' intelligence, existing needs, and past experiences.
2. The intended purpose should be kept in mind at all times while designing and utilizing audiovisual materials.
3. The more concrete the pictured object and the more attributes the material possesses, the more it can increase the predictability of the response from students.
4. Flexibility is important in the design of audiovisual materials.
5. Consideration should be given to the students' attitudes and assumptions toward the subject matter.
6. An understanding of cultural and social beliefs that make up the students' personalities should be considered.

Consideration of the principles and assumptions for determining and employing the most effective audiovisual materials aids instruction. Audiovisual materials can serve a multitude of functions, some of which are:

- saving time
- gaining attention and holding interest
- clarifying and supporting main points
- reinforcing or emphasizing main ideas
- improving retention

If chosen for the right reasons and used in conjunction with the teacher's objective for the lesson, audiovisual materials can be valuable aids to the teacher. Audiovisual materials should not, however, become the lecture. If a film can present the information more effectively and efficiently than a lecture, it should replace the lecture, but should be introduced by a minilecture and then followed by a lecture or discussion. Records, videotapes, films, and multimedia presentations are all special forms of audiovisual materials that become the lecture or supplement it to the extent that the teacher is temporarily not the presenter.

*Visual aids,* which differ from audiovisual materials, do not supplant the teacher but are nonverbal visuals. Visual aids can take the form of photographs, drawings, slides, overhead projections, opaque projections, objects, graphs, charts, models, and so on. Whatever type of instructional aid is chosen, it should be used because it makes learning more effective and efficient. Thus, the use of instructional aids should be carefully planned and thought out. Using them with a little ingenuity and imagination can add a new dimension to the lecture. The effective lecturer uses supporting and clarifying materials to avoid abstract, unclear, and unsupported statements, thus increasing the chances that information will be understood, accepted, and learned. We encourage you to learn as much as possible about the resources that are available to you and always to choose the aids that will make your instruction the most efficient and effective.

## Patterns for Arranging the Main Points

Once all the content and instructional aids have been gathered, it is time to consider organizing the lecture. Research provides no clear relationship between the organization of a lecture and student learning. However, most teachers and researchers agree that an organized lecture is more effective than an unorganized lecture. The lecture is a form of communication, and any communication that is organized will be more easily received by the listener. Many different patterns of arrangement can be used to provide a meaningful, clear, useful, and pleasing relationship among ideas; and understanding of the various patterns of arrangement should assist in organizing a lecture. Several of the more widely used patterns of arrangement follow.

The *time sequence or chronological pattern.* This method of arrangement begins at a particular point in time and continues forward in chronological order or backward in reverse order. The key is to use a natural sequence and not to jump haphazardly from date to date. This pattern provides a useful vehicle for tracing the steps of a particular process, set of events, or the development of ideas. The following example demonstrates an arrangement for developing a lecture in chronological order:

1. Determine the overall objective of the lecture.
2. Gather the content and supporting and clarifying materials.
3. Organize the lecture.
4. Deliver the lecture.

Reverse order begins at a point and works chronologically backward from that point. For example, a teacher lecturing on the emphasis of advertisers for the auto industry could order the lecture as follows:

1. 1980's — the advertisers emphasized fuel economy.
2. 1970's — the advertisers emphasized the ride.
3. 1960's — the advertisers emphasized . . .
4. 1950's — the advertisers emphasized . . .
5. And so on.

Another pattern is the *space sequence,* in which main ideas are arranged according to spatial relationship. Presentations that require a description of distance relationships or area utilization are best suited to this pattern. For example, a lecture in this pattern might describe sounds produced in the human vocal system or the relationships among the protons, neutrons, and electrons of an atom.

The *topical pattern* is used when neither space nor time unifies the main ideas but the topics are members of the same family — that is, the parts are related in that they do combine to make the whole; therefore, the topical pattern serves to unify them. For example, a speech may be divided into an introduction, discussion, and conclusion. Each part of the speech becomes a separate topic of the lecture. The topical pattern is a widely used form of lecture arrangement because it is simple to structure even though it may not be as effective as other, more complex patterns. A lecture on the different types of supporting and clarifying materials, for example, might follow this pattern.

1. Testimony
2. Explanation
3. Analogy
4. Illustrations
5. Statistics
6. Restatement
7. Audiovisual aids

The *problem-solution pattern* is used to define and remedy a need, a doubt, an uncertainty, or a difficulty without creating other problems. This pattern, if used correctly, should provide students with an understanding of the problem as well as an understanding of the solution and why it resolves the problem. For example, a speech teacher lecturing on communication anxiety might develop the following approach:

1. *Problem:* Over 20% of all college students suffer from communication anxiety.
   a. Communication anxiety affects relationships

     **b.**   Communication anxiety affects career choice

     **c.**   Communication anxiety affects learning

**2.**  *Solution:* A special program needs to be devised to help the students who suffer from communication anxiety.

     **a.**   Systematic desensitization

     **b.**   Behavior modification

     **c.**   Cognitive restructuring

The problem-solution pattern usually comprises two to five of the following steps.

**1.**  *A Description and Definition of the Problem.*  These include a description of the symptoms, the size of the problem, and the goals to be met in solving it.

**2.**  *A Critical Analysis of the Problem.*  This includes a discussion of the causes of the problem, the effects of the problem, what is being done to solve it, and the requirements for a solution.

**3.**  *Suggestions of Possible Solutions to the Problem.*  These include a number of alternative solutions, along with a description of each plan and its strengths and weaknesses.

**4.**  *The Selection of the Best Solution.*  In this step the description of the best solution is presented, as is the reason for selecting it over the other proposals.

**5.**  *Putting the Selected Solution into Operation.*  This step is the final stage and calls for the description to implement the plan. What has to be done to get the solution into operation?

The *cause-effect pattern,* which is similar to the problem-solution pattern in illustrating logical relationships, uses two approaches: (1) pointing out certain forces or factors and then showing the results that follow from them, or, conversely, (2) describing conditions or events and then pointing out the forces or events that caused them. For example, a lecturer might begin by recounting recent developments in computer uses in education that have provided more effective and efficient learning and then show that, as a result, students' motivation to learn has increased dramatically; or a lecturer might reverse the process and first point out that students' motivation has increased dramatically due to the recent developments of the computer. The cause-effect method of arrangement has two main points — a description of the factors that are the *cause* and a prediction or identification of the subsequent *effect.* When using the cause-effect pattern, the lecturer must be sure that the causal relationship and its effects are both evident and logical.

Whatever pattern of arrangement is selected, only that pattern should be used for the main ideas. For example, if the subject is education in the United States and four main ideas are used, then all four should be related according to a single principle controlling that relationship.

At the secondary level, or when another unit or whole is divided into parts, other patterns of arrangement may be used. The following outline illustrates how space, topical, and time patterns can be combined.

**EDUCATION IN THE U.S.**

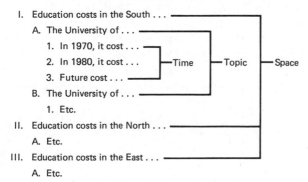

   I.  Education costs in the South . . .
      A.  The University of . . .
         1.  In 1970, it cost . . .
         2.  In 1980, it cost . . .     Time    Topic    Space
         3.  Future cost . . .
      B.  The University of . . .
         1.  Etc.
  II.  Education costs in the North . . .
      A.  Etc.
 III.  Education costs in the East . . .
      A.  Etc.

Another important consideration concerns the phrasing of the main ideas, which are the major statements of the lecture; therefore, they should be carefully worded to give emphasis and clarity to the specific learning objective. While the supporting and clarifying materials provide proof and understanding, which is the bulk of the lecture, the main ideas convey the major thrust of the message. They also provide a foundation or framework upon which details are tied. The general principle is to phrase the main ideas carefully so that they can be easily understood and easily remembered. For example, "Communication is the key to successful learning" is better than "Communication, with one or two exceptions, is the most effective and important ingredient in learning, particularly with young children."

Main ideas should be stated so that they attract attention and provoke thought; they should become punchlines of your lecture. If they lack colorful words and phrases, they will not stand out from the details and supporting materials surrounding them. The main ideas should be stated as briefly and concisely as possible without taking away from their meaning. The main ideas should be structured so that they are as uniform and similarly phrased as possible. The following main ideas are not attention getting. Neither are they uniformly and similarly phrased.[2]

1.  The amount of your income tax depends on the amount you earn.
2.  Property tax is assessed on the value of what you own.
3.  You pay sales tax in proportion to the amount you buy.

A better way to phrase these is:

1.  The amount you earn determines your income tax.
2.  The amount of real estate you own determines your property tax.
3.  The amount of goods you buy determines your sales tax.

[2] Examples adapted from Alan H. Monroe and Douglas Ehninger, *Principles and Types of Speech Communication*, 7th ed. Glenview, Ill.: Scott, Foresman and Company, 1974, p. 384.

Still another important consideration when developing a lecture is the use of transitions. Transitions provide the connections that move the lecture from one point to another, from one subpoint or supporting point to another, from the introduction to the discussion, and from the discussion to the conclusion. Transitions should not just happen; they should be planned. A transitional statement may be simply "Now let me move on to my second point," or "In addition to what I have just said, there is another point that needs to be discussed." Transitional statements need not be elaborate — they merely need to connect ideas.

A final important consideration related to developing a lecture is the use of internal summaries. These are short recapitulations or restatements, following each main idea, of what has been said. An example might be something like this: "Let me briefly summarize what I've said up to this point." The internal summary is extremely useful when the lecture is lengthy or complex.

## Outlining

Organizing and outlining are two of the most difficult (and therefore often avoided) steps in preparing a lecture. The three major parts of a lecture — introduction, discussion, and conclusion — are equally important to the success of the lecture; however, once the objective is determined, the lecturer is wise to develop the discussion first, then the introduction, and finally the conclusion. The reason for this order of development is based on the following: What is said in the discussion will determine what should be said in the introduction and conclusion.

Organization and outlining are somewhat similar terms. Organization is a strategy that one chooses from a number of possible options. The organization of a lecture can be considered analogous to a football game plan. Like a game plan, organization should be determined first by the instructional objective of the lecture. In football, the objective is obvious — to win the game. In a lecture, the objective should be to learn with the most effectiveness and efficiency. Secondly, what are the students like who are going to receive the lecture? The answer to this question is important in planning the strategies for accomplishing the instructional objective. In football, coaches and players study game films and statistics of their opponents in order to plan their game strategies. The understanding of who your students are helps in determining the best possible plan for reaching the instructional objective.

While organization is the method or order in which ideas are placed, outlining is the act of placing ideas in order. Two types of outline formats — full content and topical — are generally used. The full-content outline is detailed, with all the main ideas and secondary points written in complete sentences. The topical outline, on the other hand, uses phrases and, therefore, contains less detail.

The outline should help you view the message as a whole unit of thinking, make relationships clear, and provide proper balance and emphasis in arranging materials to meet the specific purpose. Outlining also helps to ensure accuracy and, especially, relevancy of materials.

The following rules help in preparing a full content or sentence outline.

1.    There should be three parts: Introduction, Discussion, and Conclusion.

2. Under each of the three parts of the outline start with a Roman numeral (I, II, III, and so on).
3. Be consistent in the use of symbols. The following system is most widely used.

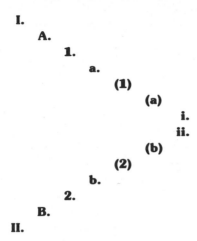

Not every heading needs to be divided as often as in the illustration; however, the symbols used should appear in this order [I., A., 1., a., (1), (a), i.], and be properly indented as illustrated in Figure 7-1.
4. Use only one single idea per symbol.
5. Each major heading (I, A, 1) should be in the form of a single sentence (questions may be used).
6. All Roman numeral (I, II, III) main ideas in the discussion part must have subpoints.
7. Usually a discussion should contain two, three, or four main ideas. In addition, no *I.* can exist without a *II*, no *A.* can exist without at least a *B.*, no *1.* without a *2.*, no *a.* without a *b.*, and so on. Of course, subpoints can go through much more of the alphabet and the number sequence.
8. Be consistent in using complete sentences or questions. A complete-sentence outline usually is better since it phrases ideas more clearly and specifically.
9. Be sure that the outline proceeds logically from one symbol to another.

Preparing the outline provides an overview of the entire lecture and makes it easy to see points in need of additional development. In addition, a well-developed outline will indicate the degree of support for each of the major points. A sample outline form is presented in Figure 7-1.

The outline at this stage should be as detailed as possible. It should be noted, however, that the outline used to develop content differs from the outline used to present content. The presentation outline, as a general rule, should contain only a few key words and phrases as reminders of the ideas to be made. If the outline used during delivery is too complex and detailed, the lecturer can easily become too involved in the notes and lose contact with the students.

Not every lecture will require a detailed, written outline. Short lectures can often be constructed and delivered from a few simple notes. But some kind of blueprint is almost always needed in constructing an effective lecture.

FIGURE 7-1 Sample of Proper Outline Form

**Introduction**
  **I.** Attention material
  **II.** Orienting material (keep in mind the instructional objective for the lecture)
    **A.** Purpose
    **B.** Presummary
    **C.** Adaptation to the students
       (Transition)

**Discussion**
  **I.** (First main idea) —————————————————————
    **A.** (Subpoint) ————————————————————
      **1.** ————————————————————
         **a.** ————————————————————
           **(1)** ————————————————————
             **(a)** ————————————————————
               **i.** ————————————————————
               **ii.** ————————————————————
             **(b)** ————————————————————
           **(2)** ————————————————————
         **b.** ————————————————————
      **2.** ————————————————————
    **B.** (Subpoint) ————————————————————
       (Transition)
  **II.** (Second main idea) ————————————————————
    And so on
  **III.** (Third main idea) ————————————————————
    And so on

**Conclusion**
  **I.** Summary
  **II.** Restatement of specific instructional objective
  **III.** Concluding statement

## Developing the Introduction and Conclusion

As stated earlier, the introduction and conclusion are developed after the body. The introduction of a lecture essentially serves the following purposes: (1) to establish teacher-student rapport, (2) to gain student attention and interest, (3) to provide students with the purpose and the objective of the lecture, and (4) to provide the appropriate background information. The overall objective is to motivate students to learn. The introduction, therefore, prepares the student for the main part (discussion) of the lecture. Of the four aims of the introduction, stating the purpose and providing background information are generally considered the most important. Without the students' attention and interest, however, no lecture can be successful.

Gaining the attention and interest of the students can usually be accomplished by pointing out the importance of knowing the information and by making it relevant to them. Of course, their attention and interest must be maintained throughout the entire lecture. Two factors help to make information more relevant to students: proximity and reality. Information with which students can identify is more apt to hold their interest. Thus, whenever possible, refer to situations and events that are recent, concrete and actual in nature, and school or community related.

The conclusion can simply be a summary of the objectives of the lecture. Here you can question students or specify what they should have learned from the presentation. Gage and Berliner (1979, p. 473) suggest that effective teachers are more apt to:

- apply ideas in the lesson to new sets of particulars
- repeat and emphasize points within the review
- announce that a test will follow
- ask students to recall specific information
- inquire as to whether students have questions about specific parts of the lesson

The conclusion should reinforce what the students are to remember, and therefore is as important as any other part of the lecture and should be treated accordingly. Finally, avoid adding new information in the conclusion. Thus, the conclusion of a lecture should reinforce the learning objective, review the main ideas, and then end with a final thought.

## Delivery of the Lecture

Now that a major portion of the planning and development of the lecture is completed, it is time to consider its delivery. Delivery includes the use of body, voice, and notes.

The effectiveness of the lecture depends on both what is said and how it is said. Basically, without solid content and valid information, there will be nothing worth communicating; without effective delivery, information cannot be clearly and vividly presented. Being effective does not mean being mechanical or basing the delivery solely on a set of predetermined rules. Effective delivery comes from practice under the direction of a competent instructor. It also stems from an awareness of self.

It is important to make the students each feel as if they are being addressed personally. This can be accomplished by talking to one person for a few seconds, then another, and so on. While talking to each individual, avoid staring. Try to think of the lecture as a conversation.

## Body

Personal appearance, bodily movement, gesture, facial expressions, and eye contact are important, significant factors in the delivery of a lecture.

*Personal appearance* (the way a person dresses and appears to others) is an important consideration even though there is no evidence to suggest clothing of a teacher affects learning. The general guide is common sense. Often first impressions are made by appearance. School systems used to have dress codes not only for the faculty but for students as well. While most school systems have dropped their dress codes, it is still wise to be aware of your appearance and what effects it has on how others perceive you. Appearance tells students and others something about your attitude toward self and them. Not much is known about the exact role of personal appearance and its effects on communication, except that appearance does influence interpersonal responses and, in some situations, is the primary determiner of others' responses. Personal appearance, which includes attractiveness, general body build, hair, and clothes, may have a profound impact on self-image and therefore affect communication with others. As trite as it may seem, looking your best does help to convey the message.

*Bodily movement* is closely related to personal appearance. Since the eye instinctively follows moving objects, movements should be easy and purposeful. The use of movement can aid in holding attention and help to convey ideas more clearly. Posture, with its direct relationship to bodily movement, should be relaxed and natural. Try to avoid being a sloucher. Bodily movements and posture can indicate confidence and convey a positive self-image.

*Gestures,* which are used to clarify or to emphasize points, are generally defined as purposeful movements of some part of the body — head, shoulders, arms, or hands. Gestures should not be forced. The key is to be spontaneous.

*Facial expressions,* according to Mehrabian (1971, p. 43), account for much of the emotional impact of a lecture. His research suggests that 55% of the affective component of what one says is related to facial expressions, and that facial expressions not only are important and powerful carriers of feelings but also portray emotions with considerable accuracy.

*Eye contact* is associated with facial expression. While facial expressions indicate feelings about a message, eye contact seems more related to feelings about the students. According to many communication experts, eye contact is the most important of all the aspects of bodily activity. Eye contact seems to indicate interest and concern for others and implies self-confidence.

## Voice

The use of voice is an important aspect of delivery that many beginning and even some experienced teachers overlook. The three essential properties of a good voice are: (1) it should be pleasant to listen to, (2) it should relate the presenter's thoughts easily and clearly, and (3) it should express feelings and emotions. These three properties are often referred to as quality, intelligibility, and variety.

*Vocal quality* is the overall impression the voice makes on the students and distinguishes voices as harsh, nasal, thin, mellow, resonant, or full-bodied. Attitude can affect the quality of the voice. The quality can tell the students whether the teacher is sincere or not.

*Intelligibility* of the voice is determined by volume, clarity of articulation and pronunciation, and the stress given syllables, words, and phrases. To determine the proper volume, awareness of the size of the room and student reactions (are there signs that students can't hear you?) are required. It is important to be aware of how you sound and to consider those who are listening to you.

*Vocal variety* gives feeling to the lecture and adds emphasis to what is being said. Generally, vocal variety is considered to include rate, force, and pitch.

Be aware of your speaking speed, for a rate that is too fast or too slow, or that never changes, can be extremely frustrating to the students. Thus, use of pauses as a rate change is an effective means of gaining attention and of adding emphasis to an important point. Essentially, pauses punctuate thoughts.

Vocal force has already been suggested in terms of the necessary volume for the students to hear you. In addition to making speech loud enough, force can aid in communicating ideas and thoughts with confidence and vigor. Force should be used in moderation to add emphasis to an important point. Changing the degree of force is an effective means of regaining lagging interest. By learning to use force effectively, a teacher can add a great potential to lecturing effectiveness.

Pitch refers to the position of the voice on a scale—high or low. Variety in pitch is accomplished either by steps or glides—a step being a change between successive sounds and a glide being a change within a sound. Variety in pitch can serve a number of functions: to provide variety in vocal expression in order to eliminate monotony, a condition that must be avoided in a lecture; or to add emphasis to key words. Many polished lecturers use a raised pitch to add emphasis to key ideas.

Obviously, any change in rate, force, or pitch serves to make the word, phrase, or sentence in which the change occurs stand out. The greater the amount of change or the more sudden the change is, the more emphatic the word or statement will be. Vocal variety is used to the greatest effect when contrasts in the voice make ideas seem more important than they would seem otherwise.

Another major consideration in lecturing is the use of notes.

## Notes

The use of notes varies from a few key words to an entire manuscript, but whatever their number, notes should not become a distraction. Earlier in this chapter we recommended the use of a topical outline for notes. The outline provides the main ideas but prevents the speaker from reading the entire lecture. When you need to be very exact in the content of the lecture, using a manuscript should be considered. The manuscript is the entire lecture written out word for word; it ensures that you are never at a loss for words. The disadvantage is that it often prevents the lecture from being flexible in adapting to the reactions of the students.

When using a manuscript, the following tips should be considered:

1. Write the manuscript for the ear. There is a difference between writing for silent reading and writing for reading aloud. The silent reader can check back to a former line for a refresher reference. The sentence or thought can be reread several times if it isn't clear the first time. Students listening to a lecture cannot do this, unless you notice that they do not understand and repeat what you have said. Sometimes, when information is important or complex, it may be necessary to repeat. This will provide students with another opportunity to understand.
2. Prepare the manuscript format for easy reading. A good idea is to type your lecture in triple space. The extra distance between lines allows for more eye freedom, and for space to mark areas or ideas that need to be emphasized.
3. Reading is often more difficult than speaking extemporaneously. The mere presence of a manuscript forces the presenter to read. It also can give a false sense of security to the information that is to be presented. The inexperienced reader often reads words instead

of thoughts. Successful reading means learning to think of what is being said. Of course, the principles of good oral delivery should be followed.

4.  Practice reading out loud and, if possible, use a tape recorder. When presenting a lecture, try to create the illusion of reading it for the first time. An effective lecture is presented with enthusiasm, vigor, and interest.

The lecture method places students in a listening role and thus makes the delivery of the lecture an extremely important consideration. We have all sat through lectures that have put us to sleep. Probably the question most important to a successful lecture is "Has the teacher really tried to lecture well?" It takes time and energy to prepare an effective lecture, and it requires that attention be given to certain skills.

Nichols (1948) found that the average student's listening ability as measured by retention is about 25%. Students' minds will wander sometimes during the lecture. A certain degree of wandering may be a sign of a good lecture, provided the wandering stimulates thinking about what has been said. No matter what kind of wandering is involved, it sometimes interferes with the lecture. Thus, you must be prepared to accept some wandering and also to provide enough attention-getting cues to keep students from straying too far off the subject. It has been suggested and generally accepted that active learning is more effective than passive learning. So getting students involved in the lecture is a good idea. To do this, Gage and Berliner (1979, p. 471) suggest inserting questions into the lecture. They further suggest that asking questions can add emphasis, can provide an opportunity for students to demonstrate that they understand what is being said, can provide a diversion because it breaks the flow of the lecture and may generate more attention and interest, and can provide a review of the materials covered in the lecture.

The enthusiasm in communication comes from our nonverbal and verbal behavior. Enthusiasm can be contagious. Although not easily faked, enthusiasm can be heightened to a degree of lively interest. Vocal variety, audibility, and nonverbal behavior (movement, voice, eyes, facial expression, and so on) are overt cues to your enthusiasm. Enthusiasm of a teacher and students relates highly to learning.

## Cautions about the Lecture Method

Gage and Berliner (1979, pp. 474 – 75) suggest two cautions to the lecture method. First, because of its seeming ease of preparation, it can be overused or used in place of other methods better suited to the objectives of the lesson. Second, the lecture method requires special public-speaking skills. Unless the teacher is willing to engage in a purposeful and continuing self-improvement program in lecturing, the lecture may not be effective. Voice, style, manner, pace, fluency, ease, and orderliness — all these and other public-speaking skills are needed for effective lecturing.

## THE DISCUSSION METHOD

The discussion method refers to an instructional procedure in which students, either in small groups or as an entire class, engage in discussion with or without the direct leadership of the teacher. Generally, most classroom discussions take place under the direct leadership of the teacher.

The discussion method is a more difficult instructional method to employ in the classroom because it requires that the teacher be a skillful leader as well as an effective communicator. As mentioned earlier in the chapter, the discussion method focuses on the higher levels of learning. It is characterized by student-to-student interaction and educational objectives related to complex thinking processes and attitude changes. It is useful for fostering critical thinking in the evaluation of ideas. McKeachie and Kulik (1975), in their review cited earlier in the chapter, suggest that the discussion method is more effective than most lectures in promoting understanding and in developing problem-solving skills.

McKeachie (1978, pp. 35–36) suggests that the discussion method is probably not effective for presenting new information to students who are already motivated to learn. However, he suggests using the discussion method when the teacher's objectives are to:

- use the resources of members of the group
- give students opportunities to formulate applications of principles
- get prompt feedback on how well objectives are being attained
- help students learn to think in terms of the subject matter by giving them practice in thinking
- help students learn to evaluate the logic of, and evidence for, their own and others' positions
- help students become aware of and formulate problems, using information to be gained from reading or lectures
- gain acceptance for information or theories counter to folklore or previous beliefs of students
- develop motivation for further learning

Stanford and Stanford (1969) indicate that the discussion method can help students solve problems, express opinions, find out what others think, express feelings, clarify points of view, examine their own opinions, and gain feelings of acceptance and belonging. The discussion method has been developed in a variety of forms. In this section, we limit the scope of the discussion method to cognitive outcomes; for example, problem solving and brainstorming.

## Characteristics of the Discussion Method

Discussion, according to Potter and Andersen (1965, p. 1), is "the purposeful, systematic, oral exchange of ideas, facts, and opinions by a group of persons who share in the group's leadership." Within this definition there are six characteristics that Potter and Andersen believe to be essential to the understanding of discussion.

1. *Discussion is purposeful.* The goals of the discussion must be understood by the teacher at the outset, for it is the teacher's role to insure that the discussion reaches these goals. In addition, the teacher must be aware that a discussion is not just a rambling but a sharing of thoughts and ideas toward a goal.
2. *Good discussion usually follows a systematic, logical plan.* It is best to insure that the discussion (unless otherwise planned) follows some kind of logical sequence. This will be further discussed later in this section.
3. *Discussion is an oral process.* Students and teachers who participate in discussions need to be proficient in both verbal and nonverbal communication skills.

4.  *Discussion calls for an open and free response of all ideas, facts, and opinions related to the topic under consideration.*   It is important, of course, to allow everyone a voice in the discussion and to set limitations so that the goal can be accomplished within a set time period.
5.  *Discussion is a group process.*   The students who are participating, whether in small, face-to-face groups or in large, more formal groups, must be interdependent with each other. Each student must perceive himself or herself to be a part of the group.
6.  *Discussion involves some form of leadership.*   The role of leader can be shared or distributed among the group members. However, in most classroom instruction the teacher decides whether to be the leader or to allow the students to participate with or without their own leader. The teacher's personality and temperament will determine how much freedom students will be given and whether the discussion method is even suitable for the objectives. Some teachers are more successful than others in using the discussion method, inasmuch as this method requires the teacher to be flexible and to relinquish some authority over the discussion so as to foster interaction.

## Preparing for the Discussion

The discussion method, like other methods of instruction, should be used in conjunction with the desired learning objectives for the lesson. Students' needs and level of knowledge should be considered in determining the learning objectives. Once the students' abilities have been analyzed and the instructional objective or objectives determined, the topic for the discussion should be developed. Essentially, the content topic serves as the vehicle for accomplishing the learning objective. The topic should be stated as a question of fact, value, or policy. The discussion method actually involves the utilization of questions not only by the teacher but by the students as well. The teacher's questions, however, need to be sequenced in order to help guide the discussion. In Chapter 6 we presented information on questioning and on responding to students. We suggest that you review this information, for it is critical to the effectiveness of the discussion method.

The topic question can be controversial or noncontroversial. Some sample discussion topics are:

What are the various hemispheres in the world? (Noncontroversial question of fact)

Which of the four paintings we saw at the art gallery is the most creative? (Controversial or noncontroversial question of value)

What should be done about controlling guns in this country? (Controversial question of policy)

Factual questions often do not lead or lend themselves to much interaction because there is a specific answer to the question. The wording of the discussion question is extremely important in aiding the amount of the interaction. Additionally, students should have the necessary information and knowledge about the topic in order to carry on an effective discussion.

Combining the discussion question with the instructions or procedures for carrying on the assignment is helpful to both the teacher and the students; for example:

After viewing a film on the impacts that humans have on our environment, please discuss in groups of five the following: (1) What are the major causes of pollution in our environment, (2) what are the effects of pollution on our society, and (3) what actions can be taken to prevent further pollution of our environment? The discussion will take place in the next two class periods. Each group will then report on its discussion.

While this example divides the class into small groups, it could have related to the class as a whole. The advantage of clearly stating the assignment, as in the example, should be obvious: It helps to prevent the discussion from wandering too far, and it also provides the students as well as the teacher with a clear idea of what is expected. Sometimes it is helpful for the discussion to be divided into a *problem-solution format*. John Dewey developed the following format, which is commonly used:

1. location, formulation, and definition of the problem to be solved
2. analysis of the problem in terms of difficulties
3. reformulation of the problem in light of analysis
4. examination of various methods to resolve the problem
5. evaluation and analysis of various solutions to discover the best one
6. choice of plan of action

At times it may be appropriate to use a *brainstorming format,* which can be applied to the problem-solving format. The technique, developed by Alex Osborn (1953), is used primarily to generate ideas. The brainstorming format can be guided by placing controls on the discussion, or it can be wide open. The teacher must decide upon the instructional objective to be accomplished before determining the procedures to be followed. Osborn (pp. 300–301) developed four guidelines for using the brainstorming technique:

1. Don't criticize any ideas.
2. No idea is too wild.
3. Quantity is important.
4. Seize opportunities to improve or to add to ideas suggested by others.

Another format is the *open discussion,* which employs few guidelines and permits discussion on anything related to the topic. This format requires that the teacher have a great deal of flexibility and confidence. Some teachers become uncomfortable when a discussion is not highly organized, logically developed, and relevant at all times to a specific topic. This format does require an ability to follow the various twists and turns that a discussion can take without losing sight of the purpose of the discussion and the learning objective that is to be accomplished. The teacher needs to be able to synthesize information quickly and to bring it together for the students.

The last consideration in the preparation stage is the *seating arrangement* or the physical setting, which can affect the interaction of the students. Sommer (1967), in comparing several different seating arrangements, found that students who directly faced the teacher participated more than students who were on the sides or in the back of the room. It is interesting to note that when students are in direct visual contact, either with each other or with the teacher, they tend to communicate more often. Takanishi-Knowles (1973), in studying third- and fourth-grade students, found that visual and verbal contact was most effective in small groups of students rather than large groups. McCroskey and McVetta

FIGURE 7-2

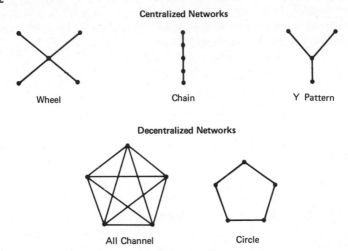

Centralized Networks

Wheel                    Chain                    Y Pattern

Decentralized Networks

All Channel              Circle

(1978) found that students had preferences as to seating arrangement depending on their level of apprehension. Research does suggest that the quantity and quality of interaction among participants in a group discussion is affected by the pattern or network arrangement of the students. The five communication networks are divided into centralized and decentralized (Figure 7-2).

Leavitt (1951) found that the central person in a network (e.g., wheel, chain, or Y pattern) usually becomes the leader and enjoys that position more frequently than those on the periphery, whose communication is somewhat restricted. That is, the central person can communicate to any of the others, but they must direct all of their communication through the center. On the other hand, the circle and the all-channel patterns are much less centralized and are sometimes leaderless. Here the teacher must decide which arrangement will increase the effectiveness of the objective as well as student involvement.

A teacher who wishes to dominate the discussion will sometimes create a network similar to the wheel. While this may be more centralized and speedy, it results in dependency on the teacher and can lower group satisfaction. The chain and the Y network allow members to communicate with one or two other persons but not with all others in the group. This can produce subgroups, decrease satisfaction, and produce little in idea sharing. The all-channel or circle networks may be somewhat slow in producing outcomes, but they are superior in terms of idea sharing and student satisfaction. Feedback is more immediate, and as a result, accuracy of communication is better. In general, the decentralized patterns, with increased eye contact and open access to communication for everyone, help to stimulate discussion and limit teachers, as well as overly assertive students, from completely dominating the discussion.

## Getting the Discussion Underway

Once the objective has been determined, the topic selected, and the seating arrangement established, discussion can proceed. Several concerns at this point should be considered: the role the teacher will play and the role the students will play in the discussion. The teacher can decide to dominate or to be silent. Both approaches have advantages and disadvantages: If teachers dominate the discussion, they remove much of the student involvement and thus limit students' creativity and learning experiences; however, if teachers remain completely silent, they run the risk of the students' becoming disorganized and wandering off the intended objective of the lesson. The outcome of either can be unproductive and dissatisfying to both teachers and students. Thus, if the topic has been carefully delineated to the students, the role of the teacher should be that of overseer and guide; that is, the teacher should enter the discussion when help is needed to control, reinforce, or add expertise in reaching the objective of the lesson. Remember to be patient, however, as the discussion method takes time.

The role of the students should be made explicit so that they know what is expected of them. It may be necessary, for example, to emphasize that only one person should talk at a time, that all students should have an opportunity to participate, that all ideas are open to criticism (both positive and negative), that discussion calls for clarification of ideas, and that cross-questioning of one another is appropriate. The class itself can also establish norms and behaviors for taking part in a discussion.

The role of the leader, whether it be the teacher, a student assigned by the teacher, or a student who emerges from the group itself, can be extremely important to the outcome of the discussion. Leader skills call for an ability to initiate the discussion, obtain participation, appraise progress, ask questions, overcome resistance, control conflict, and summarize the outcomes.

Leaders (teachers or students) generally face two kinds of problems in group discussions — the nonparticipating student and the monopolizing student. The nonparticipant is often a victim of past classroom experiences, in which students were expected to be silent. In this case students must be made aware of the value and need for participation by all. Other students may have personality problems or apprehension about communicating. In this case rewards should be provided for participation. Involvement can be initiated by asking questions, but the question must be one that the student can answer. Calling the student by name might encourage freer contribution also. As mentioned earlier, the seating arrangement can affect student involvement — either increasing or inhibiting contribution.

Very often monopolizers do not realize that they are dominating. One way to eliminate the problem before it happens is to talk about the need for equal participation. Another way is to confront a monopolizer privately and deal with the problem.

## Cautions about and Limitations to the Discussion Method

A general misconception, especially held by young teachers, is that the discussion method is simple. However, this method takes careful planning and preparation in order to be successful. It contains some limitations, which McKeachie (1978, p. 45) points out:

1.   Students must have adequate information to discuss.
2.   Discussion can easily become disorganized and ambiguous as to purpose.
3.   The instructor may dominate the discussion or answer questions for the students.
4.   The teacher may strive too much for agreement, and may feel that reaching agreement is the most important outcome of the discussion.

5.  Teachers may want students to agree with their solution, and may become overly forceful in bringing it about.

The discussion method can be an excellent way for students to take an active role in their own learning. It must be carefully planned, and the role of the teacher must be clearly identified.

# SUMMARY

The teacher has many instructional methods from which to choose. This chapter focuses on two of the most common — the lecture and the discussion. The lecture method, the more frequently used, needs careful planning and preparation in developing and organizing content. The use of audiovisual material with the lecture is a common practice, but care must be exercised in designing and utilizing it so as to insure learning. Delivering the lecture is extremely important and should employ vocal variety, audibility, effective nonverbal behavior, and enthusiasm. The lecture method is subject to overuse and misuse by teachers who are inadequately prepared both in content and their ability to deliver the lecture.

The discussion method, by providing a broad variety of classroom interaction patterns, allows students to interact with each other while the teacher assumes the role of guide, initiator, summarizer, or referee. The discussion method can help students solve problems, express opinions, clarify points of view, and gain acceptance and belonging. Discussion questions should be carefully thought out and worded. The seating arrangements of students can affect the interaction and the success of the discussion. The roles of both the teacher and students should be clearly identified and understood by the teacher as well as the students. The discussion method does have some drawbacks, and these should be considered in choosing it as a method of instruction.

## Discussion Questions

1.  What communication skills are necessary for a teacher to be an effective lecturer? Be specific and explain your responses.
2.  In what ways do the lecture and discussion methods differ with regard to their preparation? Is one easier than another to prepare? If yes, why?
3.  Discuss the advantages and disadvantages of the discussion and lecture methods.
4.  What role should the teacher play in using the discussion method? Discuss all possible ones.

## References

Gage, N. L., and David Berliner. *Educational Psychology*, 2nd ed. Boston: Houghton Mifflin Company, 1979.

Leavitt, Harold. "Some Effects of Certain Communication Patterns on Group Performance." *Journal of Abnormal and Social Psychology*, Vol. 46 (1951): 38–50.

McCroskey, James C., and Rod W. McVetta. "Classroom Seating Arrangements: Instructional Communication Theory Versus Student Preferences." *Communication Education,* Vol. 27 (1978): 99–111.

McKeachie, Wilbert J. *Teaching Tips: A Guidebook for the Beginning College Teacher,* 7th ed. Lexington, Mass.: D. C. Heath & Company, 1978.

McKeachie, W. J., and J. A. Kulik. "Effective College Teaching." In *Review of Research in Education,* Vol. 3, Fred N. Kerlinger, ed. Washington, D.C.: American Educational Research Association, pp. 446–78.

Mehrabian, Albert. *Silent Messages.* Belmont, Cal.: Wadsworth Publishing Co., 1971.

Nichols, Ralph. "Factors Accounting for Differences in Comprehension of Materials Presented Orally in the Classroom." Doctoral dissertation. University of Iowa, Iowa City, 1948.

Osborn, Alex. *Applied Imagination: Principles and Procedures of Creative Thinking.* New York: Charles Scribner's Sons, 1953.

Potter, David, and Martin P. Andersen. *Discussion: A Guide to Effective Practice.* Belmont, Cal.: Wadsworth Publishing Co., 1965.

Seiler, William J. "Audio-Visual Materials in Classroom Instruction: A Theoretical Approach." *The Speech Teacher,* Vol. 21 (1972): 197–204.

Sommer, Robert. "Classroom Ecology." *Journal of Applied Behavioral Science,* Vol. 3 (1967): 489–503.

Stanford, Gene, and Barbara Dodds Stanford. *Learning Discussion Skills Through Games.* New York: Citation Press, Scholastic Book Services, 1969.

Takanishi-Knowles, Ruby. "Relationships among Instructional Group Size, Student Engagement, and Teacher Strategies." Unpublished doctoral dissertation, Stanford University, 1973.

Travers, R. M. W. *Research and Theory Related to Audio-Visual Information Transmission.* Washington, D.C.: U.S. Department of Health, Education, and Welfare, Office of Education, 1964.

# For Further Reading

Beebe, Steven, and John T. Masterson. *Communicating in Small Groups.* Glenview, Ill.: Scott, Foresman and Company, 1982.

Klopf, Donald W., and Ronald E. Cambra. *Speaking Skills for Prospective Teachers.* Englewood, Colo.: Morton Publishing Co., 1983.

Nelson, Paul, and Judy Pearson. *Confidence in Public Speaking.* Dubuque, Ia.: William C. Brown Company, 1981.

Tubbs, Stewart L. *A Systems Approach to Small Group Interaction.* Reading, Mass.: Addison-Wesley Publishing Company, Inc., 1978.

White, Eugene. *Practical Public Speaking.* New York: The Macmillan Company, 1982.

# Communicating: Simulation, Games, and Role Playing

## chapter 8

*focus*   THREE MAJOR STRATEGIES THAT EMPHASIZE STUDENT
INVOLVEMENT

SIMULATION
Vestibule Training
Case Studies
Incident Process
In Basket/Out Basket

ACADEMIC GAMES

ROLE PLAYING

One of the most frequent charges made about teaching and training concerns a lack of relevance for today's society and for the real needs of students. In fact, students are often faced with the question "How are this course, these learning materials, and this teaching important to me?" The question of pertinence relates to more than application, however. Many times students are asked to play only a passive role in learning — to be like sponges, merely on hand to soak up whatever information is sent their way. An answer to student passivity and the relevance question is the development and use of instructional materials and resources that more fully and actively involve the student. This chapter deals with instructional strategies and approaches that are intended to do just that.

Curriculum specialist Hilda Taba (1962, p. 156) wrote that "learners need to get insights intuitively and empirically and then extend these insights by rational processes of abstracting, deducing, comparing, contrasting, inferring, and contemplating." Using her ideas as a framework, we can look at some "laws" of learning theory that were developed by Smith and Smith (1966):

1. Learning is most effective when the learner is motivated, when he has "something at stake" in the activity.
2. Learning seems to proceed more quickly and permanently when the instructional strategies are related to the learner's physical and intellectual ability.

3.  Learning is most effective and permanent when the learner understands the process and the goal toward which he is working.
4.  Learning is easier when it takes place in a social situation within the individual's frame of reference and understanding [p. 45].

This chapter focuses upon three major strategies — simulation, academic games, and role playing — that emphasize high student involvement, the ways each can be used in actual teaching and learning, and the advantages of each method in increasing the participation of learners.

## SIMULATION

Garvey and Seiler (1966) have studied the effectiveness of simulation in the teaching of high school students. Their conclusions are a starting place in our discussion of simulation:

1.  The process of education is better if the structure (a frame of reference) is emphasized in the learning experience.
2.  Structure results in students' acquiring more information and greater retention of that knowledge.
3.  Use of an actual operational setting provides instruction in quite complex situations and applications.
4.  Learning is easier, more enjoyable, and more meaningful if the learner acts as a person engaged in the actual conduct of the subject under instruction.
5.  Increased student motivation occurs in simulation and results in increased openness and receptivity which leads to better learning by students [pp. 5–7].

Maxson (1974) writes that simulation is a model of a real-life situation, with reality simplified. Simulations are experience-based exercises, developed in a setting with one or more problems that must be solved. The problems in the make-believe setting can be economic, political, social, interpersonal, ethical, or behavioral. Each problem consists of communication cues and messages designed to elicit a response from the learner.

In its simplest form, simulation can be exercises involving participants sitting at desks, receiving information, processing it, and passing it on. In its most complex form, simulation may require the construction of special equipment such as a model automobile or flight simulator to train individuals to perform complex visual and response activities.

The two keys to simulation are (1) a total or partial copy of an actual working environment, which uses real or simulated materials that the student will actually be using and in an atmosphere as close as possible to the "real thing," and (2) a capacity to control the environment to provide feedback to students without risk of negative or painful effects. Learning to fly an airplane or manage a company might be more realistic without the use of simulation, but the risks of making mistakes in the real settings are far greater than in the learning simulations. We discuss four types of simulation that can be used in instruction and training situations: (1) vestibule training, (2) case studies, (3) incident process, and (4) in basket, out basket.

## Vestibule Training

Vestibule training provides all the benefits of on-the-job training with few of its drawbacks. In this type of training, the system of work itself is duplicated in some special area other than the actual working site, but usually close to it; for example, in teaching people how to do some kind of processing of materials, a miniature processing procedure away from the main operation could be set up for students to both observe and practice. Here the student would be able to try to do everything in the regular procedure (for example, assembling a newspaper) without being under pressure to do everything right for fear of ruining the final product. Students who may be learning how to put together a radio or television production could practice every step of the procedure while not compromising the actual program.

## Case Studies

This method is a process-oriented, nondirective learning experience. It is developed through a carefully documented description of a real-life (or simulated) situation and presented in written or audiovisual form to students. The student learns through analysis and solution of the problems presented or implicit in the actual case. The objective is to learn through self-discovery and independent thinking. Under this method, the teacher acts as a coordinator and catalyst to guide the learning process. The following is an example of a case study assignment in writing:

> You are the advertising manager of a cosmetics company. You manufacture an exceedingly pure soap selling for $1 a bar.
>
> As a result of recent marketing studies, you realize that you are not reaching the age group most in need of a pure, clear soap of the kind you manufacture. This soap contains no perfume, alkali, or medications. Because of its unique patented formula, it can be used for any type of skin — dry, oily, normal.
>
> So far, magazine advertisements have stressed its use by women in the 25–30 age group. The appeal has been largely on the basis of saving money, trying to show that this soap is cheap at $1 a bar. The newspaper campaign has not been working well, even in that age bracket. You realize that the teens, boys as well as girls, are really your best market because they have more complexion problems and are more conscious of their appearances.
>
> You have bought two mailing lists, one of college students and the other of high school students. You plan a direct-mail campaign to each name using a fill-in name-and-address letter.
>
> The letter might be written on special promotional sales stationery featuring a headline. Stress that this soap is for all college (or high school) complexions with or without problems, although it is frequently recommended by doctors for people with acne.
>
> Supplement the letter with a coupon offering a trial cake for 10 cents. Mention that the soap can be bought in most drugstores and pharmacies.
>
> Your main problem is that many soaps sell at one fourth or one half the price of yours, a real handicap to overcome!

The writing of the letter by choosing ideas, words, and arguments, approaches and appeals to the audience, and testing of the effects of the letter, are all important learning outcomes in communication and advertising (for example).

## Incident Process

The incident process is a dynamic variation of the case study method. Instead of giving all the students all the descriptions necessary to analyze and solve the entire problem, the instructor presents one critical incident at a time, trying to re-create in order of occurrence each thing that happened in the way that it happened. This type of simulation may be in the form of a script, a written text, a tape recording of a conversation between two people, a memorandum or letter, or some document that highlights a problem for solution.

After the incident is presented, students must ask questions of the teacher in order to solve the problem. The learners are given only the information they ask for and they, in turn, must develop the solution to the case and the reasons they chose a particular solution. Here, as in all simulations, the learning activity is dynamic and student originated, with the instructor playing the role of information source and facilitator.

## In Basket/Out Basket

The first step in development of an in-basket simulation exercise involves putting all case-study materials into the actual form in which they occurred. As the name implies, this procedure resembles the gathering of a set of materials containing items that look like actual communication between individuals or groups dealing with a specific problem within a specific context or organization. These in-basket materials may be in the form of letters, reports, memos, charts, budget sheets, canceled checks, and so on. Some may be important documents in solving the problem, and some may be diversionary. It is up to the student to read each and decide which information is useful in the solution of the particular simulation exercise. Student responses throughout the simulation can be observed by the teacher while the student keeps a continuous record of his or her decisions made in processing the in-basket items. Feedback comes to the student afterward, when the teacher analyzes the solution students place in an out basket for implementation.

## ACADEMIC GAMES

Academic games involve students in some type of competition to reach a goal or positive result. In this manner they differ from simulations. They may, however, include simulations, many of which combine the essentials of case studies, critical-incident process, and in-basket, out-basket simulations. Academic games are often sophisticated simulations that include the elements of chance and competition. Generally, an academic game has an underlying logic or set of mathematical relationships, which if discovered by the players can determine advantages or disadvantages of winning or not winning. Games may vary from simple paper-and-pencil exercises involving a single task to those using complex computer programs and involving decisions on the total operation of a company, community, or nation.

Games have many advantages as instructional strategies. These include immediate feedback to students, opportunity for competition with others, and incentives to learn basic skills for succeeding in some goal or expectation that is inherent within the competitive nature of the gaming exercise.

Raudsepp and Hough (1977) state that games can be the stimulus for creativity because they are presented in the forms of puzzles or problems that challenge old ideas and stimulate the imagination of player-learners. Ruben and Budd (1975) present the argument that many of the processes and protocols of human communication can be better understood and learned through the experience of the learner in simulations and games. Their book provides complete directions for 49 games that can be used for classroom learning in the discipline of communication.

Many academic games are available for purchase from such publishers as Academic Games Associates, and Project Simile II. A list of selected published academic games and their general purposes as well as the names of some academic game centers and their addresses, are listed in the Appendix.

The following is a description of a game used in a survey course in Russian history:

*Game:*   Parties and Constituencies in Russian Revolution.

*Instructor:*   Bill Rosenberg, Associate Professor of History.

*Course:*   History 503, Survey of Twentieth-Century Russian History.

*Enrollment:*   About 100 students.

*Game Time:*   1½ hours (up to 2 hours).

*Preparation:*   Four or five students volunteered to work out this game as their course project; two or three took a leadership role. The instructor consulted with them in planning; he suggested readings and consultation with an instructor who had worked on gaming and simulation.

The students prepared a twelve-page document on four parties and four constituencies that took part in the Russian Revolution. This program told each group what its orientation was (for example, peasants wanted land), what its members were striving for, and what their methods tended to be. The program was given to students to read in advance of the day of the simulation.

*Purpose of the Game:*   To look at the electoral processes, in terms of (1) where groups of people stood, and (2) how they related to each other politically.

*Structure of the Game:*   There were, historically, two elections: in the middle of 1917 and at the end of 1917. One of these elections took place in the game situation after parties and constituencies had been playing their parts for an hour. The game then went on for another half hour or more.

Students volunteered for four "party groups" and four "constituency groups." A few were assigned to groups or chose not to participate. Each group consulted the program and met in caucus to decide on its actions. They could do about anything they wished: attempt to form alliances, appeal to another group for support, influence others, and even lie. Delegates were sent from caucuses to different groups and returned for further strategy discussions.

After an hour, an election was held and tallied on the blackboard. The game continued for about half an hour after the election.

*Physical Setting:*   The game took place in the usual large lecture hall, but smaller groups spilled out into the hallway and beyond the room. The usual lecture time of one hour was extended to two hours that day.

*Evaluation:*   The instructor felt that the simulation was remarkably effective as a re-creation of what actually took place in 1917. For example, the Bolsheviks were clear about what they wanted and went directly to the point of gaining power, while the Liberals were meeting in the hall and came in to ask at an advanced stage of the play whether the game had actually begun.

Evaluations of this session were elicited from students, who were uniformly positive. There were some suggestions that the instructions could have been clearer and more time might have been taken to explain in advance.

The educational use of the game might have been strengthened by planning for more student discussion afterwards. About twenty minutes or so were spent in discussion after the game in the lecture room, and there was some discussion in section meetings. However, more planning for postgame discussion might have strengthened this game as a teaching technique.

In addition to the many published sources of academic games listed in the Appendix, teachers can develop simulation exercises of their own. Some guidelines are:

1. Identify the goals (objectives) to be achieved.
2. Construct a simplified model of the game.
3. Identify the roles of individuals and groups who will be game participants.
4. Set the conditions for the players, being certain to set up specific guidelines for procedures, resources, personnel, and so on.
5. Develop specific objectives or goals for the actors.
6. Set the limits and overall rules that will govern permissible behavior.

Basically, remember that all game simulations are similar in design, in that each is a simplified, operational model of a real-life problem or predicament.

# ROLE PLAYING

Role playing, a make-believe situation in which people pretend to be something they are not, is involved in most simulations and academic games. Its purpose is to teach by demonstrating the gap between what you think you are doing and what you are actually doing. The primary uses of role playing in education are:

- training in leadership and human relations skills
- training in sensitivity to people and situations
- stimulation of inquiry and discussion
- training in effective group problem solving

Role playing can be structured in two ways: as an extension of the critical-incident process, in which a critical situation is structured with specific roles for students; or as psychodrama in which a description of a particular personality is provided and students assume these unstructured roles as actors. In both cases learning proceeds from the live interaction between individuals who are playing certain roles, whether with a script or without. Participants in role playing have the opportunity to explore their own feelings about persons with other roles in the group on a variety of subjects, to test skills in a new situation, or get feedback from the participants (both the thoughts and feelings) about how they felt in applying certain strategies in group interaction.

The setting and scenario for role playing can be completely imaginary or an actual experience of persons in the group. The enactment of role playing can involve two people or a number of people in multiple and complex situations and relationships. Role playing should always be built upon controversy or conflict with a problem to overcome. In this way, students learn through the process of actually identifying and considering potential solutions. The real learning, however, comes from discussion (or debriefing) after the completion of the role playing. The teacher can help students to analyze the problem and the roles, and to perceive how solutions were identified, hindered, and facilitated by certain people in particular roles. The teacher should guide the entire role-playing exercise so that students understand and draw conclusions about the total learning experience.

A number of important role-play techniques can be adapted to specific problems and situations. For example:

*Doubling.*   The instructor sits behind the player and interrupts to help the player express the ideas and attitudes behind the dialogue. It is a form of talking to yourself about your motives.

*Soliloquy.*   The instructor stops the action to interview a player in order to gain a better understanding of that player's attitudes and feelings.

*Multiple-Role Playing.*   In a scripted role-play situation, instruction is given about the situation, the characters, and the objectives of the exercise. Role-playing teams act out the sequence of events.

*Role Rotation.*   All members of a group try out various parts in a given problem area to obtain as many different responses as possible. The responses are then compared and analyzed.

*Imitation.*   A member plays a role the way he or she feels someone else would.

*Switching.*   A player exchanges roles with an antagonist to understand the other's point of view.

*Alter Ego.*   A player responds to another person in a socially acceptable way, then stops, and tells what he or she is really thinking.

*The Wheel.*   The teacher sits in the center of a circle and directs the same question to each role player, who reacts in what he or she feels is a normal way; then the group analyzes for the best response.

*Substitution.*   The antagonist role is changed to see how the leader reacts to various challenges and approaches.

A particularly useful technique in role playing is role reversal. In this technique, students take roles that are completely opposite those they usually have. Roles may be reversed from the beginning of a simulation, or participants may "build a case" in their typical role (for example, that of student or teenager) and then at a critical time of interaction switch roles. This approach offers students a unique opportunity to gain insight into their own behavior and its peculiarities by having to contend with the conditions they themselves have created. Through this strategy, students gain an awareness of and an empathy for other persons and their needs.

In all types of simulation, careful preparation is very important. In addition, each form calls for feedback and analytical interpretations by the teacher and the role players after the role playing is completed. Of course, the use of either audiotape or videotape recorders can improve the postanalysis of role playing for purposes of review and learning by students.

# SUMMARY

Experimental research done with simulation and role playing has shown both to be important strategies for teaching and learning. Two researchers, Guetzkow and Jensen (1966), report that "simulation techniques have demonstrated utilities both in research and teaching."

Role playing itself has been shown to be a strong means of influence in producing opinion and attitude change. Research studies by Janis and King (1966) show that people who actively participated in role playing experienced the greatest amount of attitude change toward the direction expressed in selected role-playing situations.

The use of simulation, academic games, and role playing depend solely upon communication cues and behaviors as well as instructional strategies that call for a great amount of student participation and involvement. Each of these approaches provides for experiential learning that ends up with a dramatic impact upon students. Students not only come out with feelings of greater self-satisfaction and higher levels of interest and involvement, but also are more apt to remember what they have learned and to apply it in real-life situations they will encounter.

"Cases, simulations, and games all involve getting, recalling, and using verbal and non-verbal information to solve problems. The integration and restructuring is likely to result in better retention, recall, and use of information outside the classroom" (McKeachie, 1978 p. 149).

# Discussion Questions

**1.** How can learning materials increase student involvement?
**2.** Why is simulation safer than real-life experience?
**3.** How may a teacher build a role-playing simulation upon some type of conflict or controversy?
**4.** In what ways and to what extent is feedback important in any type of simulation or role-playing learning activity?

# References

Garvey, Dale M., and William H. Seiler. *A Study of Effectiveness of Different Methods of Teaching International Relations to High School Students.* Final Report, Cooperative Research Project No. S-270. Washington, D.C.: U.S. Department of Health, Education, and Welfare, Office of Education, 1966.

Guetzkow, Harold and Lloyd Jensen. "Research Activities on Simulated International Processes." *Background: Journal of the International Studies Association,* Vol. 9, No. 2 (February 1966): 263–64.

Janis, I. L., and B. T. King. "The Influence of Role-Playing on Opinion Change." In *Attitudes,* Marie Jahoda and Neil Warren, eds. Baltimore: Penguin Books, Inc., 1966, pp. 225–39.

Maxson, Robert C. "Simulation: A Method That Can Make a Difference." *Education Digest,* March 1974: 48–50.

McKeachie, Wilbert J. *Teaching Tips: A Guidebook for the Beginning College Teacher,* 7th ed. Lexington, Mass.: D. C. Heath & Company, 1978.

Raudsepp, Eugene, and George P. Hough, Jr. *Creative Growth Games.* New York: Harcourt Brace Jovanovich, Inc., 1977.

Ruben, Brent D., and Richard W. Budd. *Human Communication Handbook: Simulations and Games.* New York: Hayden Book Company, Inc., 1975.

Smith, Karl U., and Margaret Foltz Smith. *Cybernetic Principles of Learning and Educational Design.* New York: Holt, Rinehart and Winston, Inc. 1966.

Taba, Hilda. *Curriculum Development Theory and Practice.* New York: Harcourt Brace Jovanovich, Inc., 1962.

# For Further Reading

Chapman, K., J. E. Davis, and A. Meier. *Simulation/Games in Social Studies: What Do We Know?* ERIC Clearinghouse for Social Studies/Social Science Education. Boulder, Colo., 1974.

Heyman, M. *Simulation Games for the Classroom.* Bloomington, Ind.: Phi Delta Kappa, Inc., 1975.

Phelps, Lynn, and Sue DeWine. *Interpersonal Communication Journal.* St. Paul, Minn.: West Publishing Company, 1976.

*Simulation/Gaming/News,* a magazine on simulation and academic games published six times yearly. Available from Box 3039, University Station, Moscow, Id. 83843.

Stadsklev, R. *Handbook of Simulation Gaming in Social Education.* Part Two: *Directory.* University, Ala.: Institute of Higher Education Research and Service, University of Alabama, 1975.

Yoder, D., and H. Heneman, eds. *Training and Development: ASPA Handbook of Personnel and Industrial Relations.* Washington, D.C.: Bureau of National Affairs, Inc. 1977.

# Communicating:
# Self-Instruction

*chapter* **9**

---

*focus*  INSTRUCTIONAL TECHNIQUES TAILORED TO THE NEEDS
OF INDIVIDUAL LEARNERS

THE DEVELOPMENT PROCESS OF PROGRAMS OF
SELF-INSTRUCTION
**Programmed Instruction**
**Personalized Systems of Instruction and**
**Learning Contracts**
**The Instructional Resources Concept**

Although many chapters in this book focus upon the teacher as an active, personal, and directive communicator in the classroom or training situation, we should not forget that the teacher or trainer may also take the role of the "expert" and the learning "facilitator." The question of how the teacher presents the information and materials for learning is as important as the personal qualities of the instructor as a speaker or writer. The area of information identification, organization, and presentation is the starting point of this chapter. This area represents the beginning of classroom communication, in which the instructor views the subject area; reviews various materials and concepts; chooses the concepts, ideas, and skills that will be included in the course or module; organizes the information; and decides upon the instructional strategies to be used for learning.

The way a teacher organizes the information and plans the instruction can vary from a situation of high personal and direct involvement with students (see Chapter 8) to one in which students proceed individually through carefully organized units of instruction, without group activities such as the lecture, discussion, or role-playing simulation. This chapter focuses on the second situation, namely, the area of individualized instruction whose broad definition includes any instructional technique in which learning programs and materials are precisely tailored to the needs of individual learners. The primary way of individualizing instruction presents information in a form in which it can be viewed, read, studied, or practiced by each individual student at the time when he or she is prepared for it. In other words, the time and pace of learning are determined by each individual student.

This chapter deals with the following areas of self-instruction strategies:

1.  development of learning materials for individualized instruction
2.  programmed instruction
3.  personalized systems of instruction and learning contracts
4.  the instructional resources concept

After reading this chapter you should be able to describe each type of self-instruction strategy, the advantages and disadvantages of each, and examples of each as currently used in the classroom.

# THE DEVELOPMENT PROCESS OF PROGRAMS OF SELF-INSTRUCTION

McKeachie (1978, p. 5) states that the first step in preparing for teaching is to establish objectives or purposes. These objectives should state as specifically as possible what and how students are to learn. Objectives are not simply a set of topics to be covered, although the subject will have various areas or topics that can be listed (see Kibler, Cegala, Watson, Barker, and Miles, 1981 or Mager, 1962). They should include specific statements about what the students should be able to do after studying the course, module, or unit you are teaching.

The second general step in the development process is the selection of a primary instructional approach, the instructional strategies, resources, and media that will be used to communicate the subject, and the ways in which evaluation or assessment will take place.

The final step is the planning of the specific instructional steps, the assignments students will be given, and the materials you and the students will actually use for the learning of the objectives. In this final area, you may choose instructional materials and assignments on which students can work individually at their own pace. One of these self-paced learning techniques is called programmed instruction.

## Programmed Instruction

Programmed instruction is a teaching method based upon psychological educational research indicating that students can learn complex ideas if they are taught in small, progressively difficult steps and are reinforced immediately for each correct response or answer. The immediate knowledge of the results (feedback) becomes available after each step. Studies have shown that being told immediately whether you have the correct or incorrect answer is both a powerful and stimulating reward for the student.

The small steps in a programmed instruction format (in either a book or a teaching machine) are called frames. Some programs have two or three thousand frames, others have a hundred or less. Each frame is composed of three sections: stimulus, response, and confirmation (answer). Each stimulus contains small bits of information, followed by a question about the information. The student studies the information in the stimulus and then records or writes the answer in the response section. Next the student checks the answer in the confirmation section. In this way a continuous exchange of information flows between the student and the program.

The following is an example of programmed learning:

**FIGURE 9-1  A Behavioral Research Laboratories (BRL) Demonstration Program**

1.  The numbered information you are now reading is called a FRAME. This frame is part of a larger plan that helps you learn quickly and easily. You have just finished reading Frame ___ .

    1/2

    1

2.  Where I work, we call the larger plan a PROGRAM. A program is a plan for learning. Because what you are about to learn has been planned, we call it a _____ .

    program

3.  A program consists of a number of pieces of information called frames. For example, you have just finished reading the third _____ in this program.

    frame

4.  A careful plan works, but a careless one doesn't. A careful program works, but a careless one _____ .

    doesn't

5.  Good! Already this program is working, because you _____ write the word "DOESN'T" when you completed the previous frame. You did just as I had planned!

    did/did not

    did

6.  Let me introduce myself. I am the programmer, the fellow who writes the frames that make the careful plan we call a _____ .

    program

7.  My job is to write frames so carefully that the program you read works. When a program works, you learn what you are reading. When a program does not work, all you learn is that the programmer _____ plan carefully enough.

    did/did not

    did not

8.  PRO means "BEFORE" and GRAM means "WRITE." If I write down what you learn AFTER you learn it, I am simply a reporter. If I write down what you will learn _____ you learn it, then I am a programmer.

    after/before

    before

9.  A program consists of a number of pieces of information, each of which we call a _____ .

    frame/programmer

    frame

10.  Each _____ gives you a new piece of information. When you have been given all the information you need to know, the program ends. It's as simple as that!

    frame

11.  Reading a frame is like having a conversation that teaches you something. A conversation needs two people. That's why there's a blank in this frame — to give _____ something to say.

    me/you

    you

12. Because I am a programmer, I am a kind of teacher. You can't see me because I live in San Francisco. Even so, we can have a conversation. All you need do is read this program and fill in the blank in each _____ care-    frame
fully.

13. Since I am a _____, I have planned our    programmer
programmer/reporter
conversation down to the last detail. I will say what's over here. You say what's over there.

As you can see by reading this example, knowledge is built in a step-by-step fashion. The ability to answer each new stimulus is based upon the learning experience from earlier frames. More important, students proceed at their own pace. This is particularly helpful for slow learners, because they have the extra time they need to go over the frames and responses. On the other hand, fast learners do not have to slow down for others and can proceed through the learning program as quickly as they are able to understand and satisfactorily respond to each frame.

Programmed instruction and learning is not a cure-all for every instructional problem. It has been used successfully as a supplement to other strategies for two primary reasons: (1) It frees the teacher from the presentation of repetitious, objective subject matter, and (2) it permits individual, self-paced instruction for the student.

Some topics such as science, mathematics, language, and vocational training, based on specific rules, laws, or principles, lend themselves to programmed instruction. Others, such as art, music, dramatics, and similar subjects, are more difficult to program because of the difficulty of agreeing upon what information should be presented and what specific learning behaviors for students are desirable.

Several publishing companies have prepared and published programmed learning materials. Among the areas in which programmed texts are now available are the following: reading, language arts, spelling, English grammar, mathematics, statistics, logic, astronomy, biology, chemistry, economics, political science, geography, French, German, Spanish, and basic speech.

No matter where or for what reason programmed learning is used, its effectiveness is only as good as the communication that accompanies it. The teacher's role may be somewhat restricted but is vital nevertheless, for it is the teacher who must be sensitive to the students' needs and their progress. The program is often not flexible enough to respond to all situations, and while it can provide feedback, evaluate, and reward, it cannot be human. The human aspect is what the teacher must supply to any learning environment.

## Personalized Systems of Instruction and Learning Contracts[1]

In the early 1960s individualized instruction resurfaced at all levels of education: The Montessori preschools, founded in the early part of this century, reappeared in the United

[1] Taken from William J. Seiler, "PSI: An Attractive Alternative for the Basic Speech Communication Course." A paper presented at the 1981 Speech Communication Association Convention in New York. This paper is in press with the *Communication Education Journal*.

States after a long absence; Glaser's Individually Prescribed Instruction and Flanagan's Project Plan provided education methods on the high school level; Postlethwaite developed the Audio-Tutorial Method; and Bloom wrote on Mastery Learning for the college level.

To make learning more efficient and reinforcing, Fred Keller and others developed the Personalized System of Instruction (PSI), the most influential of all the methods of individualized instruction. This method, first used by Keller, Bori, and Azzi (1964) and brought to the attention of American education by Keller (1968), has since been researched extensively. PSI, according to Sherman (1974), is usually associated with five defining characteristics: (1) mastery learning, (2) self-pacing, (3) a stress on the written word, (4) instructor assistants, and (5) the use of lectures to motivate rather than to supply essential information.

The *mastery* feature requires that students obtain perfection in some aspects of the instruction. Keller and his associates believed that accomplishments could be detected through performance. Students in the PSI method are called upon to respond frequently and with responses that have consequence. The theoretical base of PSI suggests that if activities are to produce positive consequences for the learner, repeated testing must take place, and any errors must result in a program of remediation rather than in penalties; it is important that success be rewarded. Thus, grades must reflect accomplishment, not the number of mistakes made along the way; and grading must be determined on absolute rather than on normative standards that are competitive or comparative.

The mastery requirement (whether in part or in full) leads to the second feature, *self-pacing*. Given that at least some aspect of the PSI method requires mastery, it must allow, nevertheless, for a go-at-your-own pace. Mastery cannot always be commanded on schedule, but because individual differences must be taken into account, some self-pacing is mandatory —that is, it must be completed within the time limits of the course—a semester, quarter, or whatever.

The last three features follow directly from the first two. Because some self-pacing is required, a lockstep approach of disseminating information is impossible. *Written materials,* therefore, become the major informational source, and may be supplemented by other materials such as audiovisuals, videotapes, computers, and other innovations to aid student learning. The heavy reliance on the written word requires that the materials be written clearly with objectives specified, sequenced in small steps, and, when possible, arranged from the simple to the complex.

Because the PSI method allows students to use repetitive testing to work at different speeds and to involve themselves in a wide range of materials at any point, there must be a means to supplement and amplify the instructor. This leads to the fourth feature—the use of *instructor assistants* or, as they are known in some PSI courses, proctors or tutors. These assistants are usually students who have previously taken the course.

The use of *lectures,* the fifth feature, differs from that in the traditional classroom. Lecturing, not a major teacher commitment in the PSI method, is used to supplement and to motivate. Thus, the teacher becomes a creator of classroom materials and a manager of a learning system.

PSI has many variations. Boylan (1980) found that approximately 95% of the PSI courses used mastery learning and self-pacing, that 88% stressed the written word, and that 78% used instructor assistants. According to Kulik, Kulik, and Cohen (1979) most courses that use the PSI method meet with little or no failure as long as they contain the basic-learning theory and individualized instruction with a highly personalized relationship among students as well as between students and instructors. While emphasizing five basic features, the PSI method is by no means inflexible to the needs of the users in widely differing environments.

The teacher of a PSI course selects and organizes all the materials used in the course, writes the study guides, organizes the learning-activity packages, and constructs the examinations for the course. (For an excellent source on PSI course development, see Keller and Sherman, 1974.) See Figure 9-2 for a sample PSI study guide. Note the clarity with which the unit is described, the listing of general learning objectives, the specific objective, the reading for the specific objective, and the study question. All of this information is important to the PSI method and must be communicated by the teacher.

**FIGURE 9-2:  PSI Study Guide**

# UNIT 1[2]   THE NATURE OF COMMUNICATION

The purpose of this unit is to provide you with an understanding of general communication concepts and principles. It will serve as the foundation for the other units in the course. In order to become an effective communicator, you must understand communication as a process and a system as well as understand the components and variables that are related to it. You must also understand the effects and relationship of perception and self-concept to communication.

## GENERAL LEARNING OBJECTIVES (GLOs) FOR UNIT 1

Upon completion of this unit, you should understand:

1. the common misconceptions of communication;
2. the concept of process in communication;
3. basic elements of the communication process;
4. the relationship among communication codes, functions, and situations (an overview);
5. perception and its relationship to communication; and
6. that self-concept is socially created through communication and affects communication.

## SPECIFIC OBJECTIVES AND STUDY GUIDE QUESTIONS FOR UNIT 1

**GLO #1:**   You should understand the common misconceptions of communication.

**Reading:**   Schuelke and Seiler, pp. 3–10.

**Specific Objective 1A.**   You should understand the six common misconceptions of communication.

**1A1.**   Explain why each of the following statements is false.
   a.   Communication will solve all our problems.

[2] This guide was developed at the University of Nebraska by William J. Seiler and Marilyn Fuss-Reineck.

Learning contracts, like PSI and programmed instruction, provide students with precise structure. However, the contract method is much more personalized. It gives students the opportunity to choose objectives either in terms of what they will attempt to achieve or in terms of what they may choose *not* to achieve. In a typical learning contract the teacher and the student work out a set of objectives to be mastered, the methods of achieving these goals, and the ways in which performance will be evaluated. When the student and teacher agree upon the amount of work to be done and the way in which it is to be done, they conclude their "contract" with an agreement about the grade that will be given by the teacher if all of the work is satisfactorily completed by the student.

McKeachie (1978, p. 118) points out that the contract method reduces the student's concern and anxiety about what is expected and places the responsibility for learning upon the student. In practice, there are two difficulties with the contract:

1.  The method demands a great deal of teacher time in both working out the contract and tutoring the student who may encounter difficulty with the material.
2.  Grades are often higher with contracts than for similar work done in conventional classrooms. This is due to a tendency to write contracts that emphasize quantity rather than quality of work and thus, possibly, lead to grade inflation.

The advantages of learning contracts and the Personalized System of Instruction are similar to those of programmed learning, that is, students are able to study and learn at their own pace at the place and time of their own preference. The disadvantages of PSI and contract learning relate to the large amount of teacher time required before actual instruction and learning; the impersonal, sometimes passive, role of the teacher in the day-to-day learning of students; and the resultant apathy on the part of students involved with the system. McKeachie (1978) and Cook (1974) report that PSI has higher-than-average student withdrawals. A reason could be the lack of motivation in the PSI method compared to motivation possibly provided by teaching in the conventional classroom setting and by the conventional role of the teacher as an authority, facilitator, and role model.

# The Instructional Resources Concept[3]

The Instructional Resources Concept, which is quite different from the modes of individualized instruction previously discussed, emerged from two separate areas: the conventional library and the learning laboratory. These two settings have been integrated into a new media-based Instructional Resources Center. In this approach, the instructor develops the objectives for learning in much the same way that the objectives are developed for any other course, and then provides the types of information and sources needed by students to fulfill these objectives.

At this point, the instructor enlists the help of resource, media, and information specialists to determine the available modes of acquisition and presentation of the learning materials, whether such materials and resources are available and accessible, whether new materials or resources need to be designed and developed, and which learning materials and

---

[3] Special assistance for this section was provided by Dr. Wesley Grabow of the University of Minnesota Instructional Resources Center.

resources will actually be used by students to accomplish the objectives of the course. If adequate learning materials are not available, professional media developers are available to most teachers for cooperative design of appropriate materials and media, which may include films, transparencies, slides, audiotapes and videotapes, working models, single-concept films, and actual simple laboratory experiments.

In this instructional-resource-team approach, the teacher works with information specialists, librarians, and media designers to set up teaching and learning resources rich in variety and interest to meet the needs of various students with different learning styles and abilities.

The advantages for students can easily be demonstrated. First, students benefit not only from the instructor, but also from other professionals such as media specialists and librarians working together to provide a variety of materials and resources for their learning. Second, students may find a diversity of materials and resources in one location (similar to that of a conventional laboratory) without going to a number of places to view a film, find a book, obtain a computerized bibliography, or work through an experiment. The Instructional Resources Center may also have the advantage of open access for students at both the time and pace they prefer. In this way, individual differences may be accounted for in much the same way they can in either programmed instruction or Personalized Systems of Instruction. Finally, the quality of teacher preparation and instructional materials is apt to be significantly higher in situations where the teacher is teamed with media and resource specialists in the management and providing of instruction. This approach is one of the few that allows for the use of multiple methods, machines, resources, and media to meet the problems of learners directly. On the other hand, this Instructional Resources Concept can be costly both in preparation time for the teacher and in the budget for the rental or purchase of learning materials and resources.

Because the Instructional Resources Center concept is based upon the utilization of various learning resources, it is one of the few integrated systems of teaching and learning that has the potential for a truly multimedia approach. More research needs to be done to determine what advantages there might be to the use of multiple media forms. Twyford (1969) reports in the *Encyclopedia of Educational Research* that the increasing diversity of communication media for education will create a greater need for the application of communication technology in an integrated and coordinated fashion in the classroom. He concludes with the suggestion that educational media centers will continue to be developed to meet the needs of teachers and learners in the future.

# SUMMARY

In this chapter, we have described self-instruction as an instructional strategy for teachers and discussed programmed instruction, the Personalized System of Instruction and teacher-learner contracts, and the Instructional Resources Center concept. In each of the examples, there is a fundamental approach that underlies the entire chapter: to make the organization of instruction so complete and discrete that students will be able to enter and proceed through their own learning at the time and place of their own choosing and with speeds and intensities that are self-determined. In each of these self-instruction strategies the emphasis is upon careful, thorough, and formal preparation by the teacher. In each case the instructor does the bulk of the communication before the actual learning by the student.

The teacher communication competency must be in organization, research, discovery and use of eclectic resources and materials, and phrasing of very specific directions in precise terms for student learning and performance. In these forms of classroom communication, the instructor is primarily a careful composer of messages that passively direct individual students through a series of learning experiences. In this case, as in others, the multiple communication roles and competencies of the classroom teacher are central to the learning process.

# Discussion Questions

1. Give an example of individualized instruction, and explain some of the advantages and disadvantages of this kind of learning material.
2. Explain the essential elements of programmed learning.
3. Why is the Personalized System of Instruction sometimes referred to as "mastery learning"?
4. How do learning materials and student needs affect one another and the Instructional Resources concept?

# References

Boylan, Hunter R. "PSI: A Survey of Users and Their Implementation Practices." *Journal of Personalized Instruction,* Vol. 4 (Spring 1980): 40–43.

Cook, D. A. "Personalized System of Instruction: Potential and Problems." *Educational Products Report,* Vol. 67 (November 1974): 647–51.

Keller, Fred S. "Goodbye Teacher. . . ." *Journal of Applied Behavior Analysis,* Vol. 1 (1968): 79–84.

Keller, Fred S., Carolina Martuscelli Bori, and Rodolpho Azzi. "Um Curso de Psilgia." *Ciencia e Cultura,* Vol. 16 (1964): 307–09.

Keller, Fred S., and J. Gilmour Sherman, eds. *The Keller Plan Handbook.* Menlo Park, Cal.: Benjamin-Cummings Publishing Co., 1974.

Kibler, Robert, Don Cegala, Kittie Watson, Larry Barker, and David Miles. *Behavioral Objectives and Instruction,* 2nd ed. Boston: Allyn and Bacon, Inc., 1981.

Kulik, James A., Chen-Lin C. Kulik, and Peter A. Cohen. "A Meta-Analysis of Outcome Studies of Keller's Personalized System of Instruction." *American Psychologist,* Vol. 34 (1979): 307–18.

Mager, Robert. *Preparing Instruction Objectives.* Palo Alto, Cal.: Fearon Publishers, 1962.

McKeachie, Wilbert J. *Teaching Tips: A Guidebook for the Beginning College Teacher,* 7th ed. Lexington, Mass.: D. C. Heath & Company, 1978.

Sherman, J. Gilmour. *Personalized System of Instruction: Forty-one Germinal Papers.* Menlo Park, Cal.: Benjamin-Cummings Publishing Co., 1974.

Twyford, Loran C., Jr. "Educational Communication Media." In *Encyclopedia of Educational Research,* 4th ed. London: Macmillan & International Ltd., 1969, pp. 367–80.

# For Further Reading

Behavioral Research Laboratories. *Effective Teaching with Programmed Instruction*. Palo Alto, Cal.: BRL, 1970.

Gage, N. L., and David C. Berliner. *Educational Psychology*, 2nd ed. Boston: Houghton-Mifflin Company, 1979.

# Communicating:
# Computers,
# Responders,
# and Videotape Recorders

*chapter* **10**

---

Computers are "freedom machines," in that their possibilities for doing our work more easily and quickly seem to be virtually unlimited. Besides keeping records, guiding rockets, and solving mathematical problems, the computer can do a number of things supporting the teaching/learning process. The computer and other instructional technology, including the filmstrip projector, the slide projector, the 8mm and 16mm movie projectors, the student-responder system, the audiotape and videotape recorders, and the overhead projector, are used extensively in classrooms. This chapter deals with the computer, student responder, and videotape recorder as examples of technology that are being used to improve instruction and learning. Other forms of technology are more familiar, having been in classroom use for a number of years, and are therefore not included here.

After reading this chapter, you should be able to describe particular instructional or communication technologies, the ways in which they are being used in classrooms, the problems and advantages of each, and the ways in which *you* might use each instrument in your teaching in your subject area, with your students.

# THE COMPUTER

The future of education has been and will continue to be affected by the computer. Nearly all teachers realize that the role of the computer as a tool for teaching and learning is significant. For example, the National Council of Teachers of Mathematics has stated:

> . . . each student should acquire an understanding of the versatility and limitations of the computer through firsthand experience in a variety of fields. . . .

To begin with, the computer was not designed to be a teaching tool. Its original purpose was to manipulate numbers and to perform long and tedious mathematical calculations. Using the computer for purposes of direct communication in a teaching/learning situation, therefore, requires a large amount of preparation to make sure that the people using the machine understand what it is communicating (output), how it works, and how to work it (user interface). Finally, the ways a person communicates with the computer (input) are also complex and require special knowledge and the willingness to make an occasional mistake while learning how to use the machine. The earliest use of computers in teaching (Storulow, 1967) was for problem solving, drill and practice, simulation and gaming, tutoring, and presenting written materials.

Let's take each of the areas and show how the computer can help students to learn. In each case, the computer becomes a communication channel that presents materials to the student for use in a particular and specific way. As a "communicator," the computer has two important features: memory and logic.

## Problem Solving

Problems in teaching and training are often presented as questions for students to answer. This format presents opportunities to students so that they can show what is known and not known. In Figure 10-1, an example of the problem-solving method of computer-based teaching is shown using a lesson on Writing Better Business Letters (Lippert, 1977).

As you can see, the sequence is as follows: (1) the student is presented some visual materials on a cathode ray tube (CRT), which is similar to a television screen; (2) the student is asked a question; (3) the student types or writes the answer; and (4) response to the student's answer appears on the screen or typewriter.

## Drill and Practice

A second type of application of the computer allows for repetitive exercises in which students can receive various questions, phrased in different ways, and attempt to provide the most appropriate responses with a number of tries. In this way the student learns the correct answer by a trial-and-error method. One of the important things that a computer-based instructional program can do is to provide a number of questions phrased in the same or different ways for students to answer in ways that they think are correct. The computer can also immediately respond to the answer (affirm or correct) and present another question, all in rapid succession. Since the computer is a machine, it can be used for purposes of drill and practice for almost an unlimited amount of time.

## FIGURE 10-1[1]

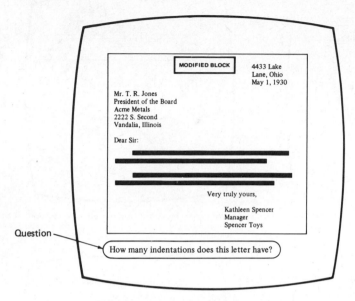

The lesson presents a letter form and asks a question.

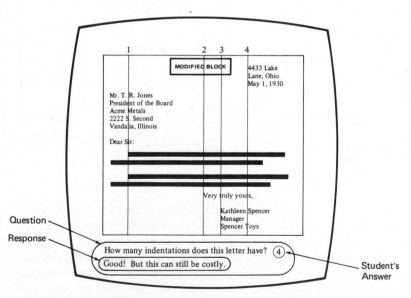

When the student replies, the lesson positively reinforces
the correct answer.

[1] Adapted by permission of Control Data Corporation, Minneapolis, Minnesota.

## FIGURE 10-2[2]

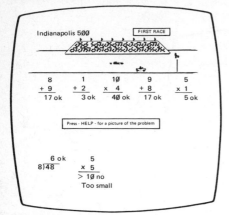

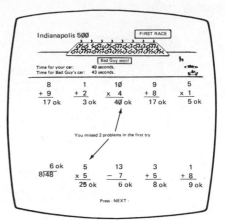

An elementary game of arithmetic drill and practice. The student makes a mistake and must correct it.

At the end of the race, the lesson points out the student's mistakes and the length of time the student took to finish the race.

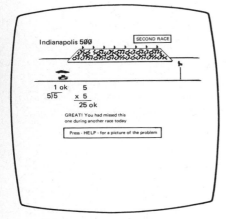

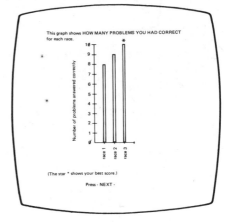

During the second race, the student races against the previous best time. The lesson repeats problems that the student missed during the first race.

After the races, a graph shows the student's improvement. (Bonnie Anderson Seiler)

[2] Adapted by permission of Control Data Corporation, Minneapolis, Minnesota.

Figure 10-2 shows how a beginning lesson in mathematics provides the student with a number of problems in a set amount of time. The student tries to correctly complete as many problems as quickly as possible. At the end of the drill period, a graph is shown to the student comparing the accuracy and time used between practice sessions. The computer provides an instant evaluation of a student's responses and reports that evaluation to both student and teacher. A teacher can also obtain separate feedback reports to determine the progress of each student and whether special help is needed.

## Simulation and Gaming

Simulation, by attempting to re-create in a controllable form some real-life task or job, helps students try out their knowledge in something that approximates a real situation, using materials with which they will eventually be working. Much of the material discussed in Chapter 9 explains the basis and approach to simulation and games as classroom communication techniques. By rereading Chapter 9 you may be able to recall the actual elements of simulation and to determine how they can be applied with the computer.

Games with learning objectives can be played on microcomputers or with the more popular video-game programs. The *1980 Catalog of PLATO Courses,* published by Control Data Corporation of Minneapolis, Minnesota, lists thirty games ranging from calculation and checkers to Paint by Touch and Wall Street (pp. 187–194).

In Figure 10-3, a rear-screen projector is used to simulate driving situations. Students are given multiple-choice questions on the computer terminal that ask what the driver's next action will be.

**FIGURE 10-3[3]**

This lesson is a driver's education test using slides of driving situations.

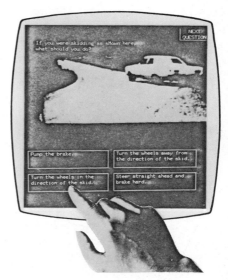

To answer the question, the student must touch the box.

Slides can be photographs or drawings. (David Frankel and Cindy Poulos)

[3] Adapted by permission of Control Data Corporation, Minneapolis, Minnesota.

## Tutoring

Perhaps the oldest method of instruction involves one-to-one communication between instructor and learner. In this situation, an instructor develops a set of rules or procedures involving a number of learning activities, materials, and resources, and then directs the individual learners to proceed through the activities at their own pace. The instructor monitors the progress of each student or, in the case of fully automated computer-based tutorial programs, the computer program assesses student progress at regular intervals.

In this procedure, shown in Figure 10-4, the computer "manages" instruction in much the same way that a teacher manages instruction in direct face-to-face interaction with the

**FIGURE 10-4[4]**

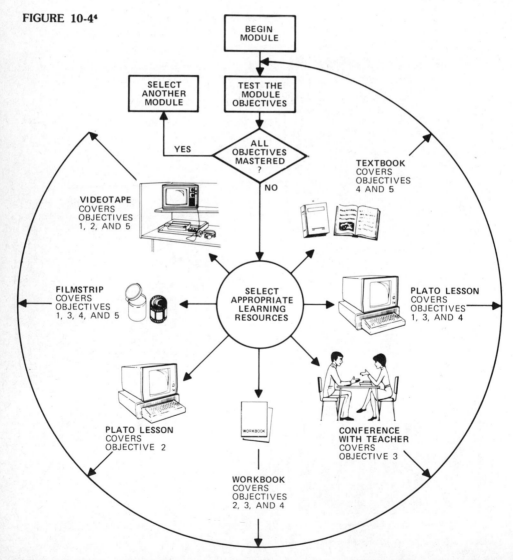

[4] From *Control Data PLATO System Overview.* Copyright © 1976, 1977 by Control Data Corporation. Reprinted by permission. PLATO is a trademark of Control Data Corporation.

student. You will notice that the lesson (or module) begins with specific objectives, moves through a number of learning experiences and resources, and ends with a test of the module objectives. This tutorial learning program is most commonly called computer-managed instruction (CMI).

## Presenting Written Materials

Much of learning depends upon reading written words from books, manuals, teachers' handouts, syllabi, blackboards, or overhead projectors. In addition, overviews, summaries, study questions, examples, pictures, charts, and problems are usually presented in written form. A computer program can carry and present written information as well. The computer is an important educational tool in this area, because it is a *unique medium of communication* in itself, quite different from traditional materials that are used in classrooms. For example, a teacher can design a written communication package in a specific subject area that might *combine* some of the following features:

- narrative description of facts, sources, skills, objectives, or "how-to-do-its"
- drill and practice exercises to help a student memorize facts, learn a concept, or master a skill
- times and places for students to ask questions in order to solve problems
- students' interaction with the computer to analyze their own performances by providing summaries of progress, correct and incorrect answers, and comparisons with other students taking the course
- options within the curriculum structure for students to select, skip, or take the pretest or any segment or part of the total course at the time they may feel a specific option is the most appropriate
- an up-to-date record of each student's performance as well as the performance of all students studying a particular course at a specific time, including such information as time needed to complete certain problems or exercises, degree of difficulty of particular objectives, and projection of need or ancillary instruction or curriculm redesign to meet student needs

As you can see, computer-based instruction can open various opportunities to both teacher and learner. Some of these are:

- providing individualized and self-paced instruction for all levels of students, an especially important factor for the very slow or exceptionally fast student
- improving the quality of presentation of learning materials through better organization, clearer use of language, examples, visual materials, and more rigorous editing and analysis of instructional directions
- using a multiple resource and media approach that attempts to utilize the full gamut of educational services and resources that may be available in a particular area (called the instructional resources concept)

Problems in using the computer as a teaching/learning machine should also be recognized. Some of these are:

- the shortage of materials, programs, and courses (software) developed by teachers for actual use.

- the copyright law, which makes it difficult for teacher-course designers effectively to develop and use a multiple-resource approach without paying high costs for materials published and/or distributed in other media forms.
- the lessening of interpersonal contact between teacher and learner. We can point out here that this generally happens with the less effective teacher anyway. Machines and automated instructional programs are never a substitute for the teacher. A computer-based program may enhance the organization or presentation of instruction and release the teacher for more personal and individualized person-to-person teaching, but in the end the teacher must take full responsibility for monitoring the progress of each student, whether machines such as the computer are used or not.

One of the difficulties in using computers in the classroom has been the lack of suitable software materials. See Appendix for a partial listing of software vendors who may provide catalogs and descriptions of various programs available for purchase or rental.

A great deal of research on the effectiveness of computer-assisted instruction exists in such communication areas as:

reading comprehension

literacy

spelling

vocabulary development

discovery and use of bibliographic sources

discovery of topics

writing (composing and editing of sentences)

interpersonal communication (computer conferencing)

Generally, computer technology has been found comparable to conventional teaching methods in (1) cost, (2) retention of information by students, and (3) positive attitudes of learners (Schuelke and King, 1982). The computer, as well as other forms of technology, will not only permit but also require increased emphasis upon individualized dyadic communication and competency-based learning as the main feature of formal teaching and learning in the future.


## THE STUDENT RESPONDER SYSTEM

The student responder system is an electronic device that gives the teacher immediate and continuous feedback from the students to indicate how well they comprehend the material being presented. This is accomplished by means of an electronic console, placed on the teacher's desk, that receives messages from individual student units. The teacher poses multiple-choice questions dealing with the lesson, and all students can respond instantaneously, simultaneously, and confidentially. Each student unit has a letter dial, which records the student's name, and an answer button, which records the answer to the question.

The teacher's console may have two display units. The answer-distribution unit

FIGURE 10-5

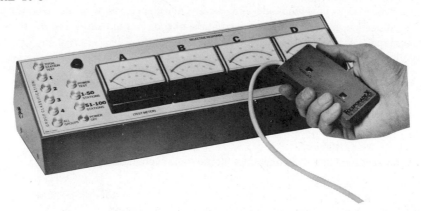

indicates the percentage of students who have answered with response letters A, B, C, or D. The answer identification unit reflects the class seating layout with a lamp for each student position. If the teacher has indicated the correct answer to the console, the lamps of the students choosing the correct answer will brighten. Only the teacher knows how each student responds, so students are not inhibited by the possibility of public embarrassment.

The advantage of using the student responder system is readily understood if we remember that good teachers are sensitive to the communication of the students. A good teacher perceives the level of understanding of the students and can intuitively determine the pace of presentation. This is, of course, an ideal situation and usually happens only in small-class situations. The student responder system, however, can simulate the rapport of a small class even in a group of fifty or more. In addition, immediate feedback is more accurate, for a glance at the console tells the teacher with certainty what percentages of the class, as well as which individual members, are not keeping up with the presentation.

The student responder also can be used at the beginning of a class session to determine how much the class has retained from the previous meeting or how well a reading assignment has been understood. A teacher who finds the class has lost the thread of continuity can quickly review the main points of the previous lesson. Similarly, at the end of a class session, the teacher can ask questions that reveal whether or not the objectives of that lesson have been achieved. At any point during the class session, a check with the student responder may reveal that the lesson is understood, and the pace can be increased.

With the response system, students are active participants in each lesson and therefore tend to remain more attentive. Furthermore, they receive positive reinforcement, a powerful element in learning, from the machine when the teacher elects to reinforce correct answers: When the correct-answer button on the console is pushed, a light corresponding to that answer on the student's unit will blink.

One optional feature of the student responder is the confidential answer mode. This feature conceals the identity of the individual student, although the number of students responding with the correct answer is known. This encourages participation by even the shyest student, while still supplying the necessary feedback to the teacher. Another optional feature provides a printed record of all student responses to questions. Experience with this feature shows that students are interested in their own performances and rarely fail to examine the printout at the end of the class session. This option is an effective teaching aid because the responses of the whole class can be read at a glance, and weak areas can be noted easily. Any question missed by a large percentage of the class indicates that the related or background material was not presented clearly.

We have seen that the student responder is a useful tool for the following reasons:

1. It helps the instructor to determine accurately what percentage of the class comprehends the lesson presented and to identify individual students needing help.
2. It increases the attention and motivation of the student.
3. It helps the teacher to determine the pace of instruction with the confidence that all class members are keeping up.
4. It achieves a semblance of small-class interaction, even in a large group.

Some of the disadvantages include:

1. The group has to be large enough to justify using the system.
2. The flow of the presentation might be interrupted by stopping the lecture to ask review questions.
3. Initial cost of the equipment might be too expensive.


# VIDEOTAPE RECORDERS

Videotape recorders provide a varied and vast means of enhancing the quality of classroom teaching, even when school budgets are restricted. The specialized knowledge of world or national experts, recorded at convenient times, can be integrated into a lesson plan, as can events recorded at an earlier time. Furthermore, rare or immovable items, such as museum pieces, can be "brought" to the classroom by the videotape projection, which is also capable of magnifying details so that every student can see. Careful selection from this rich resource can improve the classroom experience.

While film projections are also capable of performing all of the functions that have been mentioned, videotape can be recorded for immediate playback without costly processing of any kind. Videotape consists of iron oxide layered to a plastic back and is similar in appearance to audiotape. While the low cost of videotape is a great advantage, it is not the only one: Any mistakes that occur during taping can be erased easily and rerecorded at the same session; entire lectures can be taped and used for many years, permitting the teacher to use time for other tasks; and the content of the lecture can be easily revised and updated.

When the material on a tape is no longer needed, it can be completely erased and the tape used anew. Because videotape is generally low in cost, students (even in primary grades) can write, produce, and tape their own presentations. After studying and criticizing their performances, they can erase the tape and start over. Work by secondary school students includes costume and set design and manufacture in addition to writing, performing, and taping the presentation. College students produce news shows that are preparations for careers in television journalism. Students learning to produce televised programs must acquire many skills in addition to writing, performing, and taping. They learn to organize, direct, edit, and cooperate with others and assume responsibility.

Videotape has the distinct advantage of its capability of being played back immediately after recording. This feature can be used to great advantage by teachers and student teachers for self-evaluation, giving them an accurate method for assessing their performances in front of a class. Playing back an actual class session allows teachers to analyze their speech and gestures and to discern faulty organization of material. The teacher can also observe the class reaction (or lack of it) to certain teaching aids. This instant replay feature for evaluation purposes is particularly useful in teaching physical skills like gymnastics and dance or in delivery skills like public address, so that students can observe their performances as compared to those of experts and can also see their own progress.

An unresolved problem in the use of videotape, however, concerns the standardization of equipment. The first tapes marketed were two inches wide; the next sizes were one inch and three-quarter inch; since 1970, half-inch tape has been popular. Some producers feel that the narrower tapes cannot match the quality of wider tapes, yet the narrower ones accommodate 50% more tape length in cassettes. Each format has some advantage and none is clearly superior. Tape width presents a problem for the customer, since buying videotape equipment represents an investment and the various formats are not interchangeable. This restriction limits usefulness once one format is chosen, since all programs are not available on all tape sizes.

The future of video in education undoubtedly will include greater use of self-paced individual instruction. A technique that takes full advantage of visual images for individual instruction is videodisc and computer interface. An LP-record-sized optical videodisc stores audio and video information that can be played on a TV receiver. Any one of a total of 54,000 tracks can be located (or accessed) in five seconds or less by a microcomputer-controlled videodisc player. Sustik, in a study using a videodisc system in art history, reported high student interest in spite of the lack of practice with the system.

# SUMMARY

We have seen in this chapter how machines, acting as communication media, can be used by the teacher to enhance instruction. We have investigated three types of machines — computers, responder systems, and videotape recorders. In each of these classroom communication tools, the teacher is critically important. For the computer, the teacher's role is similar to choosing, developing, or utilizing a textbook. The computer software is the content that needs to be prepared in advance by a subject-matter expert. The teacher needs to be aware of design variables in both the machine and the programs. They are equivalent to the channel and message existing in all classroom communication events.

The responder system provides for individual responding by students during an actual lesson. In this case, teachers may systematically evaluate specific feedback to questions with minimal interruption of the flow of teacher-led discussion and with one-way presentations of information.

The videotape recorder and playback system require similar involvement by teachers. Content is provided by instructors who use the media to deliver prerecorded visual and audio messages. The potential for capturing real people and events for subsequent study is the greatest advantage of video recording and playback. When professionally produced programs can be added to the list of classroom resources, the potential for improved learning is even greater.

This chapter provides teachers with a basic understanding of the potential use of these communication enhancement machines.

# Discussion Questions

**1.**  Discuss how communication is processed by a computer, and explain why it requires special preparation to use the machine.

**2.**  How is the computer well suited for drill and practice exercises?

**3.**  Why does the quality of learning materials usually improve with the use of machines such as the computer or the tape recorder?

**4.**  How can a student responder system improve the teacher's sensitivity to student responses to instructional materials?

**5.**  Why is the videotape recorder preferable to film as a medium for classroom instruction?

**6.**  What are the disadvantages of the student responder system and videotape recorders?

# References

Lippert, John W. *Better Business Letters*. Minneapolis, Minn.: Control Data Corp., 1977.

Schuelke, David, and D. Thomas King. "New Technology in the Classroom: Computers and Communication and the Future." Unpublished paper presented at the American Educational Research Association convention, March, 1982.

Storulow, Lawrence M. *Computer-Assisted Instruction*. Cambridge, Mass.: Harvard University Press, 1967.

Sustik, Joan M. *Art History Interactive Videodisc Project at the University of Iowa*. Iowa City, Ia.: Weeg Computing Center, The University of Iowa. No date.

# For Further Reading

Gage, N. L., and D. C. Berliner. *Educational Psychology*, 2nd ed. Boston: Houghton Mifflin Company, 1979.

Morrow, James, and M. Suid. *Media and Kids*. New York: Hayden Book Company, Inc., 1977.

Taylor, Robert, and B. Green, eds. *Tales of the Marvelous Machine*. Morristown, N.J.: Creative Computing, 1980.

Weizenbaum, Joseph. *Computer Power and Human Reason*. San Francisco, Cal.: W. H. Freeman and Co., Publishers, 1976.

# Communicating: Assessment and Feedback

*focus*  THE ASSESSMENT OF CLASSROOM INTERACTION AND FEEDBACK

ASSESSING CLASSROOM INTERACTION:
SYSTEMATIC OBSERVATIONS

FEEDBACK
**Advantages of Feedback**
**Costs of Feedback**
**Feedback from Students to Teacher**
**Feedback to Students**
**Feedback to Parents**

Probably the question asked most often by students as well as teachers is "How well am I doing?" While students are generally concerned with their grades, especially whether they pass or fail, teachers, particularly beginning teachers, are concerned with their effectiveness. Both of these concerns are important to learning and to the communication process that occurs in the classroom. Feedback, as described in Chapter 1, is an integral part of the process of communication and instruction that allows a source or sender (teacher or student) to monitor the communication encounter (classroom interaction) and to check on (assess) the success of communication and instruction. Feedback is, as suggested in Chapter 1, continually occurring throughout the instructional process (from teacher to student, from student to student, from student to teacher, from teacher to parents, from student to parents, from parents to student, and from parents to teacher). This chapter is concerned with assessing classroom interaction and feedback. Included is an examination of systematic observation techniques used to evaluate communication behavior in the classroom. In addition, feedback is discussed in terms of written, oral, positive, negative, private, and public student-teacher conferences and parent-teacher conferences.

## ASSESSING CLASSROOM INTERACTION: SYSTEMATIC OBSERVATIONS

Classroom interaction is an extremely complex process. At present there is no one method or system to adequately measure all aspects of classroom interaction. Before any system of assessing communication in the classroom can be used effectively, two conditions must be present: (1) The teacher, whether a student teacher, a first-year teacher, or a tenured teacher with twenty-five years of experience, must have a positive attitude toward change. The teacher who does the same thing day after day and year after year is shortchanging students by increasing the chances of being less effective, potentially boring, and predictable. (2) The teacher must recognize the need to improve. A beginning teacher may soon find a need for some technique or skill that will allow for better classroom control. The experienced teacher, on the other hand, may feel a need based on observation or on feelings of dissatisfaction with the motivation or achievement of students. An observant teacher who is willing to change can make appropriate adjustments, if required. One way of determining classroom performance is to use systematic observation.

Systematic observation techniques comprise sets of categories that examine teacher behaviors. Some typical categories or behaviors are lecturing, giving praise, asking questions, criticizing, and giving opinions. Many of the systems are not concerned with content but with teacher behavior, and thus can be used with any subject or grade level.

Simon and Boyer (1970) list several uses of classroom observation techniques, nearly all of which were originally developed for research. One use is to test various assumptions about classroom communication. The second is to aid in teacher training and to assist teachers in improvement. The third is for supervisors to use in providing feedback for rating or evaluating teacher performances. In this chapter, we are most concerned with the second, because it relates most directly to training and improvement.

There are many different classroom behavior-coding systems[1] that can be used to record teacher behaviors. Nearly all the systems take time to learn and master; for example, approximately ten to twenty hours of coding experience are required (usually with the assistance of someone who has been trained) to categorize classroom behaviors accurately and reliably. This may seem to be a tremendous investment in time, and it is. However, like any professional who monitors success and failure, the teacher must make a time investment. A dancer learning a particular routine makes many mistakes before mastering the routine correctly. In perfecting the routine, the dancer will probably spend a considerable amount of time practicing under the watchful eye of a choreographer or director. Like the dancer, the teacher must continually, or at least periodically, be observed to determine if certain teaching behaviors need improvement.

A number of studies on the effects of systematic observation techniques indicate that these techniques can change teacher behavior. Amidon and Hough (1967) suggest that teachers who have used systematic observation as a means of examining their teaching behaviors have become more aware of their communication and thus more accepting, less critical, more sensitive, and more interactive with their students. Friedrich and Brooks (1970, p. 285) cite a number of sources suggesting that "the use of various systematic observation instruments leads to changes in teacher behavior and increased student learning—results which traditional methods of teacher training have been unable to demonstrate." They

---

[1] For a review of observation instruments, see Simon and Boyer, 1974. For additional instruments, see Barak Rosenshine and Norma Furst, "The Use of Direct Observation to Study Teaching," in *The Second Handbook of Research on Teaching*, Robert M. W. Travers, ed. Skokie, Ill.: Rand McNally, 1973, pp. 128–84; and G. D. Borich and S. K. Madden, *Evaluating Classroom Instruction: A Sourcebook of Instruments*. Reading, Mass.: Addison-Wesley Publishing Company, Inc., 1977.

continue by explaining that the use of systematic observation techniques provides the beginning instructor with:

(1) a model — in behavioral terms — of the kind of teaching behavior he may choose to develop, (2) the framework for conceptualizing and developing a variety of teaching roles, (3) feedback concerning progress toward the development of those teaching behaviors he has chosen, and (4) an opportunity to gain insight into principles of effective teaching through personal inquiry.

Systematic observation systems merit use because they do provide an opportunity for classroom teachers to analyze their communication. It should be noted that systematic observation does not provide evaluative data to tell whether or not a teacher is effective, but does provide a view of behaviors. It remains for the teacher to interpret the effectiveness of the teaching.

Let's go through the procedures of using a systematic observation technique. The *first* step is to decide which behaviors are to be observed. For example, teachers may wish to compare the amount they talk against how much the students do, to examine the kind of talk taking place, or to determine the effectiveness or ineffectiveness of classroom behavior. There are, according to Simon and Boyer (1970), two major domains of observation systems: the affective and the cognitive. The affective domain records the emotional climate of the classroom by coding the teacher's reactions to the feelings, ideas, work efforts, or actions of students. The cognitive domain consists of categories that examine the differences between kinds of information a teacher presents, the questions asked, or the way students respond. Table 11-1 illustrates some of the observation systems that are available, the focus of each system, the type of communication that is recorded, and the person being observed.

The *second* step is to select a system that will evaluate those behaviors to be observed. Flanders (1960) developed an interaction analysis system that codes both student and teacher talk within the affective domain. Table 11-2 illustrates the categories of the widely used Flanders system.

The Flanders system can be used "live" by an observer coding in the classroom or with an audio or video recording.[2] Despite the small number of categories, this system has been most useful in teacher training and in helping teachers to improve their classroom communication. It provides feedback to teachers about their behaviors and the effects on student participation.

Because Flanders believes that verbal behavior can be observed more reliably than nonverbal behavior, his system deals with the former. As seen in Table 11-2, the system divides teacher talk into subcategories: response (indirect influence) and initiation (direct influence). Flanders classifies teacher statements into either of these subcategories, based on the amount of freedom the students are granted. The teacher can either be direct, that is, minimize the freedom of the students to respond; or indirect, that is, maximize the freedom of the students to respond.

The system also records student talk and thereby accounts for total interaction in the classroom. Another category, in which no interaction takes place, represents silence or confusion.

The *third* step is to analyze the coding and the observations. See Table 11-3 for an

---

[2] It is assumed that the coder understands the rules and procedures of the system being used. For a complete description of how the Flanders system works, see Amidon and Hough (1967).

TABLE 11-1

| System | System Focus | | | | Type of Communication Recorded | | Subject of Observation | | |
| --- | --- | --- | --- | --- | --- | --- | --- | --- | --- |
| | Affective domain | Cognitive domain | Work process (control) | Behavior | Verbal | Nonverbal | Teacher only | Student only | Teacher and student |
| 1. AMIDON | X | X | | | X | | | | X |
| 2. AMIDON-HUNTER (VICS) | X | | | | X | | | | X |
| 3. ASCHNER-GALLAGHER | | X | | | X | X | | | X |
| 4. BELLACK | | X | | | X | | | | X |
| 5. FLANDERS | X | | | | X | | | | X |
| 6. FLANDERS (Expanded) | X | | | | X | | | | X |
| 7. GALLAGHER | | X | | | X | | | | X |
| 8. HONIGMAN (MACI) | X | | X | X | X | X | | | X |
| 9. HOUGH | X | | | | X | | | | X |
| 10. HUGHES | X | | | | X | X | | | X |
| 11. JOYCE | X | X | X | | X | | X | | |
| 12. LINDVALL | | | | X | | X | | X | |
| 13. MEDLEY (OScAR) | X | X | X | | X | | | | X |
| 14. MILLER | X | | | | X | | X | | |
| 15. MOSKOWITZ (FLint) | X | | | | X | | | | X |
| 16. OLIVER-SHAVER | | X | X | | X | | | | X |
| 17. OPENSHAW-CYPHERT | X | X | X | | X | X | X | | |
| 18. SIMON-AGAZARIAN (SAVI) | X | X | | | X | | | | X |
| 19. SMITH (Logic) | | X | | | X | | | | X |
| 20. SMITH (Strategy) | | X | | | X | | | | X |
| 21. SPAULDING (CASES) | X | | | X | X | X | | X | |
| 22. SPAULDING (STARS) | X | X | X | X | X | X | X | | |
| 23. TABA | X | X | | | X | | | | X |
| 24. WITHALL | X | X | | | X | | X | | |
| 25. WRIGHT | X | X | | | X | | | | X |
| 26. WRIGHT-PROCTOR | X | X | | | X | | | | X |

example of a typical matrix of tabulations using the Flanders system. The tabulations made in the matrix represent pairs of numbers. The first number in the pair indicates the row and the second number the column. Once the matrix is tabulated, classroom interactions can be described. The description can be done in several different ways. The first tabulation usually reports the kinds of statements in terms of percentages. This is done by dividing each of the column totals, 1 through 10, by the total number of tallies in the matrix. This indicates the proportion of interaction for each category compared to the total interaction observed in the classroom.

One of the more important pieces of data in Table 11-3 concerns the total percentage of teacher talk in comparison with student talk. Using the illustration provided to determine the percentage of teacher talk, simply divide the total number of tallies in 1 through 7 (105)

**TABLE 11-2   Flanders' Interaction Analysis Categories* (FIAC)**

| | | |
|---|---|---|
| **Teacher Talk** | **Response** | 1. *Accepts feeling.* Accepts and clarifies an attitude or the feeling tone of a pupil in a nonthreatening manner. Feelings may be positive or negative. Predicting and recalling feelings are included.<br><br>2. *Praises or encourages.* Praises or encourages pupil action or behavior. Jokes that release tension, but not at the expense of another individual; nodding head, or saying "Um hm?" or "go on" are included.<br><br>3. *Accepts or uses ideas of pupils.* Clarifying, building, or developing ideas suggested by a pupil. Teacher extensions of pupil ideas are included but as the teacher brings more of his own ideas into play, shift to category five. |
| | | 4. *Asks questions.* Asking a question about content or procedure, based on teacher ideas, with the intent that a pupil will answer. |
| | **Initiation** | 5. *Lecturing.* Giving facts or opinions about content or procedures; expressing *his own* ideas, giving *his own* explanation, or citing an authority other than a pupil.<br><br>6. *Giving directions.* Directions, commands, or orders to which a pupil is expected to comply.<br><br>7. *Criticizing or justifying authority.* Statements intended to change pupil behavior from nonacceptable to acceptable pattern; bawling someone out; stating why the teacher is doing what he is doing; extreme self-reference. |
| **Pupil Talk** | **Response** | 8. *Pupil-talk — response.* Talk by pupils in response to teacher. Teacher initiates the contact or solicits pupil statement or structures the situation. Freedom to express own ideas is limited. |
| | **Initiation** | 9. *Pupil-talk — initiation.* Talk by pupils which they initiate. Expressing own ideas; initiating a new topic; freedom to develop opinions and a line of thought, like asking thoughtful questions; going beyond the existing structure. |
| **Silence** | | 10. *Silence or confusion.* Pauses, short periods of silence and periods of confusion in which communication cannot be understood by the observer. |

* There is *no* scale implied by these numbers. Each number is classificatory; it designates a particular kind of communication event. To write these numbers down during observation is to enumerate, not to judge a position on a scale.

## TABLE 11-3

*A Typical Illustration*

|  |  | 1 | 2 | 3 | 4 | 5 | 6 | 7 | 8 | 9 | 10 | Total |
|---|---|---|---|---|---|---|---|---|---|---|---|---|
|  |  |  |  |  |  | **Second** |  |  |  |  |  |  |
|  | 1 | 2 | 1 |  |  |  |  |  |  |  |  |  |
|  | 2 |  | 5 |  | 2 |  |  |  |  |  |  |  |
|  | 3 |  |  | 8 |  | 2 |  |  |  |  |  |  |
|  | 4 |  | 1 |  | 18 |  |  |  | 1 |  |  |  |
| **First** | 5 |  |  |  |  | 53 | 2 |  |  |  |  |  |
|  | 6 |  |  |  |  |  | 3 |  | 1 | 1 |  |  |
|  | 7 |  |  |  |  |  |  | 3 |  |  | 2 |  |
|  | 8 |  |  | 2 |  |  |  | 2 | 26 |  |  |  |
|  | 9 | 1 |  |  |  |  |  |  | 1 | 10 |  |  |
|  | 10 |  |  |  |  |  |  |  | 1 | 1 | 1 |  |
|  | Total | 3 | 7 | 10 | 20 | 55 | 5 | 5 | 30 | 12 | 3 | 150 |
|  | Column % | 2 | 4½ | 6½ | 13½ | 36½ | 3½ | 3½ | 20 | 8 | 2 |  |

**Teacher talk**
Columns 1–7 = 105
105 ÷ 150 = 70%

**Student talk**
Columns 8–9 = 42
42 ÷ 150 = 28%

Indirect (1–4)[÷]Direct (5–7) = ID ratio
40      ÷      65   = 0.62
Indirect (1–3)[÷]Direct (6–7) = Revised ID ratio
20      ÷      10   = 2.0

by the total number of tallies in the matrix (150). Thus, teacher talk accounted for 70% of the total amount of the interactions. Each of the categories within teacher talk can be broken down further to determine their percentages. For example, to determine the percentage of category 4 (asks questions), divide 20 by 105; thus, about 19% of the teacher talk was category 4 type talk. To determine the amount of student talk, total the number of tallies in columns 8 and 9 (42) and divide by the total number of tallies in the matrix (150). In this illustration, student talk accounted for 28% of the interaction. Using the same process, you will find that 2% of the time was spent in silence or confusion (column 10).

To compare the amounts of indirect and direct teacher talk, total the tallies in columns 1–4 and divide by the total of tallies in columns 5–7. This yields what Flanders refers to as the ID Ratio (ratio of indirect to direct teacher talk). Thus, columns 1–4 (40) divided by columns 5–7 (65) equals .62. This means that for every indirect statement, there were 1.62 direct statements. According to Amidon and Flanders, an ID Ratio of 1.0 means that for every indirect statement, there is one direct statement.

You can also calculate what Amidon and Flanders refer to as the Revised ID Ratio, which is used to determine the emphasis given to motivation and control. For example, in Table 11-3, columns 1, 2, 3, 6, and 7 are more concerned with motivation and control than with actual presentation of subject matter. The Revised ID Ratio (20 divided by 10), as you can see in Table 11-3, is 2.0. The interpretation means that for every direct statement, there were two that were indirect. This suggests that the teacher used few direct statements for control and motivation. The interpretation as to whether this is good or bad is left to you. There are no hard-and-fast guidelines for interpreting the results. Thus, for example, if you were having problems with motivation and control and your Revised ID Ratio was 2.0, you might conclude that you need to use more direct statements to regain control and to generate motivation. The final step is to reassess your interactions to determine whether you have made the intended changes. If your Revised ID Ratio was 2.0 and you decided to be more direct, you would want to know whether a change actually occurred and whether that change resulted in altering the students' behavior.

Using systematic observations can be a tremendous help in examining the behaviors that occur in the classroom. Teachers should constantly examine and analyze their classroom endeavors and the effects these have on environment and on learning in general.

# FEEDBACK

Feedback, the positive and negative information we receive from others, is essential to the instructional process, for it allows us to assess, stabilize, or change our behavior in the classroom. Feedback consists of receptivity as well as responsiveness (the willingness to do something about it, to take action). Smith (1966, p. 322) identifies feedback as a "control" mechanism in the communication process. Simply, *feedback is information to control and correct the signals fed forward.* It is based upon the principles of cybernetics that parallel automatic control systems, such as those found in thermostats, guided missiles, balance systems of economics, or détente theories of international politics. You need not look any further than your home for an example of feedback control mechanisms. The thermometer in your home thermostat (also discussed in Chapter 7) measures the room temperature. When the thermometer reaches a specified temperature, it activates the thermostat (an on-off switch), which starts the furnace. The same process turns off the furnace. Thus, the thermometer, thermostat, and furnace act *interdependently* of each other. Feedback, however, is not a simple on-off mechanism. In the classroom, for example, a teacher communicates instructions to the students, whose behavior the teacher observes as feedback, in the form of either a direct question, nonverbal behavior, or any behavior that signals how the students have received the instructions. The feedback can also be delayed until the students have turned in their assignments. By examining the assignment, the teacher can tell whether the students understood the instructions or not. Here the teacher, students, and instructor, acting interdependently of each other, show the complexity of feedback. Barnlund (1968, p. 230) provides the following explanation:

> The interpersonal situation, involving two organisms interacting by means of verbal and nonverbal cues, is still more complex. A social engagement is a sort of system of systems; there is a flow of information between as well as within the participating individuals. Each person must monitor his own acts to produce the words and gestures he intends, and must monitor the

reactions of others to those words and gestures to see if his message prompted the reaction he sought.

Unfortunately, far too often we fail to monitor our own communication, and more importantly, the reactions of others to our communication. You can easily see what would happen to the temperature in a room if the furnace, thermostat, and thermometer acted *independently* of one another.

Thus, feedback is more than just a corrective device or an automatic response to others; it is needed by each of us, because by telling us who we are and how others perceive us and the things we do, feedback allows us to function and adjust to those around us. We have little capacity for self-assessment, according to Miller and Steinberg (1975), without the feedback of others.

## Advantages of Feedback

In a now-classic study, Leavitt and Mueller (1951) found that as the amount of feedback increased, the reception of information became more accurate. The experiment required that students try to construct geometric patterns as described to them by an instructor. The conditions were: (1) zero feedback — that is, the instructor's back was turned to the students and the students were not allowed to ask questions or make noise; (2) visible audience — the students could see the instructor's face but could not ask questions; (3) limited verbal — the students were allowed to ask the instructor questions, but the instructor could respond with only yes or no; (4) free feedback — all channels of communication were open with no limits placed on the questions asked of the instructor. Two important findings came from this study:

1. As the amount of feedback increases, so does the accuracy of communication.
2. As the amount of feedback increases, so does the confidence about performance.

Feedback, therefore, provides more accurate message transmission and more confidence in communication.

## Costs of Feedback

In a majority of communication situations, feedback provides many advantages. However, to implement and use feedback mechanisms in everyday communication, and particularly in classroom relationships, entails potential and actual costs. The Leavitt and Mueller study provides two beneficial reasons for using free feedback in an instructional setting. However, the study also shows that gaining accuracy and creating confidence takes *time*: time in limiting the amount of instruction; time in responding to students both in and out of class; time in developing feedback instruments to gather student responses; time in meeting with parents; time in meeting with superiors; and time to provide both written and oral feedback to others (including students, administrators, parents, and the public in general). However, the cost of time may be a small price to pay for improved learning and understanding.

Feedback also involves costs at the personal level; that is, it may not confirm a portion of our self-concept. Most people do not take negative feedback without relating it directly to themselves. Each of us can probably recall situations when we felt that feedback was too threatening or expensive to justify its existence. At times preventing feedback or ignoring it is easier than running the risk of negative cues. Nevertheless, it is important to use feedback to examine what works well and what does not. Then the expense can be measured against the productive gains. Feedback should be used for monitoring and better understanding instructional effectiveness; at the same time, it should be kept in perspective as to the source and to the conditions under which it is given. It is easy to overreact. In the following section we examine feedback that assesses the teacher from the students' perceptions.

## Feedback from Students to Teacher

This chapter is based upon the assumption that education should bring about changes in students. If you agree with this, then information (feedback) from students to provide a basis for improving instruction is necessary. There are several ways of providing feedback from your students: (1) conducting student evaluations of your instruction, (2) analyzing examination and assignment results to discover how well students respond and complete them, (3) observing the immediate behavior of students during class, (4) having individual-student conferences outside of class, and (5) holding parent-teacher conferences.

*Student evaluation* of instruction, one of the most direct ways of gathering information, has been researched by a plethora of studies. Aleamoni and Hexner (1980), Costin, Greenough, and Menges (1971), Frandsen (1980), Kulik and McKeachie (1975), and McKeachie (1979) have shown that student evaluations, if appropriately used, produce student ratings that do indicate teaching effectiveness. The key is *appropriately used.* McKeachie (1979) suggests that particular rating forms may be valid for different reasons, such as educational goals (for example, teaching content, teaching critical thinking, or facilitating attitudinal/motivational achievement) or intended uses (for example, improving teaching, administrative evaluations, or student choice of teachers and courses). Care must be exercised in developing rating forms to insure validity for specific goals and intended use. Friedrich and Seiler (1981) found that student evaluation reports differ, depending upon the intended use of the evaluations. Students who were told that the evaluation information would be used by a course director for improving the course rated their teachers more harshly than students who were told that the evaluations were complying with university regulations.

This literature provides a mixture of pro and con information regarding the use of student evaluations. Believing that evaluations can be helpful, we encourage you to use them. Basically, the three common uses for student ratings are:

1. to provide information for aiding instructor improvement
2. to provide information on the effectiveness of instruction
3. to provide information to students for selecting courses and instructors

After determining the objective of the evaluation, decide when and how the evaluation should be administered. In some school systems the use of student evaluation is predetermined as to its objectives, the subject matter being rated, and the person administering the questionnaire. If this is done in your school system, then it would be wise for you to become familiar with the prescribed procedures and policies. If it is not administered by the school system, we recommend that you read about student evaluations, determine your purpose, select the instrument or develop your own, and set up procedures that will allow students the opportunity to rate you freely without any constraints. It is important that ratings be done anonymously and that students believe the results will be used.

*Analyzing examination and assignment results* can be another source of feedback. Too often an instructor will grade a project without interpreting a student's performance in terms of the quality of instruction. An assignment or test reveals areas in which students did poorly or did well. This is a valuable source of information not only about how well you are doing but also on how well your students are doing. Sometimes it is useful to ask a colleague to examine your course objectives, sample papers, and tests to determine whether or not your expectations are reasonable.

*Observing immediate behavior of students during class* is an extremely valuable source of feedback. With open and free feedback, you can learn of students' misconceptions, biases, and emotional reactions. By ignoring or limiting students feedback, you are losing a great source of information. Even when lecturing, you can be aware of student reactions. The obviousness of students' sleeping or reading the school newspaper is very difficult to ignore. Often, however, many of us disregard restlessness, blank stares, talking, and other indications that students are not paying attention. We must be constant monitors, not merely for maintaining discipline but also for determining the effectiveness of what we are doing.

*Individual-student conferences* outside class serve as a valuable source for both you and the student. Later in this chapter we discuss further information to feed back to students via conferences. During these conferences you should be continually aware of the cues and information that students are providing. Even though these problems may be of an individual nature, they may reflect possible inadequacies in instruction that need correcting.

*Parent-teacher conferences* provide another source of valuable information, for they furnish not only the parents' perceptions of your effectiveness but also their perceptions of their children's successes or failures. Being observant and listening to parents can be insightful and informative.

## Feedback to Students

One of your most important responsibilities as a teacher is providing feedback to students concerning their academic performance. Feedback assumes different forms — grades or comments on assignments, papers, and tests, as well as responses to students' actions or responses in class; and types — formal-informal, written-oral, positive-negative, private-public, or a combination of any of these. School policy may dictate certain procedures to follow in providing this feedback, particularly in formalized evaluations.

Responses to comments or recitations by students are generally informal, public, oral, and either positive or negative. It is imperative to recognize that feedback to students can either motivate or inhibit, or possibly even cause them to rebel or quit. The effectiveness of feedback can be determined by using a systematic observation technique and by analyzing students' reactions to teacher behaviors. See Chapter 6 for more on teacher reacting behavior.

Feedback can be given at any time during class. It must be sincere, fair, and accurate. Students who perceive feedback as insincere, unfair, or inaccurate will become frustrated and may even ignore teacher comments. The way teachers present verbal and nonverbal communications can affect the way students receive their feedback. A study by Woolfolk (1978) found that teachers who used positive words accompanied by negative nonverbal behaviors in their feedback were more effective than teachers who used negative words accompanied by positive nonverbal behavior. Woolfolk concludes that perhaps teachers whose behaviors are positive and contradict their verbal statements are seen as timid, anxious, fearful, not confident, or unassertive and, therefore, not to be taken seriously. Those teachers whose behaviors were negative with positive verbal comments were seen as confident, firm, and sincere. Thus, how feedback is expressed may be as important as the feedback itself.

Thompson, White, and Morgan (1982), in studying teacher-student interaction patterns in classrooms with mainstreamed mildly handicapped students, found that about half the teachers' feedback and initiations were nonacademic. They further found that the teachers used more disapproving than positive feedback. They suggest that "regular education teachers need to become more skilled at dealing appropriately with these students, particularly if increasing numbers of difficult-to-manage children are to be mainstreamed" (p. 234). This means that teachers need more training in developing an awareness of what and how they communicate with their students.

Broman and Shipley (1976, p. 118) suggest the following ways to say "very good": Excellent, I knew you could do it, Super, That's better than ever, Great, Superior, The best, Spectacular performance, Glowing, or Now you have it. They point out that it is easy to give praise when things are going well, and that the student who seldom receives praise is the most likely to need it. However, the student whose self-concept is low often sees flattery as insincere. Thus, great care is required in communicating responses to this student. Broman and Shipley suggest the following ways to express encouragement:

The second time will be better.

That's coming along nicely.

You have just about mastered that.

One more time and you will have it.

You are on the right track now.

You're doing that much better today.

You have really been working hard today.

Keep working at it — you will get it.

That's quite an improvement.

That's the right way to do it.

Keep up the good work.

You are really going to town.

I have never seen anyone try harder.

You are really improving.

Sometimes it is wise to share your praise privately with students by providing comments or a brief note informing them how you see their work.

Telling students that they are not doing well or that you are unhappy with their performance is equally important. Generally, we suggest that you deal with criticism or negative feedback privately whenever possible. To do otherwise might threaten students' egos and make them defensive. Describing and discussing the things that students are doing incorrectly is better than telling them that they are wrong.

The most formalized feedback undoubtedly is the grade report, which is generally private and can contain both positive and negative information. Report cards vary in type or form and in the amount of information they transmit to students, from a list of grades to a host of additional information such as attendance, attitude, social behavior, use of time, coopera-tion, initiative, resourcefulness, and so on. Tables 11-4 and 11-5 are examples of report cards using normative approaches. The five-category system of letter grades (A, B, C, D, F) is still widely used throughout the United States. The letter-grade and the three-category (1, 2, 3) systems of reporting are most often used by comparing the relative achievement of a student to the other students in a class.

A criterion-referenced system differs greatly from a normative-approach report card (Tables 11-4 and 11-5). The criterion-referenced report (see Table 11-6) describes each subject in detail as to what the student has mastered and what has not yet been mastered. In

**TABLE 11-4    Example of a Computer-Generated High School Report**

| Student Number | | Grade | Sex | Counselor |
|---|---|---|---|---|
| 12345612  Smith, John | | 10 | M | Jones |

| 1st Semester Report Card | Absences to date | Full Day | Part Day |
|---|---|---|---|
| From 8/23/79 to 12/22/79 | 10 | 8 | 2 |

| Period | Subject | Units | Comments | Grade |
|---|---|---|---|---|
| 1 | French 5 | 5.0 | 1 | B |
| 2 | Speech | 5.0 | 2,0 | B+ |
| 3 | Algebra 1 | 5.0 | 4,5 | C |
| 4 | English 3 | 5.0 | | A |
| 5 | Biology 1 | 5.0 | 8,9 | C |
| 6 | P.E. | 2.5 | 1 | A |

| Grades | | Comments: | | | |
|---|---|---|---|---|---|
| A | Superior | 0 | Citizenship commendable | 5 | Attendance poor |
| B | Better than average | 1 | Effort is commendable | 6 | Underachieving |
| C | Average | 2 | Recent improvement shown | 7 | Low test scores |
| D | Barely passing | 3 | Conduct needs improvement | 8 | Needs outside help |
| F | Failure | 4 | Effort needs improvement | 9 | Parent conference needed |

TABLE 11-5    Example of an Elementary School Report Card

| Name | Grade | Homeroom | Quarter | Year |
|---|---|---|---|---|
| Doe, Jane | 5 | S–4 | 2 | 1979–80 |

**Teacher Comments:**
Excellent student in math.
Very conscientious in French.
Jane is a student with a great deal of potential, and with the right kind of motivation she should excel in all subjects.

| Subject | Teacher | Achievement | Effort | Uses Time Wisely | Works Cooperatively | Shows Initiative & Resourcefulness | Prompt in Completing Requirements | Attendance | |
|---|---|---|---|---|---|---|---|---|---|
| Social Studies | | 1 | 1 | 3 | 1 | 1 | 1 | 2 | |
| Language Arts | | 2 | 1 | 1 | 2 | 1 | 1 | 1 | |
| Science | | 1 | 1 | 1 | 1 | 1 | 1 | 1 | |
| Reading | | 1 | 1 | 1 | 1 | 1 | 1 | 1 | |
| French | | 1 | 1 | 1 | 1 | 1 | 1 | 1 | |
| Drama | | P | 1 | 1 | 1 | 1 | 1 | 1 | |
| Music | | | | | | | | | |
| Graphic Art | | | | | | | | | |
| Clothing | | P | 1 | 1 | 1 | 1 | 1 | 1 | |
| P.E. | | 2 | 2 | 2 | 2 | 2 | 2 | 2 | |

**Ratings:**
1   Above grade      P   Pass ⎫ electives
2   At grade         F   Fail ⎭
3   Below grade

**Effort and Other factors:**
1   Special commendation
2   Satisfactory
3   Improvement needed

this type of evaluation, each subject has a list of objectives to be accomplished by the student. Obviously, specifying what is to be done in some subject areas is easier than in others. While the system is difficult to set up, it does tell the students and parents exactly what a student can and cannot do. Under this system the competition of getting an A, as in the norm-referenced system, is removed. The student, thus, competes with the objective and his or her own ability to master the objective in terms of absolute standards.

It is important that you fully understand whatever system is used, and that you report as reliably and accurately as possible. In addition to report cards, conferences provide a method of giving both positive and negative feedback to students. The conference is generally informal and private; information can be both oral and written. Unfortunately, teachers tend to call conferences with students only when something is wrong or when there is a problem. The handling of a conference can make a difference on the outcome, depending upon whether the impact is positive or negative. If the conference concerns a problem or disagreement with a student, caution should be exercised in handling it. Remember that there are always two sides to every issue.

TABLE 11-6 **Example of a Report Using a Criterion-Referenced Measurement System**

| **Speech Communication – Grade 9**<br>**Student: Doe, Jane** | **Teacher: Jones** |
|---|---|
| *Skill** | *Date Mastered* |
| Understands and can identify the four basic speech terms of: source, message, channel, and receiver. | 10/2 |
| Can define speaker credibility by labeling and defining the following components: trust, expertness, competence, composure, and character. | 10/15 |
| Is able to describe and write examples of the following kinds of supporting materials: testimony, analogy, statistics, and restatement. | 10/21 |
| Can identify from examples the following patterns of organization: chronological, space, cause and effect, topical, and problem-solution. | |
| Is able to write a speech using one of the following patterns of organization: chronological, space, cause and effect, topical, or problem-solution. | |

* The use of criterion-reference reports is usually much more comprehensive than our sample. However, the format is generally the same as shown.

Each of the four principal types of conferences — counseling, appraisal, complaint handling, and reprimand — requires special skills and should not be taken lightly. We urge you to become aware of each and to develop the skills that are needed to conduct them effectively.[3]

## Feedback to Parents

In place of impersonal notes, telephone calls, or other types of messages, the parent-teacher conference is probably the best way to communicate with parents. The use of a person-to-person conference can help mutual understanding of problems, whereas the use of more impersonal exchanges might widen the gap and possibly aggravate the problem. However, notes, letters, or telephone calls should not be ruled out completely as forms of feedback. When the problems are minor or when you wish to convey praise or even to establish rapport with parents, these methods can be quite useful. The key to a successful conference is to be prepared.

Depending on the grade level the amount and kind of communication with parents can vary. We believe that open communication between teachers and parents is essential. For example, communicating with parents can prepare them to help their children. Also, when

[3] For additional information on how to handle the types of conferences, we recommend Charles J. Stewart and William B. Cash, Jr., *Interviewing: Principles and Practices,* 2nd ed. Dubuque, Iowa: Wm. C. Brown Company, Publishers, 1978.

parents understand their children's learning problems, they can often reinforce desirable behaviors in their children, thus making teaching more enjoyable.

A letter to parents might be most helpful at the beginning of the school year; it serves as an early indication of a teacher's willingness to communicate with them and thus opens the door to free-flowing communication between them and the teacher. The letter might include:

- an enthusiastic greeting to the student
- a summary of the subjects and objectives for the year
- an invitation to the parents to visit the classroom
- a list of additional materials that might be needed by each child
- tips to aid parents in helping their child at home
- an invitation for parents to share their skills and abilities with the class
- your home phone number and how you can be reached at school

Calling each student's parents during the first weeks of school could be a means of reassuring them that the teacher cares about their child and that their child is in good hands.

As suggested earlier in this section, the face-to-face conference is probably the best opportunity for parent-teacher communication. Because initial planning and preparation help to make such a conference successful, teachers should know in advance the areas to be covered so that nothing of importance is omitted. If a special problem goes beyond the teacher-learner classroom situation, it may be to the teacher's advantage to consult in advance with a specialist, such as the school psychologist, speech therapist, or nurse. Try to make the room for the conference as informal as possible. Informality and an open atmosphere should help the teacher as well as the parents to relax.

Some suggestions to help in conducting the conference follow:

1.  Before the conference, critically examine the room. What kind of impression will it give to the parents? Remember that its appearance reflects on the teacher.
2.  The greeting of the parents can help set the tone for the conference. Make sure everyone is introduced and the parents are thanked for coming. The initial contact can be critical to the success of the conference.
3.  Provide the parents with some direction as to the purpose of the conference and how it is to proceed.
4.  Begin and end the conference with a positive comment about the child. Maintain a positive approach insofar as possible. Thus, be constructive rather than destructive. Negative aspects should not be ignored, but they should be presented in perspective and with care so as not to make parents defensive.
5.  Provide samples of the student's work when possible.
6.  Listen carefully to the comments and criticisms made by the parents. Avoid quick final judgments and dogmatic statements, which will probably close off discussion. The general rule is to listen more than talk. Try to get the parents to make suggestions.
7.  Always try to be specific when presenting evaluative comments. Let parents know which skills need work and what difficulties should be given priority.
8.  Remember that not all conferences concern students who have difficulties. Parents whose children are doing well want to know what their children are learning and to hear some praises for their child.
9.  Avoid being argumentative. The conference should not be a debating session. It is

important to point out areas of agreement and to establish grounds for common understanding. It should not be teacher against parents but the teacher and the parents trying to help the child.

10. Don't spend much time writing or taking notes during the conference. Note taking can inhibit the flow of the discussion.

11. Guide the conference insofar as possible so as to stay on the relevant issues of the conference. Getting sidetracked on unimportant issues can waste an entire conference.

12. Bring the conference to a smooth ending. If additional conferences or some type of follow-up are necessary, make arrangements for them but do try to close on a positive note.

Parent-teacher conferences can be a stressful part of a teacher's job, but if planned carefully and with the use of common sense, they can be quite enjoyable. After each conference, try to evaluate the effectiveness of the conference.

The teacher can ask a number of questions about the conference to determine its success. Some examples are:

1. Did everyone seem at ease and relaxed?
2. Was the purpose of the conference clear to everyone?
3. Was the objective of the conference met?
4. Was the time limit of the conference met?
5. Was the emphasis of the conference positive rather than negative? Were specific examples to illustrate the student's work provided?
6. Was an atmosphere of defensiveness created?
7. Did the conference end on a friendly, positive note?

It is important to review the conference proceedings and results to get an idea of areas that need improvement, if any, for the next conference.

# SUMMARY

Assessment and feedback communication are essential to the instructional process. Teachers must not only be capable of evaluating and providing feedback to students, parents, and administrators, but also be able to examine their own behaviors critically. Teachers must be willing to change, when necessary, to meet the needs of their students; they must also have the desire for continuous improvement. Systematic observation techniques for assessing classroom behaviors can be a tremendous help to teachers who wish to know how they are performing in the classroom. The use of systematic observation techniques requires some training and skill in interpreting them, but the time invested is well worth it.

Feedback is essential to all communication, but it plays a vital role in the communication of the classroom teacher. Feedback involves teachers letting students and their parents know how they are doing; it also involves students, students' parents, and teachers' superiors letting teachers know how they are doing. Providing feedback and allowing for feedback takes special skills and a willingness to open all avenues of communication.

# Discussion Questions

1. Why is the assessment of a teacher's classroom interactions necessary?
2. What should teachers assess when evaluating their classroom interactions?
3. What role should feedback play in learning?
4. In what ways can feedback benefit the teacher?

# References

Aleamoni, Lawrence M., and Pamela Z. Hexner. "A Review of the Research on Student Evaluation and a Report on the Effect of Different Sets of Instructions on Student Course and Instructor Evaluations." *Instructional Science,* Vol. 9 (1980): 67–84.

Amidon, Edmund, and John Hough, eds. *Interaction Analysis: Theory, Research, and Application.* Reading, Mass.: Addison-Wesley Publishing Company, Inc., 1967, pp. 121–40.

Barnlund, Dean C. *Interpersonal Communication: Survey and Studies.* Boston: Houghton Mifflin Company, 1968.

Broman, Betty, and Sara Shipley. "Very° Good: 68 Ways to Say It." *Instructor,* April 1976: 118ff.

Costin, Frank, William T. Greenough, and Robert J. Menges. "Student Ratings of College Teaching: Reliability, Validity, and Usefulness." *Review of Educational Research,* Vol. 41 (1971): 511–35.

Flanders, Ned A. *Analyzing Teaching Behaviors.* Reading, Mass.: Addison-Wesley Publishing Company, Inc., 1970.

Flanders, Ned A. "Teacher Influence, Pupil Attitudes, and Achievement." Final Report, Cooperative Research Project No. 397, U.S. Office of Education. The University of Minnesota, 1960 (now out of print).

Frandsen, Kenneth D. "Some Problems in the Use of Student Evaluations." *ACA Bulletin,* Vol. 33 (1980): 36–37.

Friedrich, Gustav, and William D. Brooks. "The Use of Systematic Observation Instruments for the Supervision of Teaching." *The Speech Teacher,* Vol. 19, No. 4 (November 1970): 283–88.

Friedrich, Gustav, and William J. Seiler. "The Influence of Differing Administrative Instructions on Student Ratings of Instructors." *Central States Speech Journal,* Vol. 32, No. 2 (Summer 1981): 111–17.

Kulik, James A., and Wilbert J. McKeachie. "The Evaluation of Teachers in Higher Education." In *Review of Research in Education,* Vol. 3, Fred N. Kerlinger, ed. Washington, D.C.: American Educational Research Association, 1975, pp. 446–78.

Leavitt, Harold J., and Ronald A. H. Mueller. "Some Effects of Feedback on Communication." *Human Relations,* Vol. 4 (1951): 401–10.

McKeachie, Wilbert J. "Student Ratings of Faculty: A Reprise." *Academe,* Vol. 65 (1979): 384–97.

Miller, Gerald, and Mark Steinberg. *Between People.* Chicago: Science Research Associates, Inc., 1975.

Simon, Anita, and E. Gil Boyer, eds. "Mirrors for Behavior: An Anthology of Classroom Observation Instruments." *Classroom Interaction Newsletter,* Vol. 3, No. 2 (January 1968).

Simon, Anita, and E. Gil Boyer, eds. *Mirrors for Behavior II,* Vols. A & B. Philadelphia: Research for Better Schools, Inc., 1970.

Simon, Anita, and E. Gil Boyer, eds. *Mirrors for Behavior III: An Anthology of Observation Instruments.* Wyncotte, Pa.: Communication Materials Center, 1974.

Smith, Alfred. *Communication and Culture.* New York: Holt, Rinehart and Winston, Inc., 1966.

Thompson, Ray H., Karl R. White, and Daniel P. Morgan. "Teacher-Student Interaction Patterns in

Classrooms with Mainstreamed Mildly Handicapped Students." *American Educational Research Journal,* Vol. 19, No. 2 (Summer 1982): 220–36.

Woolfolk, Anita E. "Student Learning and Performance under Varying Conditions of Teacher Verbal and Nonverbal Evaluative Communication." *Journal of Educational Psychology,* Vol. 78, No. 1 (1978): 87–94.

# For Further Reading

Doyle, Kenneth S. *Evaluational Instruction.* Lexington, Mass.: D. C. Heath & Company, 1975.

Gage, N. L., and David C. Berliner. *Educational Psychology,* 2nd ed. Boston: Houghton Mifflin Company, 1979.

Gagne, R. M. *Essentials of Learning for Instruction.* Hinsdale, Ill.: The Dryden Press Inc., 1974.

Staton-Spicer, Ann. "The Measurement and Further Conceptualization of Teacher Communication Concern." *Human Communication Research,* Vol. 9, No. 2 (Winter 1983): 158–168.

# APPENDIX

| Game | Number of Players | Age Level | Purpose |
|------|------------------|-----------|---------|
| GHETTO | 7–10 | 10–adult | understand social system and urban ghetto |
| DEMOCRACY | 6–11 | 10–adult | learn relation between electorate and legislature and negotiation |
| LIFE CAREER | 2–20 | 13–17 | learn choice options for future career |
| GENERATION GAP | 4–6 | 10–17 | learn processes of conflict resolution |
| INFORMATION | 8 or more | 10–adult | learn processes of teaching, drilling, and reviewing information |
| BLACKS AND WHITES | 10–14 | high school | experience social and economic pressures of racial prejudice |
| THE CITIES GAME | 4–20 | high school | learn processes of negotiation and political bargaining |
| NUCLEAR ENERGY GAME | 12–25 | high school | learn issues of community land-use planning |
| STARPOWER | 10–35 | 10–adult | learn processes of social power and wealth |
| BAFA BAFA | 18–36 | 12–adult | demonstrate cross-cultural simulation |
| PROPAGANDA | 12 | 12–adult | learn logical fallacies, persuasion through language |
| CRISIS RESOLUTION GAMES | 12 | 12–college | learn aspects of value decisions in personal behavior |
| BALDICER | 10–20 | 12–adult | understand world food problems and food distribution |

The following is a list of academic game centers and their addresses:

Academic Games Associates, Inc.
430 East 33rd Street
Baltimore, Md. 21218

Academic Games Project
Division of South Florida Education Center
3600 S.W. 70th Street
Fort Lauderdale, Fla. 33310

Board of Cooperative Educational Services
Center for Educational Services and Research
845 Fox Meadow Road
Yorktown Heights, N.Y. 10598

Creative Studies Inc.
167 Corey Road
Boston, Mass. 02146

Education Development Center, Inc.
55 Chapel Street
Newton, Mass. 02158

Games Central
c/o Abt Associates, Inc.
55 Wheeler Street
Cambridge, Mass. 02138

Instructional Simulations Inc.
2147 University Avenue
St. Paul, Minn. 55114

Learning Games Associates
Research and Development Office
1490 South Boulevard
Ann Arbor, Mich. 48104

Project Simile II
1150 Silverado
La Jolla, Cal. 92037

Teaching Research
Oregon State System of Higher Education
Monmouth, Ore. 97361

The following is a list of software vendors:[1]

Advanced Graphics
James Garon
920 West Romneya, #6
Anaheim, Cal. 92801

Apple Computer, Inc.
10260 Bandley Drive
Cupertino, Cal. 95014

Applied Economic Analysis
4005 Locust Avenue
Long Beach, Cal. 90807

Aquarius Computing, Inc.
(TRS–80)
8 Yorktown Avenue
West Chester, Pa. 19380

Astro-Learn
P.O. Box 788
Lakewood, Cal. 90713

Atari
1265 Borregas
Sunnyvale, Cal. 94058

Automated Simulations, Inc.
P.O. Box 427, Department DH2
Mountain View, Cal. 94040

Baker, Robert
5845 Topp Court
Carmichael, Cal. 95608

B & B Consultants
946 Pomeroy Avenue
Santa Clara, Cal. 95051

Barton Enterprises
1604 Marsh Lane
Carrollton, Tex. 75006

Bell & Howell
Microcomputer Systems
Audio Visual Products
7100 North McCormick Road
Chicago, Ill. 60645

Bluebirds, Inc.
2267 23rd Street
Wyandotte, Mich. 48192

Brain Box
Suite 12A
70 East 10 Street
New York, N.Y. 10003

Dr. William M. Butler
Department of Chemistry

[1] Taken from Jostad, Karen and Marge Kosel. "Search for Software," *AEDS Monitor*, Vol. 19, Nos. 7, 8, and 9 (January 1981): 21–23.

University of Michigan
Ann Arbor, Mich. 48109

Carta Associates, Inc.
640 Lancaster Avenue
Frazer, Pa. 19355

Cavri Systems
26 Trumbull Street
New Haven, Ct. 06511

Center for Quality Education, Inc.
802 Merchants State Bank Building
5217 Ross Avenue
Dallas, Tex. 75206

Cload Magazine
Box 1267
Goleta, Cal. 93017

Commodore Pet
Commodore International
3330 Scott
Santa Clara, Cal. 95054

Compak, Inc.
P.O. Box 14852
Austin, Tex. 78761

Com Press, Inc.
P.O. Box 102
Wentworth, N.H. 03282

Computer Headware
Box 14694
San Francisco, Cal. 94114

Computer Ware
1512 Encinitas Boulevard
Encinitas, Cal. 92024

Conduit
P.O. Box 388
Iowa City, Ia. 52244

Cook's Computer Company
1905 Bailey Drive
Marshalltown, Ia. 50185

Cove View Press; Software
Box 637
Garberville, Cal. 95440

Cow Bay Computing
Box 515
Manhasset, N.Y. 11030

Creative Discount
Software (Edusoft)

256 South Robertson
Suite 2158
Beverly Hills, Cal. 90211

Creative Publications
P.O. Box 10328
Palo Alto, Cal. 94303

James J. Creevay
J/C Industries
Box 441186
Miami, Fl. 33144

Curriculum Applications
16 Plymouth Street
Arlington, Mass. 02174

Cursor
Box 550
Goleta, Cal. 93017

Cybermate
RD #3, Box 192A
Nazareth, Pa. 18064

Dilithium Press
P.O. Box 92
Forest Grove, Ore. 97116

Dorsett Educational
Systems, Inc.
Box 1226
Norman, Okla. 73070

Dr. Daley
425 Grove Avenue
Berrien Springs, Mich. 49103

George Earl
1302 South General McMullen
San Antonio, Tex. 78237

Educational Activities, Inc.
1937 Grand Avenue
Baldwin, N.Y. 11510
and
P.O. Box 392
Freeport, N.Y. 11520

Educational Microsystems
P.O. Box 471
Chester, N.Y. 07930

Educational Programming Systems
1328 Baur Boulevard
St. Louis, Mo. 63132

Educational Programs
Disney Electronic
6153 Fairmont Avenue
San Diego, Cal. 92120

Educational Software
801 East 6th Avenue
Helena, Mon. 59601

Edusoft
256 South Robertson
Suite 2156
Beverly Hills, Cal. 90211

Edutek
415 Cambridge, #14
P.O. Box 11354
Palo Alto, Cal. 94306

Edu-Ware Services, Inc.
22035 Burbank Boulevard
Suite 223
Woodland Hills, Cal. 91367

EMFW
Ed Warshawer
Box 438
Oakhurst, N.H. 07755

En-Joy Computer Programs
4400 Carpinteria Avenue, #24
Carpinteria, Cal. 93013

Faulk & Associates
2531 Commonwealth
Fullerton, Cal. 92631

Fireside Computing, Inc.
5843 Montgomery Road
Elkridge, Md. 21227

J. Fox
27 Prince William Road
Morganville, N.J. 07751

M.D. Fullmer & Associates
1132 Via Jose
San Jose, Cal. 95120

Hardhat Software
P.O. Box 14815
San Francisco, Cal. 94114

Dr. S. Harter
Box 17222
Tampa, Fl. 33682

Hayden Book Company, Inc.
50 Essex Street
Rochelle Park, N.J. 07662

High Technology, Inc.
Software Department
P.O. Box 14665
Oklahoma City, Okla. 73113

Huntington Computing
2020 Charles Street
Corcoran, Cal. 93212

Indiana Biolab
Palmyra, Ind. 47164

Innovative Computer Programs
Ron Graff
P.O. Box 622
El Toro, Cal. 92630

Interpretive Education
Allen Kemmerer
2306 Winters Drive
Kalamazoo, Mich. 49002

Jensen Software
1589 Blossom Park
Lakewood, Oh. 44107

JJR Data Research
Box 74
Middle Village, N.Y. 11379

J & S Software
140 Beid Avenue
Port Washington, N.Y. 11050

Kyde Tyme Project
Ted Perry
2331 St. Marks Ways
Sacramento, Cal. 95825

Mad Hatter Software
900 Salem Road
Cracat, Mass. 01826

Charles Mann & Associates
Micro Software Division
7594 San Remo Trail
Yucca Valley, Cal. 92284

Math Software
1233 Blacktorn Place
Deerfield, Ill. 60015

Med Systems Software
P.O. Box 2674
Chapel Hill, N.C. 27514

Micro-Ed, Inc.
Box 24156
Minneapolis, Minn. 55424

Micropi
George Gerhold
2445 North Nugent
Lummi Island, Wash. 98262

Microsystem 80
Borg-Warner Educational Systems
600 West University Drive
Arlington Heights, Ill. 60004

Micro Users Software Exchange
330 North Charles Street
Baltimore, Md. 21201

Midwest Visual Equipment
6500 North Hamlin Avenue
Chicago, Ill. 60645

National Software Marketing
Elliot B. Kleiman
4701 McKinley Street
Hollywood, Fl. 33021

PEC
P.O. Box 42831
Las Vegas, Nev. 89104

Gene Perkins
5224 Winifred
Fort Worth, Tex. 76133

Personal Software
592 Weddell Drive
Sunnyvale, Cal. 94086

Petsoft Ltd.
5 Vicarage Road
Edgbaston
Birmingham, England

Petware
Peter Ruetz
368 Albion Avenue
Woodside, Cal. 94062

Programmers Software Exchange
P.O. Box 199
Cabot, Ark. 72023

Project Local
200 Nahatan Street
Westwood, Mass. 02090

P.S. Software House
Marketing and Research Company
P.O. Box 966
Mishawaka, Ind. 46544

Quality Education, Inc.
5217 Ross Avenue
802 Merchants Street Bank Building
Dallas, Tex. 75208

Quant Systems
P.O. Box 628
Charlestown, S.C. 29402

Queue
5 Chapel Hill Drive
Fairfield, Ct. 06432

Resource Center Media Company
121 East 941/2 Street
Bloomington, Minn. 55420

Jay Scott Salinger
5312 Bloomfield Drive
Midland, Md. 48640

School District of Philadelphia
Henry R. Altschuler, CAI Systems
5th and Luzerne Streets — 5th Floor
Philadelphia, Pa. 19140

Scott, Foresman and Company
Electronic Publishing
1900 Lake Avenue
Glenview, Ill. 60025

Society for Visual Education
1345 Diversey Parkway
Chicago, Ill. 60614

The Socratic Computer Journal
P.O. Box 738
Wheat Ridge, Colo. 80033

Softagon
P.O. Box 774M
Morristown, N.J. 07960

Softape Software Exchange
10756 Vanowen Street
North Hollywood, Cal. 91605

The Software Exchange
6 South Street
Box 68
Milford, N.H. 03055

Software Industries
Ted Carter
902 Pinecrest Drive
Richardson, Tex. 75080

The Software Stockpile
9434 Ironwood
Des Plaines, Ill. 60016

Southern States Systems
Thomas D. Mock
P.O. Box 152
Stafford, Va. 22554

Stone's Southern School Supply Company
329 West Hargett Street
Raleigh, N.C. 27602

Taylor
P.O. Box 1180
Plattsburgh, N.Y. 12901

Teach Yourself by Computer (TYC)
40 Stuyvesant Manor
Geneseo, N.Y. 14454

Texas Instruments, Inc.
Personal Computer Division

P.O. Box 10508
Lubbock, Tex. 79408

T.H.E.S.I.S
P.O. Box 147
Garden City, Mich. 48141

Trans-Data Corporation
161 Almeria Avenue
Coral Gables, Fl. 33134

TRS-80 Software Exchange
Roger W. Robitaille
P.O. Box 68
Milford, N.H. 03055

Westinghouse Learning Corporation
1500 First Avenue North
Coralville, Ia. 52241

Williamsville Publishing Company
P.O. Box 250
Fredonia, N.Y. 14063

Wise Owl Workshop
1168 Avenida De Las Palmas
Livermore, Cal. 94550

World Institute for Computer
Assisted Teaching (WICAT)
J. Olin Campbell
P.O. Box 986
1160 South State Street
Orem, Ut. 84027

# Author Index

# Subject Index